CRUISING THE
CARIBBEAN

The Windward & Leeward Islands

Laura & Diane Rapp

HUNTER
PUBLISHING, INC

Hunter Publishing, Inc.
300 Raritan Center Parkway
Edison NJ 08818
(908) 225 1900 Fax (908) 417 0412

ISBN 1-55650-599-X

© 1994 Hunter Publishing, Inc.

Cover:
St. Lucia, the Petit Piton (J. Messerschmidt/Leo de Wys Inc.)

About the Authors

Laura and Diane Rapp are originally from Santa Barbara, California. Upon graduation from Florida International University with a degree in Hospitality Management, Laura went to work for the cruise industry and traveled throughout the Caribbean. Diane is a small business owner, science fiction writer and collaborated with Laura to write this book. Both are currently living and working in Telluride, Colorado where they enjoy the mountains but still get away frequently to the Caribbean.

Contents

Acknowledgments

We would like to extend a special thanks to Michael Hunter for supporting our project. Appreciation goes to Corey W. Rapp for his continuous support, excellent maps, and his unselfish sacrifice, allowing us to go to the Caribbean while he stayed home. Thanks to Nan Cox for her guidance and encouragement in finding a publisher. Special acknowledgment is given to the individual is-land Tourism Offices both in the United States, and on the islands. Thank you for the island information, assistance, and invaluable help during our research trip. We especially thank the following people and businesses on each island.

ST. THOMAS:
Gloria Gumbs-V.I. Department of Economic Development & Agriculture
Joost Barens-General Manager of the Ramada Yacht Haven Hotel
Naked Turtle catamaran cruise/Atlantis Submarine
Sugar Reef Cafe/Castaways Restaurant/Hotel 1829 restaurant

ST. MAARTEN:
Pelican Resort & Casino
Bayside Riding Club

ANTIGUA:
Ramada Renaissance Royal Antiguan Resort

ST. KITTS & NEVIS:
Rose Herbert Taxi Service
Sun'n Sand Beach Village
Rawlins Plantation/The White House/The Georgian House Restau-rant/Fairview Inn
Oualie Beach Hotel
Eddy's Bar & Restaurant

GUADELOUPE:
Hotel Saint-John

DOMINICA:
Dive Dominica/Castle Comfort Lodge
Reigate Waterfront Hotel
Ken's Hinterland Adventurous Tours

ST. LUCIA:
Green Parrot-Inn and Restaurant
Anse Chastanet Resort
Scuba St. Lucia

BARBADOS:
Atlantis Submarine

GRENADA:
Coral Cove Hotel
Rhum Runner-booze cruise
Nutmeg Restaurant/Tropicana Restaurant & Bar/Rudolf's Restaurant

Foreword

While employed as Ship's Purser for a major cruise line, it became apparent to me that the questions most frequently asked by passengers were not being answered by travel agents, ship lectures, or by current travel guides. Since cruise passengers are usually allotted between eight and ten hours for sightseeing and exploring in each port of call, they need a guidebook specifically oriented to that time schedule if they are to plan their time ashore. *Cruising the Caribbean* answers the most basic island questions, and lists detailed activities to help travelers enjoy their Caribbean adventure.

The experience of working on cruise ships taught me that the hardest task of a Ship's Purser, besides maintaining a continuous smile, was answering the same port questions week after week, month after month. While on board, I assembled a ports of call information book to supply answers for most commonly asked questions. The port information book was an essential tool for the Purser's office, and what you are reading now is an expanded version for all cruise passengers and travelers to the Caribbean islands.

To keep the size of the guidebook small enough to carry while exploring ashore, the islands featured in this edition were limited to the 11 most frequented by cruise ships in the Windward and Leeward chains. The chapters are presented in the same order as they appear on the Caribbean map from north to south, beginning with Puerto Rico and ending with Grenada.

Each island chapter supplies information on history, shopping, transportation, shore excursions, beaches and sports activities. The suggested taxi fares, tours and excursions, recommended beaches, and shopping hints are designed to answer all of the traveler's questions before arrival.

Some cruise passengers may only be interested in getting off the ship to stretch their legs on the pier, while others may want to venture out on the island for scuba diving, shopping, or island excursions. Cruise activities tend to center around broad categories. The format of this guide corresponds to these activity categories: 1) The Pier; 2) In Town (Historical Walking Tour, Shopping); 3) Transportation, Excursions (Tours, Beaches, Sports, One-Day Itinerary).

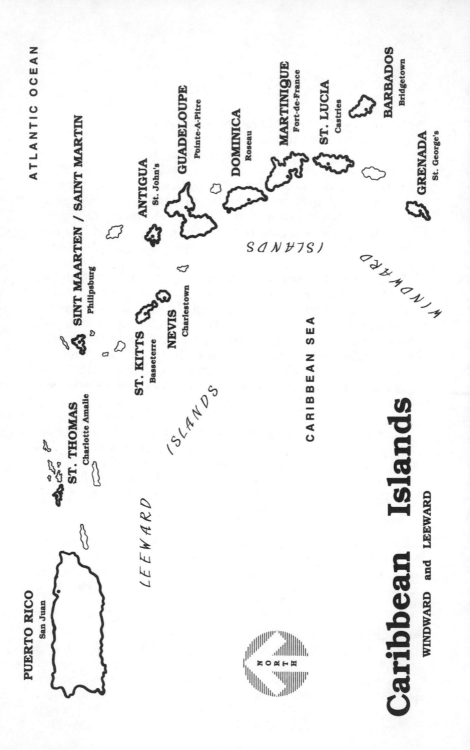

Caribbean Islands
WINDWARD and LEEWARD

The Caribbean Islands

An Introduction

Caribbean Geography:
Islands in the Caribbean were formed by massive upheavals caused by earthquakes and volcanoes. Some islands are fundamentally coral-limestone mountains pushed up from the sea bottom, while others are mountains of volcanic ash with fertile soil and rain forests.

Coral islands such as St. Thomas, St. Maarten, Antigua, and Barbados are surrounded by reefs teeming with exotic tropical fish. They are generally less mountainous, have a drier climate, and less fertile soil than volcanic islands. Vegetation on coral islands is thick, low-growing, hardy, and drought resistant. Water can be scarce, forcing certain islands to purchase water from others, practice water conservation, collect rainwater, and grow fewer crops. Coral islands have naturally protected harbors and superb white sand beaches, attracting trade and tourism. The artificial environments surrounding the major resorts are the exception, not the rule.

Luxuriant tropical vegetation and steep mountainous terrain are found only on those islands formed by volcanic eruption, such as Dominica, St. Lucia, St. Kitts and Nevis. Volcanic fumaroles are nature's pipelines, transporting water and minerals from the depths of the earth to irrigate the craggy slopes of fertile soil. Mist continually clings to the tallest peaks, producing daily rain showers which range from a sprinkle to a deluge. The rain dissipates quickly and dries in the heat of the tropical sun, but it creates the dense rain forests which make up the hothouses of the Caribbean.

Many varieties of plants were imported to the islands by settlers from all parts of the globe, anxious to recreate an atmosphere reminiscent of home. Plants grow so well in the rain forest that they become almost unrecognizable–taller, broader, greener, and producing more abundant fruits. Small garden variety ferns become giant trees, flowering bushes produce a profusion of blossoms, and hothouse plants grow wild here.

Cruisers should plan a hike into the rain forest on at least one of the volcanic islands, arranging for a guide who knows the pathways and can explain the plants encountered along the route. To truly appreciate the rain forest, you should discover the primeval atmosphere within its deepest parts, where you might hear the song of tree frogs, taste the pure spring water, and swim in a pool beneath a cascading waterfall. For any such excursion, wear lightweight clothing that dries quickly, old tennis shoes or stable walking shoes, and bring a hat rather than an umbrella for the occasional rain shower. After all, if it doesn't rain in the rain forest, you've been cheated.

Poisonous Plants:
Although snakes have been exterminated by the "mighty mongoose," the islands are not entirely benign. Ask the guide on an island tour to point out a manchaneel tree and stinging nettle, two plants to be avoided. The manchaneel tree produces a very poisonous green fruit the size of a small apple. A bite of the fruit will certainly hospitalize, and very likely kill its victim. The Carib Indians used the manchaneel to poison war arrows, and may be responsible for the tree's introduction to the islands. Even the sap or rain dripping from the leaves of the manchaneel can cause painful blisters.

The stinging nettle plant is more harmful than its cousin in the United States and Europe. Touching the nettle's hairy leaves can create an irritating rash which will last for days and put a damper on any vacation. Visitors may never encounter these plants, but you should exercise caution when wandering through the tropical vegetation.

Island Coastlines:
Waters encircling volcanic and coral islands contain many of the same fish, but the ocean plant life differs vastly. The volcanic islands produce soft corals, sponges and sea fans that gently wave in the current, while underwater pinnacles formed by the volcanoes soar hundreds of feet from the sea floor. The terrain can be as exotic under the water as it is on top.

The waters around coral islands contain magnificent staghorn and brain corals which take thousands of years to grow. Scuba divers and snorkelers should remember that corals, sponges, and sea fans are easily damaged by a careless kick from a diver's fin or by touching them with bare, acidic skin. Most islands have prohibitions against taking anything from the sea bottom, so divers and snorkelers are urged to be careful and leave the ocean floor as they found it for the pleasure of future divers. Diving can be an exciting experience on either type of island when led by an expert who knows the reefs.

Avoid touching bright orange fire corals or patches of orange or red growing on rocks and coral with your bare skin, and do not pick up or touch feathery looking fire worms. The defensive mechanisms which nature supplied such harmless looking creatures can cause a painful rash or blisters, leaving the unwary diver in severe pain.

Beaches:
Beaches on volcanic islands often consist of dark volcanic sand rather than the sparkling white sand associated with coral islands. "Coral" sand is amazingly cool to the touch as it consists of millions of particles of pulverized coral. The parrot fish, a multi-colored fish with a nose like a parrot's beak, is responsible for the sand, producing up to two tons of sand each year per fish. The parrot fish eats tiny polyps which are the living part of coral and at the same time crunches pieces of indigestible hard coral skeleton. The residue left after digestion is white sand.

Caribbean History:
An announcer on a "booze cruise" in Grenada summed up Caribbean history in this way: "The Arawak Indians found Grenada, liked it and settled in, but the Carib Indians came and kicked them out. Then the Spanish came and kicked the Caribs out, and the British came and kicked the Spanish out. When the Cubans came they kicked everyone out, so the Americans came and kicked the Cubans out. Now we welcome the Americans to our beautiful little island." With some variations, his explanation applies to all the islands of the Caribbean.

Relics from the first inhabitants of the Caribbean indicate the ancient Ciboney Indian tribes moved up the island chain from South America as early as 3485 B.C. Later the Arawak Indians, an agricultural tribe from South America, arrived, striving to escape their enemies, the fierce Caribs. But the Carib Indians pursued the Arawaks and, when Columbus began exploring the islands on his second voyage in 1493, the Caribs were the dominant tribe on many of the islands.

The Spanish claimed all the islands of the Caribbean, whether they had set foot on them or not. They concentrated their efforts in gathering gold and treasure from the New World, so those islands with little treasure attracted less attention. The Spanish quickly wiped out the remaining Arawaks, but when they used the same tactics on the Caribs, the Indians fought back and successfully repelled the Spanish on some islands.

By the 1600's other European countries were lured by the prospect of wealth, and established settlements and ownership claims in the Caribbean. During the next 200 years, Europeans played "settlement ping pong," where islands seemingly changed flags to appease passing warships. The French, Spanish, and British were the major players, leaving the Dutch, Danish, and Germans to slip in wherever they could.

Few settlers dreamed of making the islands their home; instead they planned on staying long enough to become wealthy, before returning to Europe. But the sugar trade changed the settlement picture. Sugar became the "white gold" of the Caribbean and, to grow sugar cane profitably, large land areas needed to be cultivated with cheap labor supplied by slaves. Establishment of plantations made settlements in the islands more permanent. The European owners built grand homes in European styles, planted formal gardens and fashioned European-style communities within the islands. Slaves on the plantations occupied housing designed to be easily moved from place to place. Later these wooden "chattel houses" became the only property slaves owned. (See Chattel House Village, Barbados.)

Sugar prosperity ended in the early 1800's, when northern sugar beet production was perfected and began to compete with island-grown sugar cane. Finally, the emancipation of slaves marked the death of the sugar cane industry as a whole. Most islands freed their slaves well before the United States, and former slaves became the basis for the majority of the population. Today individual islands celebrate Emancipation Day with festivals, often expanding into several days of Carnival, with jubilant dancing, parades, and calypso music.

Sugar cane is currently produced on just a few Caribbean islands, but it is an important ingredient in rum production, which thrives on many islands. Volcanic islands with rich soil and a good water supply may depend on agriculture for a majority of their national product, but tourism is quickly becoming the number one industry in the Caribbean as a whole. Less developed islands are recognizing the need to attract tourists, and are studying the preferred ways to utilize resources without destroying their land and culture.

New cruise ports have been built, or are in the planning stages, to provide special docking facilities for cruise ships on many of the islands. Island ports of call are offering more duty-free items from year to year, and are improving tourist attractions. Restored sugar mills have been incorporated into hotels and restaurant buildings, while ruins of windmill towers dot the landscape, creating an atmosphere of romance and nostalgia. Rain forests are protected by conservationist governments, while guided tours into the primeval atmosphere stimulate the sense of adventure and excitement for city dwellers on vacation. Artificial reefs are created by intentionally sinking old ships, and laws protect fragile coral and sealife, encouraging scuba diving and snorkeling enthusiasts.

As the cruise industry expands, introducing new ships and more options for the tourist, new island adventures and attractions emerge. Repeat cruisers may see an island they have already visited in a different way, and islands which were previously inaccessible may emerge as exceptional new tropical destinations.

Language:
A close relationship exists between England, Canada, America, and the Caribbean islands. The official language on most islands is English and, even where it is not, many islanders learn English as a second language to accommodate the tourists. American passengers have no difficulty bargaining or asking directions in English, though, when visiting French islands such as Martinique or Guadeloupe, you may wish to use a pocket language guide to assist with basic communication.

Creole, also called Patois, is a West Indian slang spoken among the locals on each island. The dialect changes from island to island, and sometimes from village to village on the same island, but the basic slang is understood all over the Caribbean. The language blends French, English, Dutch, African and West Indian words which are spoken in a lilting, musical manner unique to the islands.

Holidays:
The Windward and Leeward islands are made up of separate countries which celebrate their own unique island holidays, including Independence Day, Emancipation Day, and special days or weeks set aside for Carnival. Standard international holidays such as New Year's Day, Christmas, and Boxing Day (the day after Christmas) are celebrated on the islands as well.

When cruise ships arrive in port on a holiday, most often a few stores will be open for shopping. Even if stores close on a holiday, the beaches remain open to visitors and taxi drivers are available to transport passengers around the island for sightseeing or exploring. If shopping or visiting a particular museum on an island is important to you, plan ahead and check the island's special holidays before booking a cruise date. A listing of basic holidays is included in the chapter for each island. Dates given are for 1994. Keep in mind that these dates will often change from year to year. If a holiday falls on a weekend, banks, museums, and government offices may close on the Monday or Friday.

The Pier

Each island has a unique pier to accommodate commercial vessels, or has specially designed terminals for cruise ships. Some have narrow wooden piers stretching out from land to meet ships, while others have cement docking areas next to town where ships can pull alongside allowing easy disembarkation. Occasionally ships anchor in the harbor and tender passengers by small motorized boats from the ship to the dock.

Piers may have a variety of amenities including shopping, telephones, island information centers, and taxi stations. Each island chapter outlines the specific facilities at the pier, with tips on the walking distance to town, and special amenities found at the pier or port area.

Pier Phones:
Cruise ship ports are designed to accommodate the needs of passengers by offering phones for local or U.S. calls. Calling Stations are offices where travelers can make long distance calls from private booths, but these are only available in the larger ports. These calls can be paid in cash, traveler's checks, or can be charged to a credit card.

AT&T has a long distance service for their cardholders called "U.S.A. Direct." This service is available on clearly marked telephones, or by dialing a special number from regular pay phones. Some islands also have a PhoneCard system where the caller can purchase a phonecard in the island's currency for $10, $20, or $40 worth of long distance time. As the card is used, the dollar amount of the call is electronically subtracted from the value of the card until it becomes void. These colorful cards are available at the cruise terminals, and make a good souvenir when you finished with the call. The PhoneCard machines are clearly identified, and instructions for placing a call are printed directly on the telephone. Be aware that it costs between $2 and $5 just to place a call to the U.S., so purchase a card with sufficient credit and plan your calls accordingly.

Calls made from the islands become more expensive as you travel further south, and become very expensive in the French islands. The location of phones for cruise passengers and the types of phone systems available are covered in the chapters that follow.

In Town, Shopping

Currency:
Due to the large number of American tourists visiting the Caribbean each year, many stores, restaurants, and taxi drivers accept and return change in U.S. currency. However, some islands will only give you change in their own currency, so carry only small amounts of U.S. currency unless you want to end up with a pocketful of foreign currency in change. You can change excess foreign currency to U.S. dollars at banks and international airports, but foreign coins are not usually accepted. It can be advantageous to use credit cards for most expenses as the card companies offer the best exchange rates.

To avoid carrying cash on vacation, read the fine print in your cruise ship brochure concerning the policies for cashing traveler's checks, personal checks, or obtaining cash advances on credit cards. Most ships have limited cash resources, but ban'.s in the larger ports of call can accommodate passengers. In an emergency, casinos often have credit card machines where you can secure a cash advance. Remember to set aside sufficient cash to tip shipboard personnel at the end of the trip.

Cruise ships often have safety deposit boxes available for passengers to store personal valuables, credit cards, traveler's checks, and extra cash. When leaving cameras, jewelry, and cash in the stateroom, store them in a drawer, closet, or simply out of sight. Cabin stewards and other ship's personnel value their jobs, and can generally be trusted to protect personal items left in a stateroom. Avoid leaving jewelry in an ash tray, under trash on a counter, or in the bathroom. Busy cabin stewards dump trash and tidy rooms very quickly, and may not notice a stray piece of jewelry in an odd location.

To avoid attracting the attention of thieves while exploring on land, don't wear excessive jewelry or carry expensive cameras. Carry small bills to pay for taxis, and take only one credit card and a few traveler's checks for island shopping. Taking precautions eliminates risks and ensures the peace of mind necessary to enjoy a vacation.

Individual island chapters that follows contain currency information, approximate exchange rates, the location of banks and their banking hours. Antigua, Barbados, St. Kitts, Nevis, Dominica, and Grenada all accept Eastern Caribbean (E.C.) currency, so any change received in E.C. on one island should be saved for the next island.

Postage:
St. Thomas and Puerto Rico are the only islands that are part of the U.S. postal system and so permit you to mail postcards or letters with U.S. postage. Elsewhere you need to purchase island stamps.

As a convenience, stamps are often available at the Purser's Office or Information Desk on cruise ships. If you want to purchase your own stamps you can find the location of post offices and the price of postcard stamps in each island chapter. Stamp collectors should not miss the Philatelic Bureaus on islands such as Dominica and Grenada.

Historical Walking Tour, Museums & Historical Sites:
On the islands of Puerto Rico, St. Thomas, and Grenada historical walking tours are outlined and accompanied by maps. Other island chapters provide information about significant buildings, forts, and museums worth seeing, although some may require a taxi for transportation to the site.

Shopping:
The allure of buying jewelry, china, and a myriad of foreign goods at half the cost of home has caused many husbands to spend their vacations lugging shopping bags through store after store behind wide-eyed wives waiving credit cards at every clerk. An exaggeration, perhaps, but the phenomenon of duty-free shopping has created an entirely new industry in the islands.

What does duty-free really mean? Simply stated, import taxes (duty) normally added to the price on foreign goods, are waived. Some islands waive the duty only for tourists and require identification when purchasing goods; therefore, you need to carry your ship's boarding pass, passport, or driver's license while shopping on these islands. In each chapter, information about the duty-free shopping area and how to ensure a duty-free price is supplied.

The amount of savings "duty-free shopping" provides the buyer depends on the amount of duty charged at home; but do any of us know how much that really is? Smart shoppers will do some research at home before the cruise, and jot down prices of specific items they wish to buy. Another place to compare prices is at shops in the embarkation port of Puerto Rico, where many ships leave and return. Puerto Rico is an American port, but offers duty-free items. Knowing you will return to Puerto Rico at the end of your cruise, you can bargain for the best price on an item while in the other islands.

Good buys still exist in the islands, but do not assume everything bought in the islands is a bargain. Ask where the merchandise was manufactured. If the answer is the United States, then the item is cheaper at home. If the merchandise was manufactured in Europe or Japan, there may be a great saving over U.S. prices. The very best buys are on goods actually made on the island, so stores offering such products are listed in each chapter.

Here are some suggestions to prepare you for a successful shopping adventure:

- Make a list of specific items you want to buy, and establish a maximum price range. Having an established price limit makes bargaining easier.
- Visit shops at home and write down prices of name-brand merchandise you expect to find in the Caribbean. This may be

the most valuable time you spend before your trip, and will give you confidence when bargaining.

- Ask a jeweler at home to weigh a gold necklace or bracelet and compute the price per gram of gold. He may also be able to give you some great tips on looking for quality gemstones. Unset stones purchased in the Caribbean are not added to your U.S. duty allotment, and your local jeweler can mount them in a setting when you return home.
- When entering a specialty store in the islands selling watches, T-shirts, jewelry, souvenirs or liquor, look for items on your list first. This narrows your focus, so you will not feel over-whelmed by the abundance of merchandise.
- Some jewelry stores display chains on the wall by style, length and price. If you want a 10-inch diamond cut chain, ask to see those styles first. Why waste time looking at all the other chains?
- On the larger islands, visit major stores like Colombian Emer-alds and Little Switzerland first to get a sense of their quality and prices. These stores have a set discount with no bargaining, so you will know the top price range when bargaining in other shops. Smaller stores often carry the older styles in namebrand watches, crystal or ceramics, while the major stores carry the newest models available. (See Major Duty-Free Stores)
- Buy film, batteries, bug repellent, sunscreen products, medica-tions, and hair care products at home. These are all much more expensive in the islands.

Shops Featured In Each Chapter:
Shopping can be tedious if the same merchandise is repeated from store to store and island to island. In an effort to provide informa-tion not generally found in every guidebook, the shopping section of each chapter emphasizes shops which carry island-made prod-ucts or unique items.

When jewelry stores are specifically listed, the stores have spe-cially designed pieces, and often repair and make their own jew-elry on the premises. The shops listed in each chapter are accessible by walking or taking a short taxi ride from the pier. Exceptional shopping opportunities out on the island are described in a sepa-rate section for passengers using a taxi or rental car to explore.

Many small shops covered in the chapters will not be on the ship's list of stores, because small shops cannot afford to pay for the listing. However, smaller stores may actually offer better prices due to their lower overhead. Cruise passengers should not assume that shopping is ONLY good on Puerto Rico, St. Thomas and St. Maarten. Prices can be quite reasonable on the smaller islands where the shopping may prove to be more pleasant than on islands crowded with ship passengers. Following is a list of best buys for specific islands:

Best Buys:
- *Gold:* St. Thomas and St. Maarten
- *Watches:* St. Thomas and St. Maarten
- *Electronics & cameras:* St. Maarten
- *Tablecloths and linens:* St. Kitts, St. Thomas and St. Maarten
- *Silver & coral jewelry:* St. Kitts and Antigua
- *Batik clothing:* St. Kitts and St. Lucia
- *Coconut soap products:* Dominica
- *Imported perfumes & cosmetics:* Martinique, Guadeloupe, and French St. Martin
- *Island made perfume:* Grenada and St. Lucia
- *Spices:* Grenada
- *Handicrafts:* Barbados and Dominica
- *Crystal & china:* St. Thomas, St. Maarten, and Barbados
- *Handmade clothing:* St. Maarten, St. Lucia, and St. Kitts
- *Straw mats & baskets:* Dominica
- *Jams & jellies:* Dominica, Antigua, and Grenada
- *Passion fruit products:* Dominica
- *Rum:* Every island has its own brand of rum at very tempting prices so do some tasting before you buy.

Whenever possible, buy souvenirs from locals because it often supports a family's livelihood. T-shirts and carved coconuts are among the many souvenirs available on every island from local vendors. On Antigua island ladies string beaded necklaces and offer them to tourists at negotiable prices, often a great bargain. On Grenada spice baskets are assembled by locals and sold on the streets and at tourist attractions. The baskets make excellent gifts at very reasonable prices.

In each chapter unique shops are starred (***). These shops offer products not sold elsewhere, have a high quality of artistry, or an atmosphere that must be experienced. It was a pleasure to discover these unique stores, so be sure not to miss the following:

- The Butterfly People in Old San Juan, Puerto Rico.
- Mango Tango in St. Thomas.

- Eudovics, a master wood sculptor in St. Lucia.
- Merceline's, with white lace clothing in St. Maarten.
- The Goldsmitty in Antigua.
- Pelican Village, a craft village in Barbados.
- Caribelle Batik factories on St. Kitts and St. Lucia.
- Passman's black coral sculptures in St. Thomas.

Bargaining Tips:
Bargaining is a purchasing ritual in the islands, whether passengers are shopping for gold chains, or a palm-frond hat. Shop keepers selling products such as watches, gold jewelry, and local crafts expect to bargain, and usually price their items higher in order to have room to negotiate. However, many stores price their items with no intention of bargaining to avoid the embarrassment of haggling.

To begin a bargaining session ask the merchant if he gives discounts to cruise ship passengers; if he agrees to an initial discount, then begin to bargain. Passengers unwilling to play the bargaining game should ask the merchant for his lowest price and be prepared to go to the next store if the price is not acceptable. The same item may be offered at a better price down the street.

When shopping for gold chains and bracelets, have the salesperson weigh the item, compute the cost per gram, and then negotiate to the store's lowest price. Write the quote down on a store business card, then repeat the same process in several other shops until the best price for the item is discovered.

Prices are often quoted in both the island's currency and in U.S. dollars. If only one price is given, ask which currency is quoted before bargaining. Stores usually accept traveler's checks and credit cards for purchases, but better bargains may be had for cash. Jewelry stores in particular may quote one price for credit cards and another for cash sales. However, credit card companies often offer their customers a better exchange rate, so the difference in price may be offset. Depending upon your cash situation and the value of the item, it is often better to pay with credit cards or traveler's checks, saving your cash for taxis and tips. In either case, be sure to get a receipt for customs.

Guaranteed Stores:
Passengers should ask their Cruise Director or Purser's Office for a list of "Guaranteed Stores" on the islands before shopping. Guar-

anteed stores have a special arrangement with the cruise line to guarantee merchandise against defects through the duration of the cruise. If the item (such as a ring) breaks due to a defect, or the passenger discovers a defect in the product during the remainder of the cruise, the passenger may return the item to the guaranteed store via the Cruise Director. Once the Cruise Director has returned the item, the passenger will receive a replacement item or a refund of the purchase price. The arrangement between the Cruise Director and guaranteed store may differ slightly from ship to ship, but passengers receive extra protection when buying merchandise at a "guaranteed store."

Major Duty-Free Stores:
The following chain stores are located in the major port areas, and have virtually the same prices from port to port:

- **LITTLE SWITZERLAND** can be found in St. Thomas, St. Maarten, Antigua, St. Kitts, and St. Lucia. This chain of stores is renowned for china, crystal, Swiss precision watches, imported fragrances, and a large selection of fine jewelry, including designer pieces. Every shop is designed with elegance in mind, using rosewood display cases, Swiss lighting fixtures, wide shopping aisles, and air-conditioning. The staff is always expertly trained and often multi-lingual. Little Switzerland is the authorized distributor for Rolex Watches on the islands where its stores are located. Ask for a Caribbean price list for Rolex to discover the great savings.
- **COLOMBIAN EMERALDS** has stores on the islands of St. Thomas, St. Maarten, Antigua, and St. Lucia. In ancient times, the emerald was believed to impart mystical insight to its wearer, and the green color was a symbol of immortality. Today emeralds can be more expensive than fine diamonds, and over 90% of the world's emeralds are produced in Colombia. From collector quality to the finest investment quality, Colombian Emeralds brings stones direct from the mines and cutters to the buyer. All merchandise is guaranteed, and Colombian Emeralds has a service office in Miami. Other gemstones, jewelry, and the newest styles in designer watches are also offered.

Outlet Stores:
Manufacturers and designers with a name to sell are earning greater profits by opening stores in outlet malls across America. With duty-free status, the Caribbean has always been a favorite of

outlet stores, and the name-brand outlets can offer bargains which may astound their name-dropping customers. The following outlet stores are found on various islands:

- **BENETTON**, the international Italian fashion line made from natural fibers, sells classics in linen, cotton, and winter wools in coordinated colors and designs. Everything from sweaters, scarves, swimwear, lingerie and accessories in the newest designs can be found in their stores in Antigua, St. Thomas, St. Maarten, and Puerto Rico.
- **GUCCI**, a world famous name in distinctive handbags, luggage, scarves, and accessories, has outlets on St. Thomas, St. Maarten, Antigua, and Puerto Rico.
- **POLO/RALPH LAUREN** offers a broad selection of men's and women's casual clothing and accessories from the famous designer. Stores are located in St. Maarten, and Puerto Rico.
- **LAND** leather products, handbags, belts, wallets, luggage has an outlet in Antigua, and Land products can also be found in duty-free stores on other islands.

Customs Regulations:
Duty-free merchandise is only free of duty imposed by the country where the goods are purchased. Foreign made electronics, jewelry, alcohol, cigarettes, linens and perfumes may be subject to a U.S. duty when returning home. Before leaving on a cruise, travelers should be aware of the duty regulations, and take care to keep sales slips and record all purchases on their declaration to customs if they exceed duty restrictions.

To receive specific information and updated regulations, contact U.S. Customs Service, P.O. Box 7407, Washington, DC 20229 for a pamphlet entitled "Know Before You Go" which will answer specific questions.

The following explanations are based on the "Know Before You Go" pamphlet:

- U.S. Customs allows passengers $400 worth of duty-free items for personal use or gifts from a foreign country, 1 liter of alcohol (for family members over 21 years old), and 200 cigarettes (one carton) per person during any 30-day period. Purchases over the limit may be subject to a 10% duty tax upon clearing U.S. customs. (See following chart and examples) Gifts not exceeding a value of $50 per day, may be sent to friends and relatives in the U.S. from foreign ports.

- Family members traveling together are allowed to combine their duty allotments (except for liquor allowances if children are under 21 years of age).
- Items purchased from "Beneficiary Countries" have an increased duty allotment of $600 per person, but the $400 maximum for other foreign countries must be included in this total. (See following chart and examples.)
- When visiting the U.S. Virgin Islands the duty allotment is increased to $1200 per person plus one extra bottle of liquor if it is made in the U.S. Virgin Islands, and an extra 800 (5 cartons) cigarettes only when purchased in the U.S. Virgin Islands. Passengers who purchase merchandise in the U.S. Virgin Islands as well as other foreign ports must deduct the amount purchased in the other ports, not exceeding $600 (including on-board purchases) from the total $1200 allowed from the U.S. Virgin Islands. (See following chart and examples.)
- The duty for purchases over the limit on items purchased in the U.S. Virgin Island is taxed at a flat rate of 5% instead of 10% for items purchased over the limit on other islands. Friends and relatives may receive gifts sent from the U.S. Virgin Islands with a value of $100 per day free of duty.

The chart below shows the maximum U.S. Customs allotment for items purchased on the specific islands covered in this book:

Country	Maximum Allotment
Antigua & Barbuda	$600
Barbados	$600
Dominica	$600
Grenada	$600
Guadeloupe	$400
Martinique	$400
Puerto Rico (U.S.)	no limit
St. Kitts & Nevis	$600
Saint Lucia	$600
St. Maarten	$400
St. Thomas	$1,200
On board ship	$400

- Items actually made in the U.S. Virgin Islands, including jewelry, are considered duty-free when returning to the U.S.

- Unset gemstones are not generally considered part of the U.S. Customs allotment upon re-entry to the United States. (Large purchases of stones may be considered commercial use and become taxable.)
- Purchases made in Puerto Rico are duty-free and not added to other purchase allotments due to Puerto Rico's status as an American Commonwealth.
- Items made from endangered species such as tortoise shell jewelry, ivory products except antiques, and certain skins, feathers, eggs, and furs are prohibited from being imported into the United States. State laws may further prohibit importation of products made from certain animals, so check the individual state regulations.
- Food products (except bakery items and cured cheeses) are only allowed if canned or sealed by the manufacturer. Fruits, vegetables, plants, plant cuttings, seeds, and unprocessed plant products are prohibited. Drugs, and drug paraphernalia are prohibited; firearms and ammunition are subject to restrictions and permits.

U.S. Customs Tips:
Customs regulations may seem difficult to understand, but cruise passengers traveling to the Caribbean rarely exceed the duty restrictions. Passengers who do not purchase watches, jewelry, cigarettes or alcohol in large quantities usually do not exceed duty limitations. If you visit St. Thomas and other islands, an easy rule of thumb is not to exceed $800 per person on St. Thomas, and $400 on all the other islands combined with on-board purchases.

When packing island purchases, do not pack alcohol bottles in your luggage to avoid custom officials. Passenger luggage is handled quite roughly; the bottles can easily break and ruin your clothes. On the customs declaration form, declare the total amount of purchases made in the islands and the ship, and only list the purchased items if they exceed the island restrictions. Have this card filled out before reaching the custom officials to save time. If an official asks to open your luggage, do not hesitate; be honest and helpful to avoid costly customs penalties.

Transportation

Taxis are eagerly awaiting ship passengers at every island. The majority of vehicles used as taxis are mini-vans, but some independent taxi drivers use large passenger vans or standard four-door cars. Mini-vans are preferred for sightseeing, and are more comfortable than cramming into smaller cars. American tourists may have to cope with the strange feeling of driving on the left-hand side of the road on many of the islands.

Taxi drivers taking passengers into town for shopping, or out on the island for sightseeing and beach combing, may wait to fill up their vans with passengers before departing. Therefore, you will need to allow more time and have patience with the "islanders way of doing things." Taxi drivers, as a whole, are not out to cheat the "one-day visitor." When bargaining or asking for a taxi fare, do not approach the driver with a defensive attitude or assume he will try to gouge you. Most islands have established rates for trips around the island, and drivers are required to follow their Taxi Association's rate guidelines. The drivers are just making a living, and are not out to hustle the typical tourist. Be cautious, but not paranoid; most island drivers enjoy meeting new people and showing off their island.

Each island chapter gives specific taxi information including a Taxi Chart with current rates, tips for bargaining with drivers, and the time needed to reach island attractions. Taxi guidelines fluctuate from one island to the next, but you can usually negotiate lower rates when the group consists of at least four people. As most taxis are mini-vans capable of handling more than four, the more passengers in a group for island excursions, a ride to the beach, or a quick trip to town, the better the deal for everyone.

If your group arranges a round-trip discounted rate with one driver, it is recommended that you pay the entire amount at the end of the trip to ensure the same driver will come back for the return trip. Do not cheat by taking another driver back to the ship, which may cause problems with the taxi association, cruise port officials, and could be a legitimate cause for your arrest. Cruise passengers who take advantage of taxi drivers are illegally stealing a fare from the driver, but their actions also increase taxi rates and discourage drivers from wanting to help passengers visit the island.

Local Buses:
The bus systems on the islands as a whole are not highly recommended for cruise passengers who need to get around quickly. Local buses may be inexpensive, but you will probably not want

to put up with the delays and crowded conditions that often are part of bus travel in the islands.

Rental Cars:
Renting cars on the islands is an adventurous way to get out and explore the terrain. However, on a majority of the islands the road conditions leave a lot to be desired!! Some roads have potholes large enough to swallow a small car, and others are so steep and winding that even locals are extremely cautious when driving. Unless you are proficient at driving on both the left and right sides of the road, and can remember which side to stay on when faced with a tight situation, driving in the islands may prove difficult. A rental car may enhance your experience on some islands, and cause only problems on others. Each chapter discusses the advantages and perils of renting a car on the particular island.

Rental agencies usually require a credit card to cover a damage deposit, and a valid driver's license. On some islands, visitors must also acquire a temporary island license which rental agencies will help to purchase. In every case, purchasing collision insurance is highly advisable in case of an accident. If you are uncomfortable with driving on the left, try riding with a taxi driver first to become comfortable with the feeling before renting a car. Each chapter supplies rental car agency names and phone numbers. Advance reservations will save time when acquiring the car.

Island Excursions & Activities

All tour prices will be quoted in U.S. dollars unless otherwise noted in each island chapter.

The Best Attractions on Each Island:
- Puerto Rico: The Rio Camuy Cave Park
- St. Thomas: Watersports, Coral World Underwater Park and Observatory, sailing trip to St. John
- St. Maarten: Beaches!!, side trip to Anguilla
- Antigua: Lord Nelson's Dockyard, resort beaches!
- St. Kitts: Island tour (to fall in love with the island), trip to Nevis for plantation houses and old mills
- Guadeloupe: Waterfall hike, scuba diving at Pigeon Island
- Dominica: Waterfalls!!! and rain forest, scuba diving with Dive Dominica
- Martinique: Trip to St. Pierre and Mont Pelée

- St. Lucia: Scuba diving at Anse Chastanet, visit to the drive-in volcano
- Barbados: Beaches!!, Barbados Wildlife Monkey Reserve, Atlantis submarine
- Grenada: Botanical Gardens, La Sagesse Resort's private cove

Contact the Shore Excursion Office on your ship if you are interested in taking an island tour, snorkel trip, or boat excursion. If you prefer to adventure on their own, read the three sections on excursions and activities before planning your activity.

Most new cruise passengers are afraid to venture out on the islands without a tour group for fear they will get lost or miss the ship. Time tables for distances to specific locations, and recommendations for taxi fares and rental cars are provided, allowing you to explore safely and spend your time efficiently.

Beaches

Beaches are one of the most popular destinations for ship passengers, but there are important factors to consider before heading off to the beach. Most beaches in the Caribbean are open to the public, so you are welcome to explore them at will. Locals roam the beaches of many islands, offering to braid your hair or sell you everything from seashells to aloe vera plants for sunburn. They are usually harmless, but if you are annoyed by their approach a firm NO will usually send them on their way.

Many resorts on the islands have beautiful beaches, changing facilities and beach-side restaurants. If you are interested in a beach offering comfortable facilities within walking distance, choose a beach-side resort. But remember you are at a resort; conduct yourself as if you were a hotel guests and not "tacky tourists." Hotels are glad for cruise passengers to use their facilities if they act appropriately and patronize the bar or restaurant.

Each chapter contains a beach chart illustrating the individual sports and facilities available at each beach as an easy, quick reference.

When spending time at any beach, avoid bringing cameras or other valuable personal belongings. Locker facilities are not usually available, and valuables left on the beach may encourage theft. To avoid problems while at the beach, purchase a "beach safe," a small waterproof cylinder that hangs around the neck to protect cash and cabin keys. Another popular item is a disposable camera for those who don't want to bring an expensive camera to the beach. Both items are relatively inexpensive, and found in stores across the U.S.

Bring along bug repellent spray when heading off to the beach. Many of the islands have sand fleas or small biting bugs that will ruin a day outdoors if you aren't properly prepared. A small can of repellent can be quite expensive in the islands, so buy a brand of 100% DEET repellent before the cruise!

One last factor to consider is the intense Caribbean sun. Suntan lotion in the islands is much higher priced than in U.S. stores, so buy a supply before the trip. Choose a sunscreen protection level higher than you normally use to counteract the strong sun.

Island & Ocean Sports

All rates for island and ocean sports will be quoted in U.S. dollars unless otherwise noted in each island chapter.

Caribbean islands offer a wide variety of sports for cruise passengers. Ocean sports such as windsurfing, water-skiing, diving, and snorkeling are among the most popular, and can be found at public beaches around the islands. Golf, tennis, and horseback riding are among the activities available on many of the larger islands. The information supplied in the Island and Ocean Sports Section combined with the Beach Section, including the Beach Chart for quick reference, should answer questions concerning prices, availability, and island location.

Certified scuba divers will find numerous diving operations in the islands. If you are not certified but interested in diving, contact the ship Shore Excursion Office for available beginner scuba lessons. St. Thomas, Dominica, St. Lucia, and Antigua have quality dive operators who also offer introductory courses for first-time divers—perfect for cruise passengers who want to try the sport.

If you are interested in special activities like scuba diving or horseback riding, call ahead to reserve the activity. Phone numbers are available throughout each chapter and you can contact the operators themselves, or have your travel agent arrange the activity.

Tour operators try to work with last minute requests from ship passengers, but advance reservations are highly recommended.

"One-Day" Itineraries

Based on my experiences exploring the islands, I have created "One-Day" Itineraries which outline a full day's activities and sites to visit on each island. The itinerary will usually take between six and seven hours to complete. You may follow the directions step by step, or use the section as a reference guide when planning your own itinerary. If your port time is shorter, condense the itinerary by eliminating one or two parts to fit your particular port schedule.

How to Avoid Disappointment When Booking a Cruise

"Throughout my experience working as a purser, the majority of problems were the result of misleading information, or the lack of information supplied to passengers by travel agents. This section may help you avoid problem areas common to cruise passengers."

Once you have made the decision to take a cruise, the next step is to locate a qualified travel agent to help you select the type of cruise that is right for you and your pocketbook. It is important to find a qualified agent, knowledgeable about the cruise industry, who has a reputation for booking successful cruises.

One of the best places to find travel agencies specializing in cruises is the Travel Section of any major city newspaper or in the phonebook. Friends or family members who have recently booked a cruise can be an even better source. Speak with an agent in person, rather than only on the phone. A personal visit to the agent's office will help you to judge the professional quality of the establishment.

Travel agencies provide customers with various cruise line brochures, but you should first decide where you want to go, then select the appropriate cruise line. It is also important to read the fine print in the back of the brochures containing vital information that could affect the cruise. Information such as luggage insurance, cashing personal checks on board, and liability limitations of the cruise line can all be critical factors when selecting a cruise line.

Staterooms:

When choosing a stateroom on the ship's layout, remember that staterooms vary in many ways. Cabins either have two twin beds that may convert into one, or one standard queen or king-sized bed. The age of the ship may also contribute to the comfort of the rooms, type of beds available, and the overall condition of the cabins. Newer ships have far fewer problems with their rooms, although older ships have a certain style that is lacking in the new "megaships." Fortunately cruise lines have learned from their design mistakes over the years, and most of the newer ships have standard cabins with two twin beds that convert into one. Older ships have a smaller percentage of cabins with queen-sized beds and twin beds that convert into one, but these ships may visit more ports of call to encourage bookings. Specialized cruise lines such as Seabourne and Renaissance tend to have larger staterooms equipped with standard queen-sized beds, if you are willing to pay the price.

Cabin Layout:

The cabin layout is different with every ship and individual cabin category, so once you have selected a cruise ship, you should carefully study the cabin arrangements in the brochure. If you are concerned about booking a cabin that suits specific needs, the travel agent can make the necessary arrangements. For example:

- Some Veranda categories or outside cabins may have obstructed views due to the ship's lifeboat locations.
- Avoid cabins below the main entertainment deck or lounges as the sound may transmit into the cabin.
- To avoid seasickness, choose a cabin mid-ship, which will reduce the motion of the ocean.
- Passengers who suffer from claustrophobia should select a cabin with an outside window, but be sure to tell the travel agent to specify the medical problem when making the reservation.
- Honeymooners or anniversary couples should be aware that most cabins have twin beds which convert into one. However, on many older ships the beds may not convert at all. Have the travel agent request a specific cabin number with beds that convert or with queen-sized bed.
- If the cabin selection is important, request at least three specific cabin numbers from the ship's layout. Have the travel agent specifically request the cabin selections when making the reservation and get confirmation of the cabin number before ar-

riving on the ship. When the tickets arrive, check the cabin numbers assigned. If the new cabin is unsatisfactory, have the travel agent call the cruise line and make the necessary adjustment. If the travel agent cannot secure the cabin reassignment, cancel the reservation! In most cases the cruise will be fully booked and the ship's personnel will not be able to reassign a cabin upon your arrival at the cruise ship, so take precautions to avoid disappointment with the cruise.

Special Rates:
If you are not particularly concerned with the category of the room, its size, or the type of beds, take full advantage of special rates offered by travel agents. Though short notice can save money, cruisers gamble on special rates because such upgrades are not guaranteed.

Travel agents are not employees of the cruise lines and cannot promise special guarantees on cruises. There are no guarantees in the cruise industry, and all cabin specifics such as beds and cabin layout are upon request basis only. All requests are just that, requests. Travelers must decide what is the most important element for their vacation. If the concern is for cabin type or bed configuration, carefully select the cabin number. If lower prices or special deals are most important, be satisfied with the cabin assigned. Once you have made the cruise and cabin selection, the travel agent should submit all the specific requests to the cruise line in writing.

"What time is the midnight buffet?"
All too often weekly cruise passengers board their ship, and seem to ask ship personnel some of the silliest questions. Fortunately, these passengers help to entertain the staff, and provide material for ship comedians like Lewis Nixon, who use their questions in his comedy act. I have collected a few of the funniest questions so that new cruisers reading this book can avoid becoming the new joke among crew staff members.

- The most often asked question directed to crew members is, "Do you actually live on the ship?" Yes, all of the crew members have to live on board to work and serve cruise passengers.
- Shore excursion personnel have reported cruisers asking, "If I go snorkeling, will I get wet?"

- Never ask a ship's engineer, "Does this ship run on generators?" Cruise ships either use turbine steam engines (T.S.S.) or have large motor engines (M.S.) to run the ship.
- "Do these stairs go up or down?" No comment.
- A dining room waiter will die laughing if you ask, "What do you do with the ice carvings after they have melted?"
- If one of your cruises ever reaches the port of Nassau in the Bahamas, think of this lady's story. When a female passenger arrived in Nassau, she asked a crew member on the dock, "Where are all the missiles?" The crew member looked at her strangely and said, "What missiles?" The lady responded, "The missiles, I thought we were going to N.A.S.A.!"
- If a cruiser gets the opportunity to meet the ship's Captain, refrain from asking him, "If you are here, who is driving the ship?" The Captain is asked that question at least 20 times every cruise. The deck officers are the ones who steer the ship, not drive it, and the Captain oversees the docking procedures when arriving or departing each port of call.
- "How long does a 30-minute massage take?"
- The most amusing question was asked at sea, on the water, the ocean, while the ship was moving, "What altitude do you think we're at?" Sea level might be a good guess!

All questions are not necessarily ridiculous, however, so if you have a question don't hesitate to ask a crew staff member.

On a Serious Note:
When you board the cruise ship, please refer to the vessel as a ship, not a boat. Ships carry boats. When exploring the ship, remember the nautical terms for the right and left side of the ship are, respectively, starboard and port. Aft is to the rear of the ship; the stern is the back end.

Boat drills are given on every cruise ship either the day of debarkation or, if the ship departs very late, the drill will be given the next day. Joke around, and have fun with the drill, but when the announcement is played, listen carefully because it is the only time the instructions are given. This information may end up saving your life in case of an emergency.

Puerto Rico
The Enchantment Isle

Island Description:

Puerto Rico went through a series of name changes before receiving its final title. The island was originally called Borinquen by the Taino Indians, meaning the Land of the Nobel Lord. When Columbus landed on his second voyage to the new world in 1493, he renamed the island San Juan Bautista, and the capital port was named Puerto Rico (rich port). At some point in the island's history, the island and the capital switched names. The Spanish, who were primarily interested in gold and treasure, quickly established the largest and oldest Spanish colonial settlement in the Caribbean islands. Although the island's natural supply of gold quickly petered out, the colony thrived, and today Puerto Rico remains rich in Spanish history, tradition, and culture.

Puerto Rico's variety of vegetation, ranging from lush rain forests to fertile lowland meadows and white sand beaches, offers the visitor an opportunity to escape the city's congestion and appreciate Puerto Rico's natural beauty.

Over three and a half million tourists visit Puerto Rico yearly, spurring government and business to commit $350 million to expansion of airports and seaports, and $600 million in construction and renovation of hotels. An additional $2 billion for development of new tourism projects includes a waterfront renewal project for cruise ship terminals and improvements in the city of Old San Juan. Although renovation can be an inconvenience, the new cruise ship terminals and improved tourist attractions in Old San Juan will make Puerto Rico a more enjoyable port of call.

San Juan, the metropolitan capital city is located on Puerto Rico's northern coastline with a population of over 1 million people. Most visitors to the Caribbean pass through San Juan at some point during their journey, because San Juan offers one of the largest international airports and commercial harbors. Cruise ships dock at the great walled city of Old San Juan, situated on a peninsula bordered by San Juan Bay and the Atlantic Ocean. Well-preserved historic sites, museums, churches, fortresses, colonial mansions and plazas are among the unique architectural treasures that led the United Nations to designate Old San Juan as a "World Heritage Site." Due to the size of Puerto Rico, about 3,500 square miles, the outer island takes time to properly explore. If Puerto Rico is your embarkation port, you may wish to plan your travel itinerary to allow for an extra day before or after your cruise to enjoy sightseeing. (See Author's "One-Day" Itinerary for suggested tours.)

The Island People:
The people of Puerto Rico are a blending of Taino Indian, African blacks, mixed with Spanish culture and American idealism. The result is a proud people with a laid-back attitude. Do not expect fast service, even in fast-food restaurants, as everything takes its own time, and island time keeps its own clock.

The national symbol of Puerto Rico is the "coqui," a tiny tree frog whose melodious chirp is often mistaken for a bird's song. This species of tree frog lives only on the island of Puerto Rico. When asked about the coqui, a taxi driver said that the frog is so unique to the island of Puerto Rico that if it were ever taken away from the island it would surely die. He went on to say that the people of Puerto Rico are like the coqui: if they ever left their isle of enchantment, they too would perish.

Language:
Spanish is the predominant language throughout the island although most businesses have English speaking personnel. If you plan to venture out on the island, take a Spanish phrasebook as a reference guide.

Holidays:
Post offices and banks normally close on the holiday itself or, if the holiday falls on a weekend, the nearest Monday or Friday. Holidays and Festivals occur throughout the year, so pick up a copy of *Que Pasa* at the tourist information center for a current calendar of events.

> **January:** 1st–New Years; Jan. 6th–De Hostos Day; 17th–Martin Luther King, Jr. Birthday.
> **February:** 21st–President's Day.
> **March:** 22nd–Emancipation Day.
> **April:** 1st–Good Friday; 3rd–Easter; 20th– Jose De Diego Birthday.
> **May:** Memorial Day.

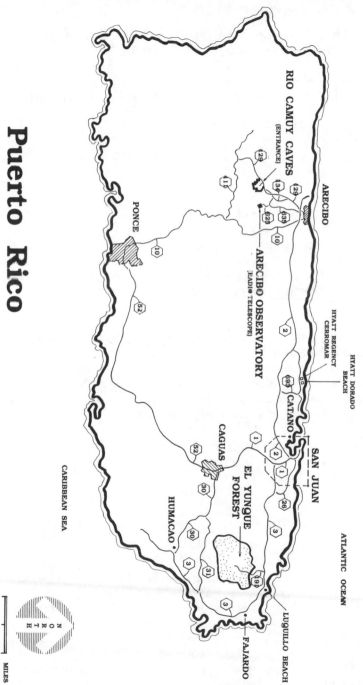

Puerto Rico

July: 4th–U.S. Independence Day; 20th–Muñoz Rivera's Birthday; 25th–Constitution Day; 27th–José Celso Barbosa's Birthday.
September: 5th–Labor Day.
November: 11th–Veteran's Day; 24th–Thanksgiving; 19th–Discovery Day.
December: 25th–Christmas.

The Pier

Cruise ships dock at one of many piers located along Calle Marina in Old San Juan. A costly waterfront renewal project is well underway, creating new, modern, air-conditioned cruise terminals offering phones, gift shops, and customs clearance. Arts and crafts from local artists will be sold across the street from cruise terminal #4 in a newly constructed building by the end of 1993.

Pier Phones:
Every cruise ship terminal building has phones available for cruise passengers; local calls require a 10 cent deposit, other phones allow passengers to make long distance calls. If you want to arrange activities on other islands before you arrive, it is best to make reservation or confirmation calls from Puerto Rico as its rates are by far the cheapest of all the Caribbean Islands

If dockside telephones are busy, a Calling Station is located across the street from cruise terminal #4, and a U.S.A. Direct Calling Station is located on Calle Recinto Sur just across from the U.S. Post Office.

In Town

The entire peninsula comprising Old San Juan is eight blocks across, with the best shopping and historical sites located close to the pier area. A free trolley car runs along Calle Marina with stops at the Tourist Information Plaza, and the center of town. (See map, and look for a yellow sign, "Parada," designating stops on the streets of Old San Juan.) Local vendors are always found in the park at the Tourist Information Plaza, and a sampling of rum can be obtained inside the building.

Currency:
Currency is the U.S. dollar and most establishments accept credit cards and traveler's checks. For emergency cash, casinos often have an ATM machine available, and there is an established bank across the street from the Tourist Information Plaza.

Postage:
The U.S. Post Office is located across from the Tourist Information Plaza, a short walk to the left from any of the piers. (See #A on Historical Walking Tour.) Postal rates are the same as U.S. rates, but do not stock up on extra U.S. postage unless you plan to send mail from St. Thomas. All the other islands are foreign countries issuing their own postage and will not accept mail bearing U.S. postage.

Casinos:
If your ship stays in port after 4 PM, the best locations for gambling can be found at:

Isla Verde–El San Juan Hotel; the Sands Hotel; the Ambassador Plaza Hotel.
Condado–the Condado Plaza Hotel; the Ramada San Juan Hotel.

Blackjack, craps, roulette, slot machines, and video poker are offered at the casinos, though live poker is not available. The larger hotels, the Sands and the Condado Plaza, also have discos for evening dancing and nightly musical shows.

Historical Walking Tour

Old San Juan contains the best examples of 16th and 17th century Spanish colonial architecture in the Caribbean. History buffs will marvel at the fascinating museums, forts, and beautifully restored homes all within walking distance of the port. The best way to explore the city and beat traffic congestion is to walk through Old San Juan's winding cobblestone streets. The following walking tour guides the visitor past historic buildings, museums, and the more interesting shops in Old San Juan. Depending on how long you linger at each stop, the tour should be completed within two to three hours.

A. Begin the walking tour from the cruise ship terminals on Calle Marina. With your back to the water, walk to the left until

Old San Juan

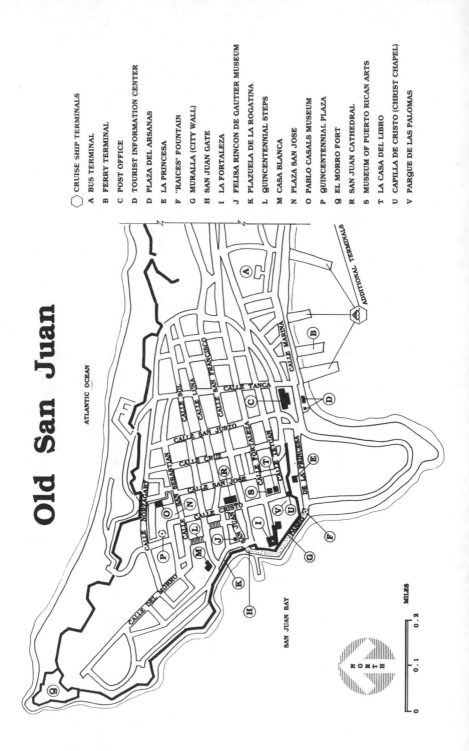

ATLANTIC OCEAN

SAN JUAN BAY

NORTH

MILES
0   0.1   0.2

○ CRUISE SHIP TERMINALS

A BUS TERMINAL

B FERRY TERMINAL

C POST OFFICE

D TOURIST INFORMATION CENTER

D PLAZA DEL ARSANAS

E LA PRINCESA

F "RAICES" FOUNTAIN

G MURALLA (CITY WALL)

H SAN JUAN GATE

I LA FORTALEZA

J FELISA RINCON DE GAUTIER MUSEUM

K PLAZUELA DE LA ROGATINA

L QUINCENTENNIAL STEPS

M CASA BLANCA

N PLAZA SAN JOSE

O PABLO CASALS MUSEUM

P QUINCENTENNIAL PLAZA

9 EL MORRO FORT

R SAN JUAN CATHEDRAL

S MUSEUM OF PUERTO RICAN ARTS

T LA CASA DEL LIBRO

U CAPILLA DE CRISTO (CHRIST CHAPEL)

V PARQUE DE LAS PALOMAS

you reach the **Tourist Information Center** located in a pink building surrounded by a small park, usually filled with local craft vendors. Due to San Juan's refurbishing efforts, some exhibits may be closed or hard to find. Pick up the current copy of *Que Pasa*, and ask the tourist center if any museums are currently closed.

B. Leaving the Tourist Information Center, follow the waterfront to the left past the Plaza de Arsanas (a new bandstand area scheduled to provide open air music events). Walk along the Paseo De La Princesa, a new tree-lined boulevard, past **La Princesa**, a former 19th century prison. The Puerto Rican Tourism headquarters is located within the newly restored La Princesa, as is a changing art exhibit open to the public weekdays 8 AM to 4:30 PM at no charge.

C. The Paseo De La Princesa adjoins an impressive new plaza containing the large bronze fountain entitled "Raices." The **Raices fountain** depicts the origins of Puerto Rico's mixed heritage and symbolizes friendship and a new future. From a distance the ensemble is meant to resemble a ship being steered out to sea with frolicking dolphins leading the way into the 21st century. Using San Juan Bay as a backdrop, the magnificent fountain was designed by architect Miguel Carlo, and finished in May of 1992 to celebrate the New World's 500th birthday.

D. Follow the Paseo De La Princesa to the right along the waterfront. **La Fortaleza**, the governor's mansion is above, supported by the massive **Muralla** (city wall), composed of sandstone blocks up to 20 feet thick. Completed in the late 1700s, the wall surrounds the entire colonial city of Old San Juan, flanked by the El Morro Fort at one end and the San Cristobal Fort at the other.

E. The paseo ends at the **San Juan Gate**, one of six massive doors which for centuries were closed at sundown to cut off access to the city. After passing through the San Juan Gate, you will find a small park on the right which is the waiting area for the guided tours to La Fortaleza, the governor's mansion.

La Fortaleza, built between 1530 and 1540, is the oldest governor's mansion in the western hemisphere. Still used today as the governor's residence, La Fortaleza is only shown by guided tour. Tour times can change so check with the guards to confirm the time of the next tour. Tours are normally conducted on the hour in English, and on the half hour in Spanish weekdays, (except holidays) 9 AM to 4 PM. If you prefer to continue on the walking tour, the route returns to this general area later.

F. Across the street from the San Juan Gate, visit the **Felisa Rincon de Gautier Museum**, the home of San Juan's first female mayor, who held office for 22 years. The museum contains personal memorabilia, an impressive display of awards, keys to hundreds of cities worldwide, and a collection of lace fans (upstairs). Open weekdays except holidays, 9 AM to 4 PM. (no charge).

G. To continue the walking tour climb the stairs next to the San Juan Gate to the top of the city wall. Follow the wall to the right, through **Plazuela de la Rogativa** (small plaza of the religious procession) dedicated to a priest who led a procession of singing women, carrying candles through the streets during the 1797 attack by British troops on El Morro Fort. Supposedly the British saw the candle flames, mistook them for Spanish reinforcements, and retreated.

H. Just past the Plazuela de la Rogativa, turn to look back across the wall (a good place for a picture of La Fortaleza). Continue on the street to the right, Calle Sol, then climb the Quincentennial Steps on the left. At the top of the stairs turn left onto Calle San Sebastian and follow the street to the end. Enter a gate labelled **Casa Blanca** (white house) and follow the garden pathway leading to the house entrance.

I. Although the governor never lived in the home, Casa Blanca was built as a reward for the island's first governor, Juan Ponce de Leon. His descendants lived in the home for over 250 years after his death. Occupation by the military caused the residence to deteriorate, but it was finally restored and furnished with antiques of the period to depict family life in 16th and 17th century Puerto Rico.

Wander through the spacious, meticulously furnished rooms, which are cooled only by ocean breezes and experience how the Spanish Colonials lived—an experience which should not be missed. (The top floor also contains an exhibit of Taino Indian culture, labeled only in Spanish.) Casa Blanca is open Wed-Sat 9 AM to noon, then 1 to 4 PM, with a charge of $2 for adults and $1 for children.

J. Leaving Casa Blanca, walk back along Calle San Sebastian to Calle Cristo. To the left is the Plaza San Jose with a statue of Ponce de Leon. Located across the plaza is the small **Pablo Casals Museum**, a charming exhibit of pictures and memorabilia, including the cello used by the world famous musician, Pablo Casals, who lived in Puerto Rico during the last 20 years of his life.

K. From the Plaza San Jose walk uphill towards Calle Norzagaray through the **Quincentennial Plaza**. Completed in 1992, the $16 million project transformed a former parking lot into a fountain plaza to commemorate the 500th anniversary of Columbus's discovery of the New World. Two needle-shaped columns point at the North Star (the explorer's guiding light), and a fountain with 100 streams represents the first 100 years of New World exploration.

L. The Quincentennial Plaza is the cornerstone of a $50 million restoration project of the historic Ballaja Sector at Calle Del Morro. Walking to the left along Calle Norzagaray the route intersects with Calle Del Morro, the road leading to El Morro Fort.

M. Built by the Spanish in 1595, **El Morro** fort contains mostly empty rooms, so be sure to obtain a free map at the entrance and put your imagination to work. Built as an observation point as well a defensive location, the views of San Juan Harbor, La Fortaleza, San Cristobal, and the old city are dramatic. An interesting feature of the upper level is an incongruous Victorian-style lighthouse inside the walls. It is the oldest lighthouse in Puerto Rico, built in 1848, and is still in working condition.

The great ramp (72 steps down the tunnel) leads to the lower levels containing, a dungeon, cannons, a sentry box, a vaulted tower, the garrison, and a steep circular stairwell, leading back to the top. This is not recommended for the elderly or very young. The small air-conditioned museum once served as storage and sleeping quarters. El Morro is operated by the U.S. National Park Service, open daily at no charge.

N. Return via Calle Norzagaray and Quincentennial Plaza to Calle Cristo and walk straight downhill. On the left (after passing several streets) is **San Juan Cathedral**, one of the oldest churches in the western hemisphere, built in 1540. The cathedral contains the marble tomb of Ponce de Leon, killed during his quest to find "the fountain of youth" in Florida.

Walk to the left and towards the back of the cathedral to view the relic of San Pio, a Roman martyr encased under a painted wood replica within a glass coffin. Be sure to read the story about how San Pio came to rest in Puerto Rico. Open daily until 4:30 PM.

O. Walking down **Calle Cristo** is like stepping into another century where some of the oldest, historically important buildings can be seen on small streets radiating from the town center.

Take special notice of the blue cobblestones used to line the streets of Old San Juan. The stones were first brought to Puerto Rico as ballast, or weight, on Spanish ships. The stones were then replaced with gold and treasure on the return trip to Spain. The British and French used red brick ballast on other Caribbean islands to build their streets, but the blue cobblestones of Old San Juan are exceptional.

The shopping area begins on Calle Cristo after passing Calle San Francisco. The time spent here may depend on what catches your attention. (See Shopping.)

P. Near the end of Calle Cristo on the left is the **Museum of Puerto Rican Arts and Crafts**. This is a museum which is also a great place to shop, offering local hand-made items at surprisingly good prices. Next door is the **La Casa del Libro**, a small museum containing a collection of rare books and manuscripts from Europe and the Americas to illustrate the history of fine printing.

Q. At the dead-end of Calle Cristo is the often photographed **Capilla de Cristo** (Christ Chapel) dedicated to the Christ of Miracles. Legend says the chapel stands in honor of a youth whose life was spared in 1753 when his horse was miraculously stopped during a horse race before hurtling over the city wall. Historical records indicate the youth was actually killed, and the chapel was built to protect against future tragedies of the same nature. Open only on Tuesdays, 10 AM to 4 PM.

R. Next to the chapel is the **Parque de las Palomas** (Pigeon Park) home to hundreds of pigeons ready to leave their mark on unsuspecting tourists. The walking tour ends here.

If you want to return to the ship, walk back on Calle Cristo to Calle Fortaleza and turn right. Continue walking to Calle San Justo, turn right and walk downhill to the Tourist Information Plaza. The pier area is located to the left of the plaza along the waterfront. A free ride is available on the trolley car which travels along Calle Fortaleza; look for a "Parada" sign.

For those who prefer to shop, Calle Cristo and Calle Fortaleza offer the best of Old San Juan. (See Shopping.) If the walking tour has stimulated an appetite, there are charming restaurants located in several of the side malls, or fast-food frenzies can be quenched at establishments bordering Plaza de Armas (Calle San Francisco and Calle San José).

Shopping

Old San Juan

The best shopping can be found on two streets in Old San Juan, Calle Cristo and Calle Fortaleza, as described in the following:

Shopping On Calle Cristo

TATA. At the end of the 202 Cristo Street Mall, this store is the sole distributor for Guatemalan handbags and belts in all of San Juan. The styles are distinctive and reasonably priced.

BOVEDA. A trendy boutique with tasteful jewelry and clothes nicely displayed.

***GALERIA BOTELLO.** 208 Cristo specializes in local and Latin American artists, with many unique pieces by its founder, Angel Botello. The gallery is housed within a beautiful colonial mansion, nearly 200 years old. The roof is supported by giant beams and the floor is paved with antique bricks from the original construction of the mansion.

CAFE PARADISO is located in a side mall on the same block. With soothing guitar music and an inviting ambience, the cafe is a good place to enjoy a quiet drink or lunch.

Also found on Calle Cristo: **Ralph Lauren Factory Store, Benetton, London Fog** (a good place to buy an umbrella for those frequent island storms), and a **Fendi/Gucci** store.

Shopping On Calle Fortaleza

***THE BUTTERFLY PEOPLE** is at 152 Calle Fortaleza, upstairs. The store is unique, and will delight any visitor with its incredible murals made entirely from shimmering butterflies protected by plexiglass. Classical music will entice the visitor to spend hours appreciating the exquisite creations. All displays are for sale and the butterflies have been bred especially for the purpose of art. No photography is permitted.

The Butterfly People Cafe on the lower level offers cool fruit drinks and light cuisine.

SAN JUAN SCENES on the corner of Calle San Jose and Calle Fortaleza has locally made ceramic reproductions of classic house fronts from streets in Old San Juan, painted in the same colors as the originals. Open daily, and late on Mondays to offer cruise passengers an opportunity to shop.

***PUERTO RICAN ARTS & CRAFTS.** 204 Calle Fortaleza could qualify as a local's art museum. It contains the very best work by Puerto Rican artisans. Elegant Santos (sculptures representing patron saints), delicate pottery, handmade dolls in island costume, masks, jewelry, tile scenes, hammocks, and paintings are available. Open 9 AM to 6 PM, Monday-Saturday (12-5 PM Sundays, only November-January).

BACHUE, at 206 Fortaleza Mall, features locally crafted nativities, roosters, and tile scenes, as well as other Latin crafts, toys, and souvenirs.

BAREDS is a chain of stores which can be found in several locations. They carry Lalique, Lladro, Waterford, Swarovski crystal, Gucci watches, stylish fine jewelry as well as other imported items found in the Little Switzerland stores on other Caribbean islands.

Transportation, Excursions

Taxis:
Old San Juan has one of the largest port areas in the Caribbean, and taxi stations are situated at each and every docking terminal. It is not necessary to take a taxi to explore Old San Juan, but if you want to see more of San Juan, the capital, a taxi is a must. Taxis are metered for trips around San Juan, with a $3 minimum fare. The price shown on the meter is for the whole taxi, so passengers sharing the taxi also share the cost. If you want an island tour, prices can be negotiated with the taxi driver. The majority of taxi drivers speak English and will be more than willing to bargain.

Taxi Chart:

Destination	Cost
Condado Plaza	$7.00
Isla Verde	$8.00
Airport	$9.00-11.00*
Taxi charter	$12.00 an hour

*50¢ a bag
All rates are for the whole taxi, one to four persons.

Taxi Facts:
- Tipping taxi drivers is customary– approximately 10% of the fare.
- It is not necessary to arrange a pick-up time with a taxi driver if passengers are taking in the sites around San Juan.
- Taxis can be found at any large hotel, and flagged down on any busy street.

Local Buses:
The Metropolitan Bus Authority operating in San Juan has bus stops (Parada Metrobus) marked by magenta, orange and white signs. The Covadonga Parking Lot located to the right (ocean behind you) of the cruise ship terminals is the best location for catching a bus. A map of Old San Juan and the bus routes is available at the Tourist Information Plaza, located to the left of the pier terminals on Calle Marina. Bus A7 has a route from Old San Juan, through Condado and Isla Verde, for passengers wishing to spend a day at the beach or at the blackjack tables. (A7 buses cost 25 cents per person.)

As in most large cities, the buses can be crowded and quite slow. On the positive side, a bus trip can be an interesting adventure and you can get to know some of the locals for only a quarter.

Rental Cars:
Puerto Rico follows the American system of transportation, driving on the right. In San Juan, locals also follow the New York City system of driving–fast with limited attention to rules of the road. Drive cautiously and always be alert!!

Renting cars in the Old San Juan area can be difficult because agencies are located at the large hotels in the Condado area, and the limited number of cars available may be reserved for hotel guests. Cruise passengers should contact one of the agencies listed below prior to arrival in San Juan to ensure a car rental. Requirements for renting a car include a valid driver's license and a credit card. The fees range from $30 to $60 per day plus gasoline and insurance. You should definitely purchase collision insurance to avoid a potential problem.

Be aware that driving in the city of San Juan can be very hectic, confusing, and frustrating if you don't know the roads very well. The opposite is true once you reach the roads outside the city, but you must drive aggressively and have a detailed city map in order to get in and out of the city. Most rental agencies supply an island map, but be prepared to get lost while attempting to leave San Juan. Another factor to consider is that the traffic around the city becomes busy between 4 and 6 PM, so if you need to be back on your ship before 5 PM, plan ahead!

Rental Agencies: The area code for Puerto Rico is (809), a long distance phone call from the United States.

AAA 791-1465, 791-2609
Avis 791-0426
Budget 725-1182; Condado office, 791-3685
Hertz 791-0844, 791-0840
National 791-1805, 791-1851

Self-Guided Tours

1. Take a Historical Walking Tour of Old San Juan. The close proximity of the cruise ship terminals to the streets of Old San Juan makes it an easy walk through Puerto Rico's historical past. (See Historical Walking Tour for a guided tour description.)

2. The **Bacardi Rum factory** located across the San Juan Bay is an interesting side trip for passengers with limited time to tour. You can easily get there on your own by starting at Pier 2 on Calle Marina. The Ferry to Catano takes a .50 cent token purchased from the booth located in the center of the station. The ferries leave every 1/2 hour from the right-hand side entrance station 'A'. Deposit the token in the slot before the swinging doors, and wait for the ferry to arrive. Once you arrive in Catano, go outside the terminal and ask for the taxi van going to Bacardi. (There are usually one or two vans designated for the short trip to the factory.) For $1 per person and a five-minute taxi ride, you will arrive at the Bacardi tent for a free rum drink while waiting for the guided tram tour. The main Bacardi plant is under renovation, which will include a new elevator, lounge area, and Bacardi museum. Final renovations are scheduled for completion by the summer of 1993.

The factory gives free half-hour tours starting at 9:30 AM, 10:30 AM, and 11:30 AM, then provides tours every half-hour between 12:30 PM and 3:30 PM. The plant is open Monday through Saturday except holidays.

Including the two ferry trips and the Bacardi plant tour, the total trip will normally take 1 1/2-2 hours. Be sure to bring money for purchasing an assortment of rum products and souvenirs at the Bacardi gift shop. Shoppers can get better deals on Bacardi rum at the factory than in any of the stores around Old San Juan or elsewhere in the Caribbean.

The Bacardi trademark is the bat. When the family opened their first distillery in Cuba and found bats living in the tin roof rafters, they chose this as a symbol for the new company. At that time, the bat was known to symbolize good luck, intelligence, and family union. Now the trademark is being phased out because management believes people today see the bat as a negative symbol, associated with Dracula. But the canopy structure where people begin and end their tour at the plant was built to resemble a bat. Look hard and you can recognize the abstract bat in the design.

Organized Tours & Activities

All prices are quoted in U.S. dollars

1. The Sands Hotel, in nearby Isla Verde, has Calypso Tours offering a variety of tours for its guests and other visitors. To make reservations for the following tours, contact (809) 791-6100.

- A Deserted Island Trip: a 48' catamaran leaves the hotel at 8:30 AM (returning at 5:30 PM) for a cruise to the deserted island of Icocas for a day of snorkeling and fun in the sun. Lunch, pina coladas, soft drinks, and transportation are included for $69 per person.
- Private Snorkeling Trip: a maximum of 6 people have the whole day to visit three islands off the coast of Puerto Rico. Beer, sodas, lunch, pina coladas, and transportation are included for a pampered day at sea. 9 AM to 5:30 PM, $89 per person.
- Rio Camuy Cave Park. A trip to the most spectacular cave system on Puerto Rico leaves at 8 AM and returns at 5:30 PM. Times and tours vary, so advance reservations are a must for $45 per person. (Also see Self-Guided Tours.)

2. Horseback Riding Tours at Luquillo Beach are available for both experienced and inexperienced riders. Complimentary rum punch and round-trip transportation are offered if you reserve your ride 24 hours in advance. Professional instructors take passengers on a guided horseback ride through the hills of Puerto Rico's countryside, across a spring water river near the El Yunque rain forest, and finish the ride at Luquillo Beach for a gallop on the sand. Morning rides depart at 9 AM, returning at 1 PM, with afternoon rides departing at 1:30 PM and returning at 5 PM. Call (809) 723-3113 and ask for a current price ($50-60) and reserve a ride for your day in Puerto Rico.

3. Blue-Water Scuba and Snorkeling Tours offers an all-day Desert Island Trip to one of the three islands surrounding the Puerto Rican coastline. Passengers can either snorkel or, if certified, scuba dive the beautiful coral reefs. The boat departs at 9 AM and returns between 5 and 5:30 PM. Reservations are required 24 hours in advance, and the price of the dive package ($50-60) includes scuba equipment. The group also offers a half-day snorkel trip starting at 9 AM, returning around 1pm, for $35 per person. By calling prior to your arrival in San Juan, the group can arrange to pick up passengers at the cruise ship terminal area. For scuba divers inter-ested in diving the islands of Icacos, Palomino and Palominito, Blue-Water Scuba provides the opportunity of diving some of the best reefs in the Western Hemisphere. Call (809) 723-3113 for reservations.

Puerto Rico Beaches:

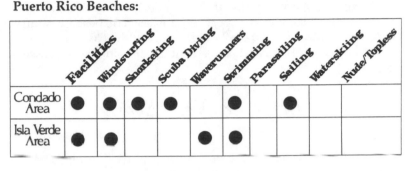

	Facilities	Windsurfing	Snorkeling	Scuba Diving	Waverunners	Swimming	Parasailing	Sailing	Waterskiing	Nude/Topless
Condado Area	●	●	●	●		●		●		
Isla Verde Area	●	●			●	●				

Beaches

Puerto Rico has over 272 miles of white sand beach, but the best beaches are those farthest away from downtown San Juan. If you want to spend the whole day at an exotic beach, you would be well advised to wait for another island.

1. A beach in close proximity to Old San Juan is **Alambique Beach** on Isla Verde. Some of the best hotels in San Juan are along this beach, but these hotels may not allow cruise passengers to enter their hotel properties. One such hotel is the El San Juan, though directly next door is the Sands Hotel which welcomes visitors to their beautiful property. The Sands offers a large pool with a Happy Hour between 6 and 8 PM, and a casino that opens at 4 PM. If you are in San Juan at night, the hotel also presents a "Las Vegas" style show with a two-drink minimum for $18 per person. Passen-gers disembarking in San Juan with time to spend before their flight home may leave luggage with the bell captain while they enjoy the beach, pool, or restaurant The Sands Hotel does every-thing it can to make your visit enjoyable.

There is a public entrance to Alambique Beach (left-hand side of the Sands Hotel) where taxis can drop off passengers who do not wish to use hotel facilities. The Isla Verde hotels offer a variety of watersports, swimming, and plenty of beach for passengers longing for a day at the beach. A 20-25 minute taxi ride brings you to either location.

2. A 15-20-minute taxi ride from the cruise ship terminals transports you to the **Condado Area**, lined with hotels and casinos, and with an inviting strip of beach for relaxing in the sun. San Juan Water Sports, with an office at the Condado Plaza hotel, offers a variety of activities for the sports enthusiast. The beach is similar to Miami Beach and frequently crowded, but the Condado area is close to Old San Juan, and convenient for arriving cruise passengers.

Island & Ocean Sports

Golf:

One of the most challenging golf courses in the Caribbean is the East course at the **Hyatt Dorado Beach**, designed by Robert Trent Jones, with a par of 72. The Hyatt Dorado Beach also has a West course, a little shorter in total length but beautifully manicured and maintained. Green fees are $75 per person, cart rental is $34 for two people, and club rentals are $15 per person. The hotel property is a 30-minute drive from Old San Juan off Route 22 to 693. Chartering a taxi to the golf course and back to the ship may cost approximately $30-40 round-trip (chartered taxi $12/hour). Arrange a price before leaving, and share the cost with a friend to minimize the expense.

Tennis:

The **Carib Inn** is the closest and easiest location for cruisers interested in playing tennis. Located near Condado, the Carib Inn has eight courts available. The hotel charges $10/hour for the court, and $5/hour for racquet rentals.

Horseback Riding: (also see Organized Tours)

Calypso Tours at the Sands Hotel offers a horseback ride on Luquillo Beach for $60 per person. Rates include transportation from the hotel. Allow approximately four hours for the tour, and contact Calypso Tours for morning and afternoon departure times. Call (809) 791-6100.

Windsurfing:

For windsurfers of all levels, the waters off Condado offer some of the best conditions on the island. San Juan Water Sports at the

Condado Plaza, offers board rentals for $25/hour, and instruction is available.

Sailing:
San Juan Water Sports at Condado Plaza, has Sunfish boats available for $35/hour, and Lazer boats for $45/hour. For those who have never sailed before, the instructors at San Juan Water Sports will make it seem so easy you won't want to stop.

Kayaks, an interesting alternative to sailboats, are available from the Water Toy Shop on Alambique Beach, Isla Verde. Rates are $15/hour and $25/half-day.

Jet Skis/Wave Runners:
The Water Toy Shop on Alambique Beach, Isla Verde has both single and double jet skis for rental. Single jet ski rates are $35/half-hour, $50/hour, and $200 half-day. Double jet ski rates are $50/half-hour, $65/hour, and $260/half day. Rentals include launching of jet skis, lifejackets, oil, gasoline, and supervision. Have twice the fun by sharing a double jet ski.

Calypso Tours at the Sands Hotel offers wave runner rentals for $50/half hour, and $90/hour. Check with the tour desk in the lobby, or the sports stand near the pool.

Scuba Diving: (also see Organized Tours)
San Juan Water Sports at Condado Plaza, offers a two-tank dive to the islands off the coast of Puerto Rico, and includes transportation and lunch for $89 per certified diver. Dives must be arranged prior to arrival to ensure availability. Allow two-three hours for the dive trip, with boats leaving at 9 AM, returning in the early afternoon. For more information, and scheduled dive packages, contact (809) 721-1000, ext. 31, and ask for Robert.

One-Day Itinerary

San Juan is a unique ports of call in the Caribbean because it is the beginning and end to so many cruises. I have outlined two itineraries for two different types of cruisers stopping in San Juan.

1. RIO CAMUY CAVES:
Passengers arriving in Puerto Rico a day before their cruise, or a day after their cruise have the opportunity to spend the whole day exploring the outer areas of the island. One of the unique sights on

Puerto Rico is the Rio Camuy Cave Park, located 2 1/2 hours west of San Juan. Here you can visit one of the largest cave systems and sinkholes in the Caribbean. Due to the difficulty in renting a car, driving the congested roads of San Juan, and battling the detours from recent construction on the highways, it is highly recommended that you take a guided tour with a local tour operator. Companies to contact are listed below. Neither price includes entrance to the park or lunch.

Sunshine Tours–Richard Morales $40 per person. 791-4500, 728-0606
Angelo Tours–Angelo $40 per person. 784-4375, 723-0896

The tour operators will begin their tours quite early in order to get to the caves, visit the Arecibo Observatory and drive back to San Juan within approximately 6 to 7 hours. If interested, contact the companies in advance to ensure space on the tour.

On your own:
If you cannot arrange to take a guided tour, contact the Rio Camuy Cave Park by phone to receive updated directions to the park. Call (809) 898-3100/756-5555. Current directions are as follows:

Take Highway 2 west of San Juan towards Arecibo. After approximately 1 1/2 hours on the road, (past the signs for the turnoffs to Arecibo) make a left onto Route 129 towards the Rio Camuy Caves. In 30 minutes, Route 129 will guide you to the main entrance of the caves (a turn-off on the left). There is a parking fee to enter the park, but price depends on number of people in the car. In Spanish, the cave park is called Parque de las Cavernes del Rio Camuy, in case you need to ask for directions. The construction on Routes 129 and 134 may cause you to make a short detour, but be alert when driving, follow the road signs, and you will find the cave park.

Rio Camuy Cave Park is a 300-acre ational park currently offering two attractions–Clara Cave and the Tres Pueblos Sinkhole. Both sites offer visitors the opportunity to view mammoth stalagmite and stalactite formations, with canyons and caverns reaching several hundred feet in diameter and depth. The park has future plans to expand and develop surrounding areas to increase the park's attractions demonstrating the extensive cave systems below the ground. The Tres Pueblos Sinkhole allows visitors to view the Camuy River, the third largest underground river in the world. Plan to spend two hours exploring the park and enjoying Puerto

Rico's most fascinating natural wonder. Do not forget a camera with a flash for pictures inside the cave.

Entrance to Clara Cave is $6 for adults and $2 for Tres Pueblos Sinkhole. Senior citizens receive a 50% discount on both entrance fees, but visitors must ask for the discount. The park is open Wednesday through Sunday, 8 AM to 4 PM, and offers a snack bar and gift shop for food and souvenirs.

Arecibo Observatory:
A trip to the caves would not be complete without a stop at the Arecibo Observatory located 20 minutes from the cave park. The observatory allows visitors Tuesday through Friday between 2 and 3 PM only, and Sundays between 1 and 4 PM only, so if you are not on a guided tour, plan your time accordingly. Driving on your own to the gate may be difficult, so follow Route 129 back towards Arecibo and make a right onto Route 134. Another right onto Route 635 will lead you to Route 625, ending at the observatory. (See map for directions.)

Visitors usually spend 45 minutes viewing the world's largest radar/radio telescope operated by Cornell University and the National Science Foundation. A 600-ton suspended platform hovers over a 20-acre dish set in a sinkhole 565 feet below. The visitor facility includes an educational center with an audio and visual presentation explaining how scientists monitor radio emissions from distant galaxies, pulsars, and mysterious quasars.

The Arecibo Observatory was recently in the news because it has been designated as the home base for SETI, the Search for Extraterrestrial Intelligence. SETI has begun an intensive study of sending signals into space in order to determine the possibility of life in outer space. If a scheduled trip to the observatory is not included in the organized tour, ask the tour company if a side trip can be arranged, for the opportunity to visit one of the most fascinating man-made structures in the Western Hemisphere.

2. EL YUNQUE RAIN FOREST:
If you can get a flight in and out of San Juan on the day your cruise ship arrives, you may only have four to six hours to spend sightseeing. I recommend taking a four-hour tour to the El Yunque National Forest and Luquillo Beach. Depending upon when your ship disembarks, or their airline flight departs, you could spend up to two hours wandering along the historical streets of Old San Juan

for sightseeing or last-minute shopping. (Also see Historical Walking Tour.)

San Juan offers a little something for everyone depending on how much time you have to spend. If the rain forest does not interest you but a day at the Isla Verde beach does, take the Walking Tour first, then spend the day at the Sands Hotel on Isla Verde enjoying the sand and sun. Whatever your preference, take the time to see all the sites and surroundings Puerto Rico has to offer visitors.

An excursion to the El Yunque Rain Forest and Luquillo Beach is one of Puerto Rico's most popular tour attractions. The El Yunque rain forest is a 28,000-acre Caribbean National Forest, and the only tropical rain forest in the U.S. National Forest system. Luquillo Beach, located only 15 minutes from El Yunque, allows visitors to enjoy one of the 272 miles of beach offered on Puerto Rico. To enjoy these areas, either join an organized tour group or rent a car. If an organized tour is preferred, the following companies should be contacted to ensure space availability. Most tours will spend up to an hour at each location.

Gray Line Sightseeing Tours of Puerto Rico 1727-8080, $16 per person, 4-hour tour.
Sunshine Tour Guide 791-4500, 728-0606, $25 per person, 4 1/2 hour tour.
Angelo Tours 784-4375, 723-0896, $30 per person, 4-hour tour. Morning or afternoon.

On your own:
If you are renting a car to explore on your own, follow Highway 3 east of San Juan for approximately 30 minutes, then make a right onto Route 191 (the turn-off to El Yunque National Forest). Luquillo Beach is 15 minutes from the Route 191 turn-off continuing east on Highway 3. A sign for the beach will guide you left towards the beach. There are plenty of vendors with food for lunch, and the park has rest room facilities on the beach.

Whether on a tour or on your own, El Yunque offers a variety of sites for every visitor. The first stop at the Yokuhu Tower gives visitors a view of nearby cities Luquillo, Fajardo and, on a clear day, the isle of Culebra. If hiking interests you, there are three possible hikes through the forest that begin at the Palo Colorado Ranger Station. Pick up a map from the ranger and decide how long a hike you prefer. Time for hiking is not usually scheduled on the organized tours, but visitors traveling on their own can plan for the necessary time needed to enjoy a hike through the rain forest.

1. La Mina Falls off the Big Tree Trail is the easiest hike, consisting of a 45-minute walk to a refreshingly beautiful waterfall. The hike can also begin at the main Ranger Station just to the left off Route 191 at the beginning of the drive to El Yunque.

2. The Mt. Britton Trail takes on hour to reach the Mt. Britton Lookout Tower and is recommended for hikers who have a half-day to explore El Yunque. The hike starts on the El Yunque Trail, then makes a left up to the tower.

3. For the truly adventurous and those with a couple of hours for hiking, the **El Yunque Trail** to the top of the mountain is worth the time and effort. The hike takes two hours and you can view the sights at the El Yunque Lookout Tower, and the Los Picahos Lookout Tower, only 15 minutes off the main trail to the right (20 minutes before the El Yunque Tower). The hike to the top of the mountain provides the best views of the rain forest, flora and fauna, and the opportunity to be serenaded by the coqui, Puerto Rico's tiny tree frog.

Whether you choose to hike or not, take the time to drive through the rain forest. It is one of Puerto Rico's unique adventures.

St. Thomas

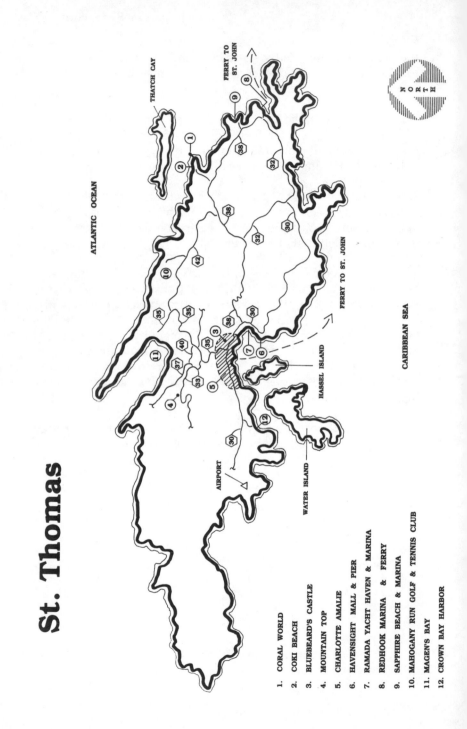

1. CORAL WORLD
2. COKI BEACH
3. BLUEBEARD'S CASTLE
4. MOUNTAIN TOP
5. CHARLOTTE AMALIE
6. HAVENSIGHT MALL & PIER
7. RAMADA YACHT HAVEN & MARINA
8. REDHOOK MARINA & FERRY
9. SAPPHIRE BEACH & MARINA
10. MAHOGANY RUN GOLF & TENNIS CLUB
11. MAGEN'S BAY
12. CROWN BAY HARBOR

St. Thomas

The American Paradise

Island Description:

During his second voyage in 1493, Columbus was so struck by the countless islands of exceptional beauty that he named them the Virgin Islands. The name was in honor of the legend of St. Ursula, the beautiful Christian daughter of a third century King of Britain. Although pledged to lead a life of saintliness, a ruthless pagan prince demanded to marry Ursula. To save her father and his kingdom, she agreed to the marriage on the condition that 11,000 of the most beautiful virgins in the two kingdoms must be her companions for three years, at the end of which time she would marry the prince.

Ursula's plan was to create an army of amazon women who would pledge their allegiance to Rome and thereby gain support against the prince. Ursula's army made the long journey to Rome, but the enraged prince ambushed the returning virgins with his own army and slaughtered them all in a great battle. As a martyr Ursula achieved sainthood, and the incredible beauty of the slaughtered virgins is symbolized today by the Virgin Islands.

The early history of the U.S. Virgin Islands was much the same as that of other Caribbean islands, embroiled in battles between Spanish, French, and English until persistent Danish settlers took possession of St. Thomas and St. John. The Danes later purchased St. Croix from the French in 1733, and the group of islands remained under Danish military rule for 251 years.

Due to its splendid harbor near popular sailing routes, St. Thomas drew the unwanted attention of pirates, who plundered ships laden with golden treasure. Notorious privateers such as Blackbeard and Captain Kidd were real island inhabitants at various times. To protect the harbor at Charlotte Amalie, a large chain was strung across its mouth and raised when needed to block the entry of attacking marauders.

As coral islands the waters and bays are surrounded by incredible coral reefs teeming with tropical fish. The white sand beaches are cool to the touch because the sand is composed of pulverized coral produced by the feeding habits of the abundant multi-colored parrot fish. The turquoise blue water maintains a pleasant 70 to 85 degrees, which makes watersports and scuba diving popular.

Today tourists may visit Bluebeard's Castle and Blackbeard's Castle—each now part of hotel complexes. The castles' stone observation towers provide visitors with a panoramic view of the island's capital, Charlotte Amalie nestled against a shimmering harbor filled with white sails that will evoke fantasies of buccaneers and pirate treasure.

The United States, eager to establish a foothold in the Caribbean in order to secure protection for the Panama Canal, purchased the U.S. Virgin Islands for $25 million in gold on March 31, 1917. The islanders assumed they would receive U.S. citizenship immediately, but the U.S. military continued to rule in the same manner as the Danes. The military regime finally ended in 1936 when the U.S. Virgin Islanders were granted home rule and U.S. citizenship.

St. John

The Danish West India and Guinea Company took control of St. John in 1694 and the first plantation was established in Coral Bay. After 15 years, 101 plantation houses were built housing 208 white settlers who controlled 1,087 black slaves. The large number of slaves is not remarkable considering the history of the Caribbean as a whole, except for the Slave Rebellion of 1733 which struck terror in the white communities throughout the islands.

A large number of slaves on St. John were from the African Amina tribe, who believed tilling the land was "women's work" and therefore humiliating. Slaves were forbidden at dances, feasts, plays, and a slave caught in town after curfew faced severe punishment. During the year of 1733, a hurricane, a drought, and an invasion by insects worsened the situation by making food scarce. Plantation owners refused rations to the already half-starved slaves, who banded together in desperation to secure their freedom.

At dawn on Sunday, November 13, 1733, slaves entered Fort Berg in Coral Bay carrying bundles of wood as part of their usual routine. Once inside, the slaves whipped out cane knives hidden in the wood and killed all the soldiers except one, who hid under a bed. The victorious slaves fired a cannon as a pre-arranged signal to the other slaves on the island. The entire island fell into the hands of angry slaves who burnt the sugar cane fields, and killed entire white families during their rampage.

Fearing similar incidents, the British sent troops from Tortola and St. Kitts, and the French sent two warships from Martinique to fight the slaves in a type of guerilla warfare waged in the hills of St. John. The rebels lasted until mid-May; realizing they were hopelessly outnumbered, the slaves gathered for one last feast in a ravine near Annaberg. After the feast the slaves committed ritual suicide rather than return to a life they detested.

Today the island of St. John enjoys a peaceful small town atmosphere, and over 60% of the island is designated as a U. S. National Park. Tourism is being handled with a conservative approach by the locals, trying to retain their quiet community and the natural beauty of the island, while still earning a living. The resorts are low key and the shopping areas are quaint, with little of the St. Thomas hustle and bustle. Repeat visitors to St. Thomas may prefer to enjoy the solitude of St. John during their time in port. (See Self-Guided Tours.)

Island People:
The protected harbor at St. Thomas and its strategic location on the trade routes to the New World attracted a wide assortment of settlers. The social melting pot of the islands was similar to that of America, but the dominant contributors to island culture were the African slaves imported to work the sugar plantations.

Islanders today are a gracious but cautious people, who cherish their privacy. They may seem reserved, but their congenial nature reveals itself when a visitors smiles and takes time to be friendly. Their fun-loving disposition is most apparent during Carnival, with its calypso music, parades, and the traditional symbol of carnival, Mocko Jumbies. The routes of Carnival go back to African slaves arriving in the islands. Their dances, called bamboulas, were based on ritual worship of the gods of Dahomey. The ritual was channeled by Christian missionaries into Carnival with parades, costumed bands, beauty pageants, music and dance. At Carnival Mocko Jumbies, dancing figures on 17-foot high stilts, appear dressed in bright colors and covered in mirrors. Everyone knows the spirit is "invisible" so when you look at a Mocko Jumbie, you see yourself in the mirrors, not the spirit.

As an unincorporated Territory of the United States, the U.S. Virgin Islands has a non-voting delegate to the House of Representatives; its natives are U.S. citizens, but they do not vote for the U.S. President and Vice President. The ruling government is modelled after the U.S. government, with three branches–Executive, Legislative, and Judicial. The Governor is elected every four years, the 15 Senators are elected every two years, and the taxes collected within the islands are kept for use by the local government.

Holidays:
Locals in St. Thomas love to celebrate holidays and will close their shops on scheduled holidays. If shopping in St. Thomas is important, plan the cruise itinerary to avoid landing on a scheduled holiday.

January: 1st–New Year's Day; 6th–Three Kings' Day (a festival for the three wise men who searched for the Christ child); 17th–Martin Luther King, Jr. Birthday.
February: 21st–Presidents Day.
March: 31st–Transfer Day (transfer from Danish to U.S. ownership); Holy Thursday (before Easter).
April: 1st–Good Friday; 3rd–Easter Sunday; 4th–Easter Monday; 18th through 30th–Carnival in St. Thomas.
May: 30th–Memorial Day.
June: 15th–Organic Day (granting U.S. Citizenship and home rule).
July: 3rd–Emancipation Day; 4th–U.S. Independence Day and Carnival in St. John.
September: 5th–Labor Day.
October: 10th–Columbus Day; 11th–Hurricane Thanksgiving Day (end of hurricane season).
November: 11th–Veterans Day; 24th–Thanksgiving Day.
December: 24th–Christmas Eve; 25th–Christmas Day; 26th–Boxing Day; 31st—Old Years Day.

The Pier

The majority of cruise ships arriving in St. Thomas will dock at the Havensight Pier, a short taxi ride from Charlotte Amalie. Havensight can easily handle three to four ships at one time, and the facilities have been designed for the comfort of cruise passengers. An entire shopping mall is part of the Havensight area for the cruisers who wish to avoid the hassle of taxis and traffic. A directory is conveniently located at dockside, and an information office is located on the dockside end of Building One. Havensight Mall contains restaurants, a bank, a U.S. Postal van, and a variety of shops to attract ship passengers.

Pier Phones:
St. Thomas is a good place to make calls home by direct dialing to the mainland, using U.S. long distance cards, or major credit cards. The service is excellent, and the prices are more reasonable than on other islands. Telephones at Havensight are located in several spots: near docking area number 3, at the dockside end of Building Three, and on the street side of Building Four. Passengers tendering into Charlotte Amalie will find telephones next door to the Visitor's Bureau at the left of Emancipation park and along Main Street.

Havensight Pier Shopping Mall

Havensight is the largest and most modern shopping center in the islands, resembling shopping malls found in the U.S. Downtown stores such as Colombian Emeralds, A.H. Riise, Cardow Jewelers, Benetton, Boolchand's, Gucci, and H. Stern Jewellers have branches in the seven buildings at Havensight. The following shops are unique to Havensight:

Building One:
BEVERLY'S. Handmade clothing, T-shirts, gold jewelry and chains by the inch.
DOCKSIDE TRADING. T-shirts, shell jewelry, souvenirs.
DYNASTY. Liquors, perfume, jewelry, watches.

Building Two:
MAMA'S. Delicious candies and sweets.
MODAMARE. Sportswear, shoes, and beach towels

Building Three:
CARIBBEAN MARKETPLACE. Features island herbs, spices, tea, and batik.

Building Six :
ATLANTIS SUBMARINE. (See Organized Tours) offers high quality fish sculptures, ocean-oriented gifts, books and videos, and Atlantis Submarine T-shirts.
THE DRAUGHTING SHAFT. Great cards, gift wrap, and art.

Building Seven:
PARADISE WRAPS. Handpainted batik fashions.

Al Cohen's Plaza

(Across the street from Havensight Mall)

***MANGO TANGO is the best place to find art, jewelry, and crafts made by islanders. Locals and cruise ship staff buy gifts at Mango Tango, such as Larimar jewelry, original art, prints, locally made dolls, baskets, and pottery. (Larimar is a gemstone found only in the Caribbean islands with a distinctive azure blue color and swirls of white which mixed together look like ocean waves.)

SHARLENE SKETCH ARTIST. Sharlene is a former Disney Artist who will create a caricature in minutes, or a pastel portrait on paper, T-shirts, or note cards.

THE GOLDSMITH is one of the most interesting jewelers on the island. The owner designs and hand-crafts most of the jewelry in his shop. Visitors will find a great assortment of gold jewelry and watches. The Goldsmith shares his store with a local artist who hand-paints island scenes on quality T-shirts.

Charlotte Amalie Pier Area

Passengers who do not dock at Havensight, tender from their ship to the Waterfront near the center of Charlotte Amalie. A short walk to the right (with the right shoulder to the ocean) leads to Emancipation Park and Vendor's Plaza. The town has more to offer than shopping, and many of the historically important buildings in Charlotte Amalie have been preserved or recently restored.

Currency:
The official currency of St. Thomas and St. John is the U.S. dollar. A Barclays Bank is at the streetside end of Building Four in Havensight Mall, and other banks are located along Charlotte Amalie's Waterfront Area. Vendors and shop keepers take traveler's checks

and credit cards, but passengers should carry small denominations of cash for dealing with taxi drivers.

Postage:
The U.S. Virgin Islands and Puerto Rico are the only islands where passengers can use U. S. postage stamps to mail items home. The postal regulations and rates are the same as the continental United States, and all first class mail travels by air. The main post office is located near Emancipation Gardens and a U.S. Postal Van is found near the end of Building Three at the Havensight Mall until 3 PM.

Historical Walking Tour

It will take about an hour to walk through the historic streets of Charlotte Amalie, ending near the town's most popular shopping malls. The malls are shaded cobblestone alleyways meandering between the major streets, where the charming shops will tempt even the most jaded.

A. Start at **Vendor's Plaza**, a new area located near Emancipation Gardens gathering all the street vendors into a central location. Previous visitors to St. Thomas will remember the chaos caused by street vendors, who would set up tables almost in the doorways of shops, and clog the already congested walkways. Vendor's Plaza was a brilliant idea which creates a pleasant open-air bazaar under colorful umbrellas. Take a few minutes to browse through the booths, check the merchandise and the prices. You will end your walking tour in this area, so you will still have a chance to buy.

B. Start the walking tour by entering the brick red building, **Fort Christian**, to the right of Vendor's Plaza. Its entrance is on the side opposite the waterfront. Fort Christian was constructed about 1672 and once housed the entire St. Thomas colony. The Fort has been designated a National Historic Site and restored to look like it did when under Danish rule. Further restoration work is underway, but some exhibits are now open to the public. A gift shop is located to the right as you enter the Fort, containing handmade items, replicas of old pictures, historical books, and island souvenirs.

On the main level of the Fort, rooms which once were dungeon cells contain a museum with antique furniture from Europe, large wicker baskets at one time used by women to carry coal

CHARLOTTE AMALIE
St. Thomas

A VENDOR'S PLAZA
B EMANCIPATION GARDENS
C FORT CHRISTIAN
D LEGISLATURE BUILDING
E VISITOR'S BUREAU
F MAIN POST OFFICE
G GRAND HOTEL
H BETHANIA HALL
I FREDERICK CHURCH
J GOVERNMENT HOUSE
K LUTHERAN PARSONAGE
L 99 STEPS
M THE 1854 HUS
N THE STRAW FACTORY
O ST. THOMAS REFORMED CHURCH
P THE SYNAGOGUE
Q CAMILLE PISSARRO BUILDING
R PALM PASSAGE
S ROYAL DANE MALL
T RIISE ALLEY

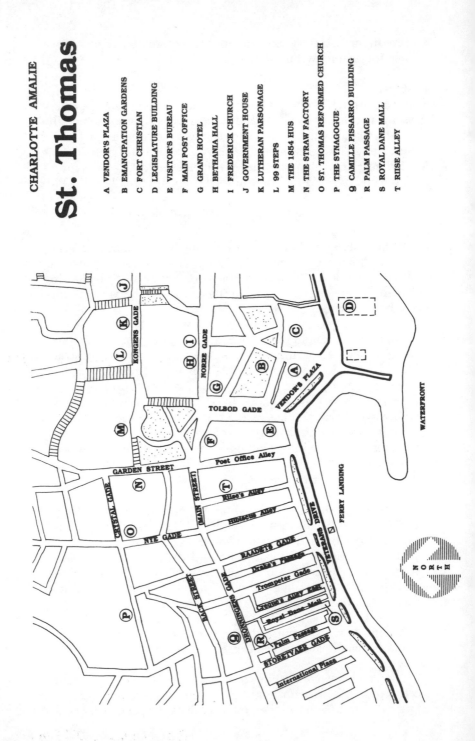

La Princesa walkway, Old San Jan

Raices fountain, Old San Juan

Market Square, Charlotte Amailie, Virgin Islands

View of Charlotte Amalie from Bluebeard's Castle

on their heads, memorabilia, old maps, personal recollections, and pictures of Transfer Day, when the Danes sold the island to the U.S in 1917. Imagine the concern felt by islanders who had been deserted by the government they knew, and were traded to a country with little comprehension of their problems.

Climb the steps to the second story for a good view of the Waterfront, Vendors Plaza, and downtown. Notice the lime-green building across the street to the left. The 118-year-old Legislature Building was once the Danish police barracks, but today is the meeting place of the U.S. Virgin Islands 15-member Senate. It is open weekdays 8 AM to 5 PM.

C. Upon departing the Fort turn left, and walk through **Emancipation Park**, which was named in honor of the freeing of the slaves July 3,1848. The governor at the time, Peter Von Scholten, was influenced by his black mistress, Anne Elizabeth Heegaard, to abolish slavery before 1859 when the Danish government had mandated the abandonment of slavery. No doubt the slave revolt of St. John influenced his decision as well (See St. John).

Emancipation Park is a good drop-off reference for taxi drivers or a good place to meet friends. The park contains a concert pavilion, a bust of King Christian V, and a replica of the American Liberty Bell.

D. Opposite the Fort in a cream colored building on Tolbod Gade is the **Visitor's Bureau**, and adjacent is a hospitality lounge with rest rooms, a luggage/package checking service, telephones and literature.

E. Little Switzerland (See Introduction, Shopping) is to the right of the Visitor's Bureau on Tolbod Gade, and occupies the former Danish Customs House building.

F. Walking away from the Waterfront on Tolbod Gade, notice the yellow painted building on your left, **Emancipation Garden Station Post Office**. The building contains two murals, a waterfront scene and a fortress vista painted in 1941 by Steven Dohanos, subsequently a Saturday Evening Post illustrator.

G. To the right, across Tolbod Gade and opposite the Waterfront is the **Grand Hotel**, a Greek Revival design structure, finished in 1840. Notice the second story pillared porticos over-looking the park. The structure was originally built with three stories, but it lost the third floor during a hurricane. Now it contains shops and offices.

H. Cross the street, Norre Gade, and turn to the right. As you walk, notice the yellow building on your left. It is currently **Bethania Hall**, the Parish House for the Frederick Evangelical Lutheran Church next door. The house was originally built about 1827 as a posh residence for Jacob Lind, and sub-sequently was a post office, a home for the elderly, and a school.

I. The next building, **The Frederick Church**, houses the sec-ond-oldest Lutheran congregation in the world. The congrega-tion was founded in 1666 when the first Danes arrived, and the original building was dedicated by 1793. Charlotte Amalie was besieged by catastrophes during its history, and the Frederick Church was hit by the same disasters. The town and the build-ing were both gutted by fire in 1826, to be rebuilt and again destroyed by a hurricane in 1870. The steadfast congregation rebuilt the church again as it stands today, in a Gothic Revival style including the addition of gables and the bell tower.

J. Turn left at the next narrow driveway and make your way to the top of the stairs to Kongens Gade (King's Street). Cross the street to the **Government House** with its red carpeted front steps. The first floor contains offices and three murals depict-ing Columbus's arrival, the Danish transfer of the territory, and a sugar plantation painted by Pepino Mangravatti in the 1930's. The second-floor is a ballroom with a balcony, and the third floor is reserved as the living quarters for the incumbent governor. The neo-classic style building was constructed in 1865-67 to replace a building dating from 1819. Go inside the lobby to see the murals in the entry or a guided tour can be arranged by calling in advance (809) 774-0001.

K. Leaving the Government House, turn right, passing the **Lutheran Parsonage** on your right. The Parsonage has been in use since 1725. Walk straight on Kongens Gade, and pass the steep stairs on the right. The stairs are the famous **99 Steps**, but there are actually 103 steps. The next house on the right is the **1854 Hus**, originally a residence but now containing restau-rants, offices and shops. Below 1854 Hus is a pink building with steps leading down to Garden Street.

L. Across the street is a good place to buy a soda and take a shopping break at **The Straw Factory**, a store containing straw hats, baskets, ornaments, carved wood items and other Caribbean-made gifts.

You are just one block uphill from the Main Street Post Office.

M. When leaving turn up (away from the water) on Garden Street and left onto the first street, Crystal Gade. On the Corner of Nye Gade is the **St. Thomas Reformed Church**, built in 1846 with massive front columns in the Greek-Revival architectural style.

N. Stay on Crystal Gade for another block and a half. On the right is the **Synagogue of Brachah V'shalom Ugemilut Chasidim** (meaning Blessing, Peace and Loving Deeds). This building is an example of an early construction technique used in St. Thomas where the bricks were made using molasses as a mixing agent. Inside, the floor is covered with sand as a reminder of the time the Israelites spent in Egypt as slaves and were forced to worship in sand-floored huts. This is the second-oldest synagogue in the New World; the building was completed in 1833. The congregation was formed in 1796 and will be celebrating its bicentennial in 1996.

O. Walk back down Crystal Gade to the first street, turn right on Raadets Gade and two short blocks return you to Main Street. Turn right and walk a block and a half, looking for the **Camille Pissarro Building**. This was the home and birthplace of the father of French Impressionist painting, Camille Pissarro, who lived from 1831 to 1903. In the passageway leading to an inner courtyard is a description of the artist's early life in St. Thomas and his later fame in Paris.

P. Cross the street and turn left down **Palm Passage** with its entire structure painted pink. This begins the shopping part of the walking tour. Passengers who prefer to return to the ship should walk through Palm Passage to the Waterfront and catch a taxi or take a tender boat back to the cruise ship.

Shopping

Charlotte Amalie

The alleyways and courtyards radiating from Main Street contain the most enticing shops in St. Thomas, but the majority of jewelry and watch stores are on Main Street (Dronnigens Gade). "Barkers" are paid to stand on Main Street and draw the attention of passing tourists to the stores they represent. The "barkers" are unique to St. Thomas and create their own type of carnival atmosphere, but if you do not wish to heed their call, simply walk on or give them a firm "not interested." The following describes some of the most intriguing shops and pleasant malls:

PALM PASSAGE is the most famous of St. Thomas's shopping malls. It is a lovely shaded courtyard painted pink and lined with exclusive designer-style shops. You may want to linger here, but should not expect to bargain in the following shops:

***PIERRE'S is the author's pick for the best jewelry store on the island. Pierre's makes its own jewelry on the premises, and carries top quality gemstones. Be sure to see the original designs in Pierre's collection, and ask for their catalogue of past designs. It is possible to create custom designs of unique jewelry with their assistance.

JANINE'S DESIGNER FASHIONS offers top European designs with savings of up to 24% on Louis Feraud of Paris, Valentino, Pierre Cardin, Y.S.L., Dior and other designers. European clothes are not inexpensive, even with the discount, but those who know the labels will appreciate the savings.

CIRCE has works of art, featuring limited reproductions of museum quality artifacts and jewelry as well as original designs.

RED FORT offers antiques from Asia, art deco designs, ethnic gold, masks, puppets, and more.

***SUN OF THE ORIENT is a wholesale leather importer featuring leather bags, luggage, wallets, and belts from Argentina, Italy, Colombia and Korea at very reasonable prices. Bargaining is possible. This shop is the author's pick for leather-made items.

JAVA WRAPS contains island sportswear at its best; the designs are appealing and reasonably priced.

Have lunch or a drink at the **COURTYARD CAFE**, then exit, turn left and enter the Royal Dane Mall.

ROYAL DANE MALL consists of three streets where tourists can meander and shop in shade and comfort.

***GUAVA GALLERY is an exceptional shop opened in 1992, though its sister shop, Pink Papaya has been going strong in St. John for years. Original artwork, fish motifs, and crafts by local artists are unique to the two shops, so you will not find the same merchandise down the street.

LINEN HOUSE has four locations in St. Thomas, but this shop has the largest supply of tablecloths, linens, and lace. Other shops are on Main Street, Palm Passage, and in the Havensight Mall.

RIISE (pronounced "rice") **WALKWAY:** After leaving the Royal Dane Mall, turn right on Main Street, walk three blocks, and look for the Riise Walkway on the right:

A. H. RIISE GIFTS is the oldest duty-free gift and liquor store in St. Thomas. It carries almost everything from jewelry to crystal and furs.

CARIBBEAN PRINT GALLERY resembles a European street art gallery. It features affordable prints and reproductions of old maps, drawings, and charming colonial scenes. Another gallery may be found in the Mountain Top Shopping Mall.

***BERNARD K. PASSMAN is an internationally known artist who has sculpted pieces for the White House and Royal family, as well as museum pieces. The gallery contains Passman original sculptures as well as black coral and gold jewelry. A visit to Passman's gallery is like visiting a museum, and you will marvel at his skill and creativity.

Shopping Outside Charlotte Amalie

If you plan to explore either St. Thomas or St. John you won't miss a duty-free shopping opportunity by stopping at any of the following shops during an island excursion:

***MOUNTAIN TOP MALL** with 28 shops to tempt visitors, has the Caribbean Print Gallery, a shell jewelry store with Larimar jewelry, a Guatemalan shop, and locally made jams, jellies, hot sauces, and coconut ships can be found in the Mountain Top Souvenir Shop. The mall boasts the best location to photograph the island of St. John and Magen's Bay. (Also see the "One-Day Itinerary.") Enjoy a famous banana daiquiri at the restaurant/bar while snapping photos which amaze friends at home.

ST. JOHN

Cruisers who have been to St. Thomas previously, or those who are jaded by crowded streets and "barkers" may wish to spend the day on the outer island of St. John. A "small town" atmosphere still exists on St. John (pronounced Sin-Jun by locals), and their handmade "sinjun baskets" are highly prized.

MONGOOSE JUNCTION is a short walk from the ferry dock at Cruz Bay. This charming arcade include shops where local artists may be observed working:

MONKEYFIST has eclectic offerings in their boutique downstairs, with paintings/prints displayed upstairs.

PINK PAPAYA features original artwork, household and gift items designed by Lisa Etre, and merchandise by other local artists. This is the sister shop to Guava Gallery in Royal Dane Mall.

THE CANVAS FACTORY contains rugged canvas luggage, bags, hats, and clothing which are hand-crafted on the premises.

R & I PATTON GOLDSMITHING has original island designs and old Spanish coins crafted into jewelry.

BATIK KITAB has designs created by local artist, Juliana Aradi, as well as batiks made with cotton, silk, linen, rice paper, and wood.

CARAVAN GALLERY offers ethnic jewelry and fine crafts from India, Africa, Asia, and around the world. Also rare hand-woven textiles by artists at work.

Mongoose Junction is named after the "mighty mongoose," a weasle-like creature roaming the island freely, and the *St. John Handbook* features drawings of the mongoose with a comical sneer on his face. Mongooses (the correct plural, not mongeese) were imported from India to various Caribbean islands to combat the local snake and rodent population. The idea was successful as far as snakes are concerned, but the nocturnal rodents often escape the attention of the day-feeding mongooses. Watch the brush while touring St. John to catch a fleeting glance of the lightning-fast creature.

Transportation, Excursions

Taxis:
Ships docking at Havensight Mall have a constant line of taxis awaiting passengers for trips around the island. The taxis usually consist of large American-made vans, and drivers wait to fill their vans before heading out from the pier area. Taxis will take passengers anywhere on the island, town, beaches, or sightseeing.

The ships arriving at Crown Bay will also find taxis awaiting their arrival on the pier. Fewer ships dock at Crown Bay, so the taxi rates given throughout the chapter will start from downtown Charlotte Amalie. A taxi from Crown Bay into town will run $4 per person.

Taxi Chart:

Destination	Cost
Bluebeard's Castle	$2.50
Charlotte Amalie (from Havensight Pier)	$8.00
Coki Beach	$7.50
Havensight Mall	$4.00
Magen's Bay	$6.50
Mahogany Run Golf & Tennis Resort	$7.00
Mountain Top	$7.00
Ramada Yacht Haven & Castaways	$2.50
Red Hook	$9.00
Sapphire Beach Club	$8.50

All taxi rates are from downtown Charlotte Amalie.

Taxi Facts:
- Taxis can be found almost everywhere on the island, at the most popular attractions, and major hotels.
- Passengers should arrange discounted round-trip fares at the beginning of the trip.
- Most taxi drivers on the island are also great sightseeing guides. Take advantage of their knowledge, and ask questions. The drivers love to tell you all they can about St. Thomas.
- Tipping drivers for a quick ride into town is not necessary; however, for island excursions, or for specially arranged pick-ups, a 10% tip is recommended.

Local Buses:
St. Thomas has a Safari Bus Service which consists of open-air buses that provide optional public transportation. The regular routes are between downtown Charlotte Amalie and the Red Hook ferry dock, passing by Havensight Mall. The fare is $2, payable to the driver when leaving the bus. The buses are also used as sightseeing transportation, so if one does not stop when flagged down it may already be booked for a tour.

Rental Cars:
Driving is on the left, and most rental cars are American made with the steering wheel on the left. This makes life more difficult for American drivers. The roads on St. Thomas are not difficult to navigate, but they were designed for smaller vehicles, not the industrial-sized vans the taxi drivers use. Those who are brave enough to try negotiating the sharp curves, should remember to honk before curves, be constantly aware of other cars, and stay to the left!!

The basic price for a 4-wheel-drive jeep or small automatic is $40-60 per day. The minimum age for rentals is 25 with a valid driver's license, and a credit card is needed for a deposit. Collision Insurance is necessary to protect against accidents on the winding roads.

A phone call to pre-arrange a rental car is only a long distance call from the United States, but most agencies will have cars available for the busy cruise port of St. Thomas.

Rental Agencies: The area code for St. Thomas is (809), a long distance phone call from the United States.

ABC Auto & Jeep Rentals 776-1222
Sea Breeze Car Rental 774-7200
Tri-Island Car Rental 776-2879
Budget Rent-A-Car 776-5774

Self-Guided Tours

1. Coral World Underwater Observatory and Marine Park is located 15 minutes from Charlotte Amalie. The five-acre park sits on the northeast shore next to Coki Beach, an excellent area for snorkeling and scuba diving. One of the highlights of the park is the Caribbean Reef Encounter, an 80,000 gallon circular tank that allows 365-degree viewing from inside the circular room. The eight-foot glass walls are exposed to the sun, air, and rain at the top, recreating a natural Caribbean reef atmosphere with exotic tropical fish, lobsters, and stingrays.

The unique underwater tower on the edge of the park is an observatory that extends 20 feet below the sea, offering views to the open sea. Several times a day a scuba diver feeds the free-swimming marine creatures in their natural environment, allowing visitors to watch the lively entertainment. Visitors can easily spend up to two hours wandering around the park enjoying all the natural exhibits and attractions.

A new addition to the park is the Seaworld Explorer. A semi-submarine allows visitors to sit in an air-conditioned area five feet below the water's surface, and enjoy the wonders of the glorious Caribbean sea life. The Seaworld Explorer gives the feeling of being submerged without leaving the surface. Two tour times are offered–20 minutes for $12, and 40 minutes for $20.

Entrance to the park is $14 for adults, $9 for children. Open daily from 9 AM to 6 PM. Re-entry to the park and locker facilities is possible if you want to spend time in the sun and sea at Coki Beach. Taxis are also available for rides back to town, or to other island attractions.

2. St. John is an outer island worth exploring for its beaches, private coves, and National Park. Only a short ferry ride away from St. Thomas, St. John is an unspoiled wonderland with excellent snorkeling reefs and white sandy beaches. **Cruz Bay**, the ferry docking town, has a sea-side shopping area specializing in island crafts and unique Caribbean items. Mongoose Junction and

Wharfside Village are two areas offering the shops that make St. John so special. (See Shopping.)

A trip to St. John would not be complete without a stop at the Visitor's Center, open from 8 AM to 4:30 PM, for information about the Virgin Islands National Park. The park encompasses more than two-thirds of the island, and has a variety of walks and tours for every visitor. Inquire at the Visitor's Center for tours available daily. The following is a list of suggested tours through St. John's National Park:

- The Annaberg Plantation has cultural demonstrations three times a week between 9 AM and 12 PM. A taxi ride takes 15 minutes to cross the island and runs $12.50 per person.
- An historic island tour is conducted three times per week by a park ranger for $14 per person.
- Another tour offered three times a week is a morning glass-bottom boat tour led by a park ranger. The tour takes about 1 1/2 hours and costs $20 for adults, $10 for children.

If you prefer to spend the whole day at one of St. John's beaches and snorkeling reefs, consider the following suggestions.

- **Trunk Bay** is the most popular beach on St. John, and with good reason. The wide sandy shore is surrounded by green-blue waters, with an underwater snorkeling trail designed by the National Park Service. There are facilities for food, bathrooms, and showers. Snorkeling equipment is available for rent on the beach for $15 per set. A taxi ride here will take 10 minutes for $7.50 per person.
- **Cinnamon Bay** is a beach situated next to a campground with facilities including a restaurant, grocery, watersports center, and rest rooms with showers. Visitors can rent watersport equipment for a day of fun in the water. The rocks off the beach make a great environment for snorkeling when the waters are calm. There is also a hiking trail to an old plantation, and a nature trail a short walk from the beach. A taxi ride here will take no more than 15 minutes for $8 per person.
- **Caneel Bay/Honeymoon Beach** are five minutes from Cruz Bay, and offer one of the nicest places to spend the entire day. Caneel Bay is one of the world's premiere resorts and allows visitors to use the beach off the main lobby, while the other six beaches along the property are reserved for guests. A walk through the beautiful grounds will entice you to come back and

stay for a week at the resort. Honeymoon Beach is an easy walk to the left of Caneel Beach, and offers some of the best undisturbed coral reefs on the island for snorkeling. A few chartered boats from St. Thomas anchor off the beach as well, so the waters may be crowded for an hour or two, but not the entire day. Both beach areas are worth visiting, and watersports equipment is available for rent from the Caneel Bay Resort. A taxi ride costs $5 per person.

The ferry to St. John leaves the Waterfront in Charlotte Amalie every two hours from 9 AM until 7 PM. The returning ferries leave Cruz Bay every two hours from 7:15 AM until 5:15 PM. The 45-minute trip costs $7 one-way for adults or children. The ferry leaves from Red Hook every hour from 8 AM until midnight, and the return ferries from Cruz Bay leave every hour from 6 AM until 10 PM. The 20-minute trip costs $3 one-way for adults and $1 for children under 12. A 20-minute taxi ride to Red Hook from downtown or Havensight Mall costs $5 per person. A Safari Bus costs $2, but may be difficult to catch when needed.

3. Two tours are available around the island through the local V.I. taxi association:

- Tour #1 is a two-hour tour to Mountain Top Shopping Mall, Drakes Seat, and Blackbeard & Bluebeard's Castles. The cost for two people is $30, or $12 per person with three or more passengers.
- Tour #2 is similar to Tour #1, but the tour is three hours and covers more of the island. The cost for two people is $40, or $20 per person with three or more passengers. Upon departing the cruise ship, ask one of the many willing taxi drivers if they will conduct an island tour. Most drivers will agree to a tour, but they may wait to fill up their van with other sightseers.

4. **Blackbeard's Hill** is a residential district with two small restaurants, and a hotel complex surrounding Blackbeard's Castle, a stone tower built in 1679. The tower, named Skytborg, was reputedly used as a lookout by Captain Edward Teach, the British pirate Blackbeard, from 1716 until he was killed in 1718. The tower was originally built by Charles Bogaert, which annoyed Governor Iverson because it was "higher than the Fort." Today the tower has been incorporated into the hotel/pool area with breathtaking views. The Mark, next door, is a Danish-style residence of ballast brick and local stone with ornate ironwork trim built in the late

1700's, and listed in the National Register of Historic Homes. Passengers can take a taxi to the castle from downtown Charlotte Amalie, or Havensight Pier for $4 per person. To save a few dollars, visitors could try hiking up the famous 99 steps to reach Blackbeard's Castle from town, but the Caribbean heat and humidity may make it inadvisable.

Organized Tours & Activities

All prices are quoted in U.S. dollars

1. Atlantis Submarine offers one of the unique experiences in the Caribbean. Passengers dive to a depth of 150 feet, spend an hour viewing colorful coral and the abundance of sealife, all in an air-conditioned submarine. A 20-minute ferry ride from the pier takes passengers to the dive site at Buck Island National Wildlife Preserve. A scuba diver meets the submarine to feed hundreds of fish in full view of the submarine windows.

Reservations for the Atlantis Submarine can be made by calling a toll-free number, 1-800-253-0493, to ensure space availability.

The Atlantis Submarine office is located in Building Six of Havensight Mall. Look for the sign in front of their office. If the cruise ship does not offer a scheduled submarine tour, check with the Havensight office for space availability on one of their daily dives. The cost for "the dive beneath the sea" is $68 for adults, $34 for children ages 13-18, and $25 for children ages 4-12. There are seven dives scheduled daily between 9 AM and 3 PM, and passengers should arrive 15 minutes before the hour for a special orientation.

Atlantis also has a submarine tour in Barbados, so passengers who are scheduled to visit both islands should take the Atlantis Submarine dive in Barbados. The Barbados dive is more dramatic, and includes a visit to a shipwreck.

2. St. Thomas is an island for ocean lovers, those who love to sail, swim, snorkel, or just relax in the sun. **Sapphire Beach Resort & Marina** has an arrangement with boat charter groups for daily sailing trips which range from $75 to $85 for a full day (9 AM to 5 PM), and $45 for a half-day (9 AM to 1 PM). The following boat trip reservations are available through the Guest Service Desk at Sapphire Beach, (809) 775-6100 ext. 2131.

- The *Morningstar* allows a maximum of six passengers to be pampered on the 40-foot sailing yacht. Lunch is included as well as snorkeling equipment and instruction for exploring the colorful reefs. Daily sails leave at 9 AM and return at 4 PM.

- *New Horizons* offers passengers the opportunity to swim, snorkel, or merely relax in the sun on a 60-foot luxury yacht. An open bar and lunch buffet will help to pass the time while sailing past St. John. Snorkel gear is provided with expert instruction, or passengers can take the dinghy ashore for beachcombing. The daily sail leaves at 9:15 AM and returns at 4:30 PM.

- On the *Halcyon*, cruisers can "take the wheel," sailing the private yacht around St. John. An open bar, barbecue picnic lunch, and snorkeling equipment with instruction are provided by the crew. Bring a towel and sunscreen, no oils please, to enjoy the day in the sun and sea. Half-day trips are available upon request.

- The *Daydreamer* is a private yacht offering a variety of sailing trips:

  1. Sail to Jost Van Dyke from 8 AM to 4PM.
  2. Sail to St. John from 9 AM to 4 PM.
  3. Take a half-day sail around the outer islands two times a day from 9 AM to 12 PM, or from 1 to 4PM.

  All trips include snorkeling equipment and expert instruction for the stops at private coves and coral reefs along the islands. An open bar, delicious food, float mats, and a fresh water shower combine to make a great day on the sea.

3. **The Naked Turtle** is a custom-built 53-foot catamaran with a spacious salon, wraparound bar, two bathrooms, fresh water showers, and an enormous play net to sunbathe or relax on over the clear blue waters of the Caribbean. Full-day sails take passengers to St. John's Honeymoon Beach for excellent snorkeling along the reef near the Caneel Bay Resort, and plenty of sun for the voyage to and from St. Thomas. The boat leaves at 9 AM, returning at 4 PM for a charge of $85 per person. The cost includes snorkeling equipment, open bar, delicious buffet lunch, and all the fun you can handle.

Half-day sails are scheduled at 9 AM-12:30 PM and 1 PM-4:30 PM. The trips include snorkeling, sunbathing, open bar and an assortment of fruit and snacks. The cost is $40 per person, and well worth the time and money. Travelers to St. Thomas can ensure space by contacting their toll-free number, 1-800-334-4760, or (809) 776-5506.

4. The Ramada Yacht Haven Marina and Castaways Restaurant is a short walk from the cruise ship pier at Havensight. You can enjoy a meal and a drink at the restaurant, or visit Underwater Safaris, a dive shop located below Castaways, offering daily sailing trips on the *Triumph*. A full-or half-day trip is available with a crew who will take passengers to the famous shipwreck, *The Cartanser Senior*. Expert instructors will assist first-time snorkelers, and snorkeling vests and flotation aids are available to ensure that everyone has the best water experience.

Complimentary drinks, snacks, and a lunch (on the full-day sails) allow visitors to relax in luxury. The yacht also has bathroom facilities, and a bimini awning offers continuous shade for those not wishing to absorb too much Caribbean sun. Spend a day sailing the high seas to a sunken wreck on the *Triumph*, then relax for an afternoon drink in the Castaways Restaurant. Half-day sails leave at 9 AM-12:30 PM, and 1-3:30 PM for $45 per person. For reservations, call (809) 774-1350, or 774-4044. (For diving trips, see Scuba Diving under Ocean Sports.)

Beaches

1. Magen's Bay, named for a lady who lived at the tip of the crescent peninsula, has been voted by *National Geographic* as "one of the ten most beautiful beaches in the world," and visitors to its mile-long shore will agree. The heart shaped beach offers an area perfect for sailing, swimming, and sunbathing. The beach has plenty of room for large families as well as picnic tables for afternoon lunches. There are locker facilities ($3/day), bathrooms, a snack bar, boutique, and a beach-side bar. A taxi ride takes approximately 20 minutes, and entry to the beach park is 50 cents per adult, 25 cents for children, and $1 for vehicles.

To the right-hand side of the beach, there are sail boats and catamarans ($30/hour), paddle cats and sunfish ($20/hour), and sailboards ($15/hour) available for rent with a one-hour deposit. Magen's Bay is one of the most popular beaches on the island, so it is best to arrive early and secure a space for spending the day on the beach.

2. Sapphire Beach Resort & Marina is the place for watersports, diving, and sailing excursions. A 15-minute taxi ride will bring the sports enthusiast to the beach of their dreams. Located at the east end of the island, the beach has views of St. John and the British Virgin Islands. Dive In, the watersport center on the beach, has floats, chairs, and snorkeling equipment ($5/hour, $8/4 hrs, $10/day) available for rent. The resort offers rest room facilities, a volleyball court, and a restaurant for a beach-side lunch. Visitors are limited in their use of the hotel, and the pool is reserved for hotel guests only.

3. Coki Beach, at the northeast end of the island next to Coral World, has some of the best reef snorkeling on the island. (Also see Self-Guided Tours, "One-Day" Itinerary.) Coki Beach Dive Club offers dives for beginners with no experience, but who want to enjoy the pleasures of the open water. There are changing areas, but no showers, and a concession stand for snacks and refreshments. A morning exploring Coral World, and the afternoon relaxing on the shore of Coki Beach is a perfect combination for a day in paradise.

Beach Chart:

	Facilities	Windsurfing	Snorkeling	Scuba Diving	Waverunners	Swimming	Parasailing	Sailing	Waterskiing	Nude/Topless
Magen's Bay	●	●				●		●		
Sapphire Beach	●	●	●	●		●	●	●		
Coki Beach	●		●	●		●				

Island & Ocean Sports

Golf:
Golfers of any level will fall in love with the **Mahogany Run Golf & Tennis Resort**. Situated on the northern coastline of St. Thomas, the course rises and drops like a roller coaster. The ultimate challenge holes, #13, #14, and #15 are called the Devil's Triangle.

Golfers who play the "Triangle" without a penalty stroke, are awarded with a "Devil's Triangle Certificate" attesting to their accomplishment. However, the beauty of the course may be enough for most golfers. Rates vary through the seasons, ranging from $33 to $60 (18 holes), and $20-$30 (9 holes) for green fees. Cart rentals are $18 (18 holes), and $15 (9 holes). Reservations for tee times can be made by calling 1-800-253-7103, (809) 775-5000, or fax your requests to (809) 775-1556.

Tennis:
Mahogany Run Tennis Club has two courts for play, $8 an hour. Play a round of golf and a set of tennis at one of the most naturally beautiful settings on the island. In addition, Sapphire Beach Resort has four courts available through the Guest Service Desk for $10 an hour. Call ahead to arrange times and court space availability.

Windsurfing:
Dive In at Sapphire Beach has windsurfers available for rent and instruction at $25/hour, plus $45 for lessons. The water is a little choppy when windy, so beginners should consider taking a lesson. For advanced windsurfers, the cross current waves in the open Marina make excellent, challenging conditions.

Parasailing:
Sapphire Beach is home to Blue Dolphin Parasailing which offers flights from a safe and secure boat launch. For reservations and current rates contact the Guest Service Desk at the hotel. (809)775-6100, ext 2131.

Sailing/Power Boats:
Dive In offers sailboat rentals and instruction for $25/hour, plus $45 for lessons. Virgin Voyages offers power boat rentals for $145/half-day, $200/full day plus fuel. Both operations are at Sapphire Beach, and reservations are made through the Guest Service Desk, and the Dive In shop on the beach.

Scuba Diving:
Underwater Safaris, at the Ramada Yacht Haven Marina below Castaways restaurant, offers daily snorkeling and diving tours. Divers with no experience can take the Introductory Scuba Safari for $59 per person. Expert instructors will guide first-time divers through the fundamentals of scuba diving. For certified divers, the group offers a one-tank dive for $49 or a two-tank dive for $79. Dive trips leave at 8:30 AM-12 PM, and 1-5 PM. All safaris include

full scuba equipment and snorkeling gear. Call ahead to arrange dive trips at (809) 774-1350.

Coki Beach Dive Club offers the lowest prices for diving, starting at $25 for a Guided Certified Reef Tour. For visitors with no experience, they offer a Resort Course & Reef Tour for $35 per person. All dives include equipment, and tank rentals are available for $10 for certified divers with their own equipment. Coki Beach is only a short swim away from a coral reef loaded with fish hungry for attention. Reservations are not required, but their phone number is (809) 775-4220.

Dive In at the Sapphire Beach Resort offers snorkel and scuba trips for all levels of divers. A Snorkel Safari from 9 AM until 12:30 PM costs $25 per person, and includes the equipment. For the first-time diver, an Introductory Resort Course is offered for $55 per diver which includes equipment and instruction. For the certified diver, a two-dive morning trip departs at 9 AM, returning at 12:30 PM for $70, and a one-dive afternoon trip is scheduled between 2 and 4:30 PM for $50. All dives require 24-hour notice, and a 50% non-refundable deposit to guarantee the reservation. Credit cards are accepted. Call (809) 775-6100, ext 2131 to enquire about the underwater experience.

One-Day Itinerary

Due to the congested roads and traffic, a rental car is not recommended. Taxis are preferable for the short-term visitor. Schedule 6 to 7 hours to follow the itinerary.

The sites, driving time from one location to the next, and the taxi fare per person are listed below. The total taxi fare per person, for two or more, is $21.50.

Coral World	15 minutes	$5.00	entrance fee $14.00
Bluebeard's Castle	20 minutes	$7.50	
Mountain Top	10 minutes	$4.50 (or less)	
Charlotte Amalie	20 minutes	$4.50	

What to Bring:
Bring along or wear your bathing suit for time at the beach, and snorkeling. If you have snorkel equipment, bring it along; otherwise, the equipment costs $15 per set to rent at Coki Beach. A towel

and waterproof sunscreen are also a necessity to protect against the sun.

Directions:
Refer to the island map for numbers corresponding with the suggested sites described.

1. Begin your journey at 9 AM, and catch a taxi to **Coral World** (also see Self-Guided Tours). Explore the Marine Park and Underwater Observatory for 1 1/2 hours, and plan to take either the 20-minute or 40-minute Seaworld Explorer Semi-Submarine tour. These two attractions are by far the best exhibits of marine-life in the entire Caribbean. Allow two hours for exploring the park (which I almost spent just in viewing the Caribbean Reef Encounter); take your time seeing all the park has to offer.

2. Change into your bathing suit, and put your valuables in a locker near the entrance. Upon leaving the park, arrange with the administration office to come back after spending time at **Coki Beach** for a drink or ice cream. Coki Beach is a few feet from Coral World and is the perfect place to spend a little time soaking up the sun, or snorkeling the reef right off the shore. If you need to rent snorkel equipment, a dive shop is located on the beach, with rental gear for approximately $15 per set. Coki Beach Dive Club and Virgin Island Diving Schools also offer scuba diving for certified divers (also see Ocean Sports). Allow for two hours of swimming, snorkeling, or just relaxing in the sun.

3. At 1 PM it is time for lunch, so hire a taxi to take you to **Bluebeard's Castle** for the restaurant with the best view overlooking downtown Charlotte Amalie and your cruise ship. Although the castle is named for Bluebeard the pirate, said to have murdered and buried his wives on the castle's terrace, there actually never was such a person. The fabricated story comes from the French legend of Barbe Blue, and was attributed to this site when graves of earlier owners were found on the terrace. The landmark tower was built about 1666, used as a lookout for Danish troops, and has been converted into a honeymoon suite for the hotel. Allow 1 1/2 hours to enjoy a St. Thomas-style lunch, then prepare to do some island sightseeing.

4. Call for a taxi, or check outside the hotel for one that may be waiting, and head off to **Mountain Top Shopping Mall**. Mountain Top is a shopping plaza with island craft stores, a balcony overlooking the north side of the island, and views of "one of the ten most beautiful beaches in the world"–Magen's Bay. There is also an excellent view of St. John and the British Virgin Islands. Spend an hour shopping and taking pictures, then take a taxi back to downtown Charlotte Amalie.

5. It should be approximately 3:30 PM, and the traffic returning to downtown Charlotte Amaile may be quite congested, but within 20 minutes you will be in the most popular duty-free shopping port in the whole Caribbean. Have the taxi driver stop at Emancipation Gardens at the far left side of town (facing the waterfront). Walk up to Main Street for shopping. (Also see Shopping.) Depending upon the departure time of the cruise ship, travelers may spend hours wandering up and down the malls and arcades off Main Street. At the completion of the tour, you will have spent between six and seven hours exploring St. Thomas.

Sint Maarten/ Saint Martin

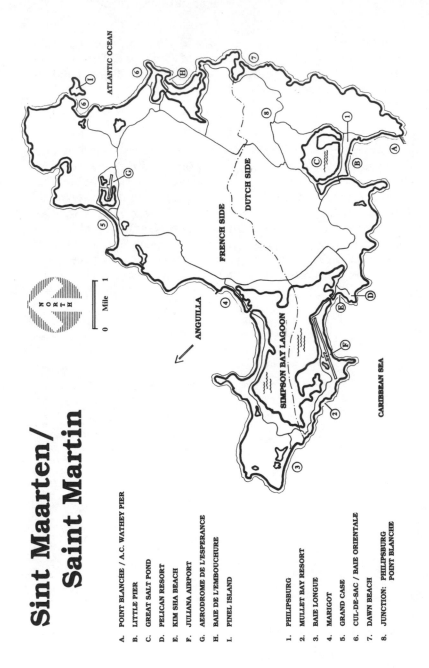

A. POINT BLANCHE / A.C. WATHEY PIER
B. LITTLE PIER
C. GREAT SALT POND
D. PELICAN RESORT
E. KIM SHA BEACH
F. JULIANA AIRPORT
G. AERODROME DE L'ESPERANCE
H. BAIE DE L'EMBOUCHURE
I. PINEL ISLAND

1. PHILIPSBURG
2. MULLET BAY RESORT
3. BAIE LONGUE
4. MARIGOT
5. GRAND CASE
6. CUL-DE-SAC / BAIE ORIENTALE
7. DAWN BEACH
8. JUNCTION: PHILIPSBURG
              POINT BLANCHE

Sint Maarten/Saint Martin

The Dutch/French Island

Island Description:
Soualiga, the land of salt, was the name given to the island by the Carib Indians before Columbus arrived in the Americas. The island was renamed St. Marten for Saint Marten of Tours by Columbus, although historians question whether Columbus discovered the island at all. According to ship's records, the route of his second voyage did not pass close enough to actually see the island. The Spanish claimed the island, but were too involved with discoveries of treasure in the new world to establish a settlement.

In the 1620's the island attracted the attention of the Dutch, who needed salt for their herring industry and for meat preservation. They settled on the island to harvest the abundant salt ponds. The strategic location attracted other European countries striving to establish a foothold in the new world. A series of skirmishes between the Spanish, French, English and Dutch caused the island to change hands 16 times.

The 1648 "Treaty of Concordia" was the foundation for the current dual occupancy of the small island. The treaty split the island between the French and the Dutch, and established unrestricted access to both sides of the island. Legend says that a Frenchman and a Dutchman decided the territory by walking from their capital cities in the morning, and the amount of the land walked by evening would belong to the respective countries. In reality the French claimed the largest portion of the island due to the stronger presence of the French navy in the vicinity. The majority of inviting beaches are located on the French side, while the Dutch side has the largest salt ponds, gambling facilities and most of the renowned duty-free shopping areas.

A small island, only 37 square miles in size, St. Maarten is geologically part of the "Anguilla Bank," a limestone coral reef in the outer arc of the Eastern Caribbean Islands. It was formed 35 million years ago when geological movement pushed the reef above sea level. The irregular coastline with its lush green hills, emerald clear waters, and white sand beaches, creates the perfect setting for a tropical paradise that claims 300 sunny days per year.

The Island People:
The peaceful coexistence of two diverse cultures for over 300 years, with roots tying them to many different countries of the world, has produced a cosmopolitan society with a reputation for warm hospitality. The salt trade made way for other commerce as the Caribbean began to produce rum, sugar, bananas, and other crops. St. Maarten's coral soil proved too poor to grow crops without slave labor, so the industrious Dutch abolished all import and export taxes in 1939 to become the hub of trade in the Caribbean. A truly duty-free port, where even the locals buy goods at duty-free prices, St. Maarten attracts tourists and buyers from other Caribbean islands as well as foreign countries.

Tourism has become the island's main source of income, and merchants understand that quality and friendly service are what visitors appreciate. The Dutch coined the phrase "The Friendly Island" to describe their gregarious people and hospitable nature. The motto appears on their license plates and promotional literature, and is noticeable in the attitude of the Dutch people.

In general the French have a reputation for brusque behavior towards tourists and one another. On French St. Martin, merchants and tour operators are encouraging locals to improve their attitude towards tourists. In any case, if treated with genuine respect, the French will respond with a warm smile and helpful demeanor.

Holidays:
St. Maarten celebrates island holidays, though most of the shops remain open Sundays and holidays when cruise ships are in port.

> **January:** 1st–New Year's Day.
> **April:** 1st–Good Friday; 3rd–Easter Monday; 30th–Queen's Birthday (Dutch).
> **May:** 1st–Labor Day; 12th–Ascension Thursday (French); 23rd–Whit Monday or Pentecost.
> **November:** 11th–St. Maarten Day.
> **December:** 15th–Kingdom Day (Dutch); 25th–Christmas; 26th–Boxing Day.

The Pier

Large cruise ships sailing into St. Maarten dock on the Dutch side of the island at Philipsburg, the capital. Smaller cruise ship lines that can maneuver their ships into the harbor of Marigot may choose to dock on the French side. Throughout this chapter, Philipsburg will be used as a starting point for excursions and activities.

Cruise ships docking at A.C. Wathey Pier, located at Point Blanche, are one mile southwest of Philipsburg. Ships may also anchor in the mouth of the harbor, and tender passengers to Little Pier located directly downtown. Tendering, transportation of ship passengers by the use of smaller boats, can take more time getting back and forth to the ship, so make the trips count and be aware of the time.

The A.C. Wathey Pier consists of a narrow concrete docking peninsula where taxis line up to take passengers into town. At the end of the dock, merchants have established a souvenir shopping area, but no other facilities are available. Little Pier, a short wooden structure, provides a covered walkway where locals display souvenirs for passengers. A short walk on the pier leads passengers to Front Street, the heart of Philipsburg's commercial center.

Pier Phones:
Whether you are at A.C. Wathey pier or tendering into Little Pier, there are few phones available for cruise passengers. The AT&T U.S.A. Direct number from St. Maarten is 001 (800) 872-2881, which will put you in touch with an AT&T operator in the states. You may then use an AT&T credit card, or call collect. Passengers can use two phones located on either side of Little Pier, or take a taxi to a major hotel and inquire about using their phone. A call from St. Maarten is an overseas call to the U.S. and will be expensive, so plan accordingly.

Arts & Crafts On The Pier:
There are always local merchants selling handmade crafts, and island T-shirts in downtown Philipsburg, and on the pier at Point Blanche. After a day of shopping in both Philipsburg and Marigot, think of these crafts as "last minute souvenirs." Bargain with the various merchants, but understand the items are only souvenirs, not valuable commodities.

In Town

Passengers docking at A.C. Wathey Pier can travel to town by taking a taxi ($2 per person), or by walking one mile (20 minutes) into downtown Philipsburg. If you choose to walk, be cautious of speeding taxis, and stay on the road leading away from the pier with your left shoulder to the ocean, until the road gradually turns left onto Front Street. In another few minutes, you will be in the center of downtown Philipsburg.

Currency:
The currency used by the Dutch is the Netherlands Antilles guilder which has an exchange rate of 1.77 guilders to U.S. $1.00. All merchants, restaurants, and taxis accept U.S. currency, traveler's checks, and credit cards on both sides of the island. The N.A. guilder is strictly used by the Dutch locals, and most visitors will receive U.S. currency in change. Banks are open 8 AM to 1 PM Monday through Thursday and 4 to 5 PM on Fridays. To find a bank, start at Front Street and Little Pier, and walk away from the ocean down one of the side streets toward the government buildings. There are several banks on Back Street and in the general area near the government buildings. Emergency cash is also available from casinos along Front Street.

French locals use the French franc with an exchange rate of 5 FF to $1 U.S. dollar. It should not be necessary to exchange currency as most merchants accept U.S. dollars. French stores post prices in francs, but will calculate the exchange rate for tourists. Banks in Marigot are located on Rue de la Republique, a short walk from the marina parking lot.

Postage:
Stamps in St. Maarten are more expensive than U.S. stamps, and whether visitors use French or Dutch stamps, the letters can only be mailed from St. Maarten. Keep in mind you have left the United States and the U.S. Postal Service. Caribbean islands will not accept mail using U.S. stamps.

The Dutch post office is located near the government buildings on the corner of Camille Richardson Rd. and St. Jansteeg. The post office has fluctuating office hours, but when open, stamps for postcards cost 70 cents N.A. (about 40 cents U.S.). The post office accepts U.S. currency, but gives change in guilders. Stamp collectors should ask at the regular window to see collectible stamps available for purchase.

The French post office is located on Rue de General de Gaulle in Marigot, and sells postcard stamps for 3.40 FF (about 70 cents U.S.). Stamp collectors may be disappointed, as these are the same stamps issued in France with no special issues for the islands.

Casinos:
While the casino on the cruise ship is closed, St. Maarten offers gambling facilities. There are six casinos connected with the larger Dutch hotels, and two casinos on Front Street, conveniently located near the shops and restaurants. Truly adventurous visitors should learn to play Caribbean Poker, a game native to the islands.

Museums And Historical Sites:
Due to its relatively peaceful history, St. Maarten is not replete with interesting historical sites. **Fort St. Louis,** perched on a hill at a 1,500-foot elevation overlooking Marigot, is the most interesting ruin on the island. It was built in 1776 to protect the French population from British attacks. To reach the fort, drive to the Sous-Prefecture parking lot, then climb a few flights of stairs to the ruins. Restoration of the fort has not begun, but superb panoramic views of Baie de la Potence, the island of Anguilla, and the harbor and town of Marigot attract photographers to the site.

The **Philipsburg Historical Museum,** at 119 Front Street, was built in the West Indian "gingerbread style" in 1888. Indian artifacts, pictures, china, and antiques are exhibited in one room while an adjacent room offers reproductions of maps and old pictures for sale. The museum is part of the **Museum Arcade,** consisting of specialty shops designed to reflect the West Indian culture. The museum is open 10 AM-4 PM, Monday through Friday, with a $1 admission charge.

The charming air-conditioned **museum in Marigot** is on the waterfront across from the pier parking area. It is informative and well organized, containing Arawak and Carib Indian exhibits as well as military and local antiquities displayed in a pleasant atmosphere. Open 9 AM-1 PM and 3-6 PM, with a $2 charge for adults.

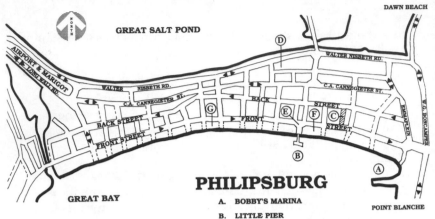

PHILIPSBURG

A. BOBBY'S MARINA
B. LITTLE PIER
C. OLD STREET
D. POST OFFICE
E. TAXI STATION
F. TOURIST OFFICE
G. MUSEUM

MARIGOT

A. MARINA PORT LA ROYALE
B. PARKING AREAS
C. FERRY PIER TO ANGUILLA
D. MUSEUM
E. FORT ST.-LOUIS
F. POST OFFICE
G. TOURIST OFFICE & TAXI STATION

PORT

WALKING PATH

SIMPSON BAY LAGOON

GRAND CASE

PHILIPSBURG & AIRPORT

RUE DE L'ALGERIE

RUE DE LA REPUBLIQUE

RUE CH. DE GAULLE

RUE DU PONT DURAT

RUE ST-JAMES

RUE DE L'HOTEL DE VILLE

RUE DE HOLLANDE

RUE DE HOLLANDE

Shopping

Best Buys in Philipsburg

Downtown Philipsburg is a long strip of land between the ocean harbor and the Great Salt Pond. Front Street runs adjacent to the harbor and the majority of stores offering gold jewelry, gem stones, watches, linens, cameras and electronics are here. Gold jewelry is one of the best buys in the Caribbean and the low prices and extensive selection offered in Philipsburg cannot be matched. Many stores carry similar gold chains, jewelry, and watches, so be sure to "shop around."

Comparison shopping along Front Street and adjoining alleyways can take two to three hours, but be sure to explore the "steegijes"– pronounced "stake-yas" (Dutch for alleyways)–to find the most unusual items. Here is a sampling of the interesting stores encountered on the steegijes.

Old Street Mall

The most attractive shopping arcade in all of Philipsburg is Old Street Mall which has been fully restored to depict an old world atmosphere. A stately entry gate with rows of colorful flags arching overhead makes a tempting scene to capture on film. Shops of interest on Old Street:

BEACH STUFF offers a wide selection of quality swimsuits, T-shirts, beach accessories. Other outlets can be found in Marigot and Simpson Bay Lagoon.

COLOMBIAN EMERALDS has two additional locations on Front Street, and Rue de la Republique in Marigot. (See Introduction Chapter, Shopping.)

DALILA is one branch of the chain of stores that can be found on several islands. The interesting displays include mobiles, Indonesian sarongs, jewelry, batik, and curios.

***VENETIAN GLASS is the only shop of its kind currently in the islands. The shop lives up to its name, offering exclusive designs by its owners from their factory in Venice. Those who know the value of Venetian glass will appreciate the prices, but everyone will admire the designs. A one-of-a-kind series is created each year, so do not hesitate to purchase a special piece, as it may not be offered again.

Promenade Arcade

IMPRESSIONS carries the largest selection of hand-painted tropical fish, mobiles, ornaments, and other collectibles in a tropical island atmosphere.

SEA BREEZE BOUTIQUE has Caribbean-styled clothing and accessories in original batik and hand-painted fabrics.

San Marcos Arcade

***COURT OF JEWELS has a deceiving name. Jewelry is available, but the shop has the exclusive distribution on St. Maarten for a line of elegant figurines made in the Dominican Republic. The stylized blank-faced characters are portrayed in island dress featuring different occupations–a good gift for the collector.

Special Shops On Front Street

BENETTON has two locations on Front Street, but the one at the end of Front Street, across from the hospital, is an outlet store with better prices than the centrally located store at 48 Front Street. (See Introduction Chapter, Shopping.)

BUTANI JEWELERS produces one-of-a-kind designer jewelry, superbly crafted by Butani's designers and manufactured in their own factory at below average prices. The store is at 86 Front Street.

GUCCI is located on Front Street. (See Introduction Chapter, Shopping)

H. STERN JEWELLERS has earned a reputation for trend-setting jewelry creations at substantial savings and is backed by a one-year exchange guarantee. Watches by top name designers are also available. Sterns is at 56 Front Street. (H. Stern also has a shop on St. Thomas.)

LITTLE SWITZERLAND is at 45 Front Street. (See Introduction Chapter, Shopping.)

***MERCELINE'S is the best clothing store in St. Maarten, with unique white lace shirts, skirts, shorts, and an assortment of children's clothing, all handmade in the back of the shop. Merceline's uses delicate white lace in attractive designs which can be customized within hours to the buyer's personal requirements. The children's clothes are adorable! Merceline's is at 99 Front Street, across from the Orange School.

POLO RALPH LAUREN has two locations, on Front Street and in Marigot. Both outlet stores offer lower priced merchandise than found in the U.S. (See Introduction Chapter, Shopping.)

***RAMS is the author's recommended store for the best buys in electronics, cameras, and accessories. With two stores, one at 28 Front Street and the other at 67 Front Street, cruisers will find good prices and honest service.

THE SHIPWRECK SHOP has the best selection of locally made items, books about St. Maarten, the islands, and sea life, curios, island art and T-shirts. The store is nicely decorated with a variety of Caribbean handicrafts, including Caribelle Batiks. (If you cannot visit St. Lucia or St. Kitts, this may be your best chance to buy Caribelle Batiks.) The owners of the Shipwreck Shop have also opened Lord and Hunter at Simpson Bay Lagoon.

TREASURE COVE is a small establishment offering upscale jewelry, watches, porcelain figurines, and collectible David Winter miniature houses. The store is at 44 Front Street.

TREASURE COVE CORAL is a new store next door to the Treasure Cove. The best buys in coral jewelry are offered, so this may be the shop to find gifts for relatives at very affordable prices.

YELLOW HOUSE offers a complete line of brand name cosmetics, perfumes, Hummel Figures, and other souvenirs. The store is just off Front Street near Little Pier on Wilhelminastreet.

ZHAVERI JEWELERS specializes in loose diamonds imported directly from the cutting centers. This store has the largest chain bar on the island with thousand of chains, bracelets, charms, etc. in 14 kt. and 18kt. gold at factory-direct prices. Zhaveri is at 85 Front Street.

Best Buys in Marigot

Marigot is truly a French town which happens to be on an island in the Caribbean. There are French-style boutiques, art galleries, and bakeries. The best buys are French perfumes, French fashions, and local crafts along the waterfront. The stores primarily sell to locals, so the town has not attracted the same high volume jewelry and electronics stores seen in Philipsburg. Near the harbor, where the tour busses drop off their crowds, Colombian Emeralds, Polo Ralph Lauren, and Beach Stuff have opened stores.

The very best shopping in Marigot is found in the open air market next to the marina. Local craftsmen have discovered the tour busses rolling in and they make sure their tables and booths are set up during peak tourist hours. Handmade coral jewelry, fabric island dolls, wood carvings, hand painted shirts, batik, original art, reproduced art, and curios are all available in the market stalls. Take some time to wander through the cheerful displays after filling up with French pastry. The shops in Marigot close for lunch, so the open air market is the only shopping available from 1-3 PM.

Special Stores In Marigot

BEAUTY AND SCENTS sells nothing but fragrances and cosmetics at duty-free prices. The store is on Rue General De Gaulle.

GINGERBREAD ART GALLERY specializes in the vibrant colors of Haitian art, which finds its inspiration in nature and the island tradition. The gallery is at 14 Marina Royale (next to Cafe de Paris).

LIPSTICK carries the largest assortment of duty-free fragrances, skin preparations, and cosmetics, including all the major brands from Europe. The store is located in the Marina Port La Royale, and 24 Rue de la Republique.

PIJAO EXPORT has been a jeweler since 1934, and claims to have the largest selection of emerald jewelry on the island. The store is at 3 Rue Kennedy.

TED LAPIDU.S.. This beautiful store is an exact replica of the Ted Lapidus boutiques in Europe, and the only one in the Caribbean selling fine leather, watches, jewelry, men's and ladies apparel, and accessories. The store is at Immeuble La Residence, Rue General De Gaulle.

Transportation, Excursions

Taxis:

Ships anchoring at A.C. Wathey Pier will find an abundance of taxis. The taxis can take passengers to town for shopping, on sightseeing tours (see Self-Guided Tours), or to one of numerous beaches on the island.

Ships tendering passengers into Little Pier will find taxis on Front Street, directly in front of the pier. These are ready to transport passengers to beaches (for rates see Taxi Chart), or to the French capital, Marigot.

Taxis in St. Maarten are unmetered but have a standard set of prices for trips to the major destinations on the island. Prices fluctuate with the number of people and one-way or round-trip passages, so discuss the rate with the driver prior to getting in the taxi. Tipping drivers is not as customary as it is in the U.S., but if you take a taxi-guided tour, or have a driver pick you up at a particular location, it is generally appropriate to give the driver an additional tip. Taxi drivers and locals are quite helpful and friendly without expecting money.

Taxi Chart:

Destination	Cost*
Philipsburg	$4.50
Marigot	$8.00
Bobby's Marina	$4.00
Pelican Resort	$8.00
Juliana Airport	$8.00
Grand Case	$15.00
Baie Longue	$11.00
Mullet Bay	$9.00
Red Hook	$9.00
Baie Orientale/Baie l'Embouchure	$13.00
Simpson Bay Lagoon/Kim Sha Beach	$7.00
Dawn Beach	$11.00

*Per couple. Add $1.00 for each additional passenger.

Local Buses:
The locals on the island use a "bus system" for traveling between Philipsburg and Marigot. The bus fare is only $1.50 per person, with various stops along the road. However, the same type of vehicles, minivans, are used for buses and for taxis. If unsure that a minivan is a local's bus, simply ask the driver. Some drivers will wait to fill up the bus before departing, but in no time at all passengers will be on their way to the French capital, for very little money.

To locate a local's bus in Philipsburg, look for "Bushalt" signs located only on Back Street, one block away from the water and Front Street. In Marigot, the signs are written in French, so look for "Arrêt" signs for the buses to Philipsburg. The drivers will let passengers off anywhere they request, but when paying the fare be sure to have small change or dollar bills.

For a trip to Marigot, the local buses are the easiest and cheapest way to travel. The bus stops are easy to find and buses are frequent.

Rental Cars:
Driving is on the right in St. Maarten, which makes it easier for Americans. The roads are well marked and in good condition.

Passengers interested in renting a car for the day should contact an agency prior to their arrival in St. Maarten. Most rental agencies have their offices at the airport, so if you decide to rent a car after you arrive, you should plan to take a taxi out to Juliana Airport. If you call ahead, the rental agency may make arrangements to deliver the car near the pier area.

The basic price for a full day rental is $25-$40 for either automatic or stick-shift vehicles. Agencies require a current driver's license, and a credit card for rentals. For passengers docking at A.C. Wathey pier, be sure to ask the rental agency if it is possible to drop off the car on the pier at the end of the day.

Rental Agencies: To call to St. Maarten, dial (011) the international access code, then (599) the country code, next a (5) for the area code, and finally the local number.

Risdon Car Rentals 23578/54239
National 44268/1-800-328-4567

Nelson's Dockyard and English Harbour, Antigua

Hawksbill Resort, Antigua

Brimstone Hill Fortress overlook, St. Kitts

Sisserou Express bus, Dominica

Avis 42316/42322
Budget Rent-A-Car 54274/54275

Self-Guided Tours

1. Visit **Marigot**, the French capital with its unique culture, gourmet restaurants, and charming boutiques. Take a local bus or a taxi, and within 20 minutes you will be exploring a little bit of France.

Do not hesitate to visit the French side. The restaurants are wonderful and you will find the European-style architecture "typically French." Toward the end of the day, a taxi ride back to Philipsburg will take a least 30 minutes due to traffic, so plan accordingly to avoid missing the ship.

2. A two-hour tour by taxi will take you around the small but well developed island. The beautiful coastal sites and island views will entice anyone to spend more time exploring St. Maarten. Taxis are available from downtown Philipsburg or from A.C. Wathey Pier for approximately $10-$15 per person. Drivers request a minimum of four people per tour. Read through the "One-Day" Itinerary section for suggested sites to visit, then request the specific locations that interest you most.

3. Highly recommended for those who have already explored St. Maarten is a trip to the beautiful British isle of **Anguilla**. Anguilla offers long stretches of beaches and clear blue water for coral reef snorkeling or diving for scuba enthusiasts (see Ocean Sports). Passengers interested in a day on Anguilla must take a taxi or bus to Marigot, then a ferry to Blowing Point. Ferries leave from Marigot Harbor every half-hour, starting from 8 AM until 5:30 PM. Returning ferries also leave every half-hour, starting at 7:30 AM. The last one leaves at 5 PM, so plan enough time for the return trip to the ship. The ferry trip takes 20 minutes, and the cost is $11 per person each way ($2 for departure tax and $9 for the ferry). Visitors to Anguilla need to take a picture ID, passport, or drivers license for departure from French St. Martin.

Upon arriving in Blowing Point, Anguilla, hire a taxi to one of the island's spectacular beaches. Shoal Bay ($25 for two people round-trip) is a two-mile white sand beach with plenty of space for privacy and sun bathing. Sandy Ground Village ($15 for two people round-trip) is a popular beach for water sports, and has a variety of restaurants for lunch. The beach is also home of Tamariain Watersports Ltd., a scuba center offering a five-star PADI international training center (see Ocean Sports).

Organized Tours & Activities

All prices are quoted in U.S. dollars

The following sailing excursions leave from Bobby's Marina, located on the road to Point Blanche outside downtown Philipsburg. The marina is an easy walk from the pier at Point Blanche, or a 15-minute walk from Little Pier.

1. Sail to Tintamarre Island, a deserted island with a coastline perfect for snorkeling. The *Cheshire Cat*, a 70' catamaran, departs at 9 AM, returning at 5 PM daily except Mondays, for a cost of $60 per person, plus $5 departure tax. The trip includes an open bar, lunch, and use of snorkel gear. Call ahead for reservations (011-599) 5-22167.

2. *No Strings* is the name of a yacht sailing to a deserted island off the coast of Phillipsburg. The yacht leaves Monday-Saturday at 9 AM, returning at 4:30 PM, for a cost of $55 per person, plus $5 departure tax. The trip includes lunch, fishing en route to the island, use of windsurfers, and open bar. For reservations call (011-599) 5-23266.

3. *The White Octopus* leaves for a sailing trip to St. Barth's daily except Sundays. The catamaran departs at 9 AM, returning at 5 PM, for a cost of $45 per person, plus $5 departure tax. The trip includes snacks and use of snorkel equipment. Reservations are requested. Call (011-599) 5-23170, or 5-22167.

Beaches

1. One of the longest beaches on the island is at **Mullet Bay Resort**. The beach is perfect for swimming, snorkeling, or simply sunbathing. A taxi ride from downtown Philipsburg, or A.C. Wathey Pier will take 20 minutes.

Mullet Bay offers an abundance of beach activities plus golf, tennis, and a full casino. There are rest room facilities, a cocktail bar, and a pricey beach-side restaurant for lunch. Passengers can rent beach chairs ($10/day), snorkeling equipment ($10-15/hour), and float-ing rafts ($10/hour).

Lagoon Cruises & Watersports is located in a lagoon next to Mullet Bay Beach and has an excellent assortment of sports equipment. Spend a day at one of the island's largest resorts, and have fun in the sun.

2. Baie Orientale/Orient Bay, is the most popular "clothing op-tional" beach on the French side of St. Martin. A taxi will take 30 minutes from downtown, or A.C. Wathey Pier. It is not necessary to arrange a round-trip ride with the taxi driver because many taxis are available at the beach.

Many ship passengers find themselves "bearing their all" on the beach, but Orient Bay also features some of the best windsurfing ($15-$20/hour), wave runners ($30/25 min), snorkeling ($10-$15/hour), and swimming (free) on the entire island. Another stretch of beach, located on the left-side of the shopping tents, can be enjoyed by people uncomfortable with the "au naturel" style of the beach. Rules of the nude beach are: no cameras, and respect one another's space. Orient Bay also has two restaurants and rest room facilities (a $1 charge). Visit the shopping tents, selling some of the best bathing suits on the island as well as souvenir T-shirts.

**Baie l'Embouchure, down the road from Orient Bay, is home of Tropical Wave, a windsurfing and snorkeling operation. (Also see Ocean Sports.) The beach offers a Beach Bistro for food and rest room facilities. The beach is situated in a private cove and the owners of Tropical Wave have created a spectacular snorkeling trail. Those not interested in the nude beach should really spend the day here.

3. Kim Sha Beach is across from Simpson Bay Lagoon, and to the right of the Pelican Resort. Known more as a locals beach, Kim Sha is an ever changing area that is close to Philipsburg, and has activities for every member of the family. Families often cruise together, and need a beach that caters to every age group. Kim Sha offers watersports, a beach for sunbathing, and a unique shopping area nearby. Visitors can enjoy the beach, walk to the Pelican Resort for lunch or gambling in the casino, and browse through the shopping area across the street at Plaza de Lago.

A taxi ride takes 20 minutes to go over the mountain to Kim Sha Beach, and large families should bargain for a lower-priced round-trip rate. Westport Watersports is located on the beach, offering the best wave runners on the island. Ocean Explorers, also located on the beach, offers one of the most unusual water experiences. They call it a Sea Walk, but even those who cannot swim will be able to walk under the water. A waterproof helmet keeps your hair dry while you walk under the water. Bring a bathing suit and a towel to enjoy a new diving experience. The cost is $35 per person, and anyone can do it.

4. One of the best locations for rough ocean-waves and calm-water snorkeling is at **Dawn Beach**. Taxis drop passengers off at the Dawn Beach Hotel, a short walk to the hotel's beach area.

Dawn Beach has snorkeling equipment ($7/hour, $15/day), boogie board rentals ($15/hour, $30/day), and beach chairs ($3.50) available at the pool area. You may also want to spend time wandering around the luxurious resort here. The pounding surf and frequent waves make the swimming and surfing more enjoyable here than anywhere else on the island. It is only 15 minutes from Philipsburg, so you can spend a half-day shopping and enjoy the remaining time at the beach.

St. Maartin Beach Chart:

	Facilities	Windsurfing	Snorkeling	Scuba Diving	Waverunners	Swimming	Parasailing	Sailing	Waterskiing	Nude/Topless
Mullet Bay	●	●	●		●	●	●		●	
Baie Orientale	●	●	●		●	●				●
Baie l'Embouchure	●	●	●			●				
Kim Sha beach	●		●	●	●	●		●	●	
Dawn Beach	●		●			●				

Island & Ocean Sports

Golf:
Mullet Bay Resort is home to one of the most challenging 18-hole golf courses in the Caribbean. The course is restricted to hotel guests, but if you are willing to purchase a golf package ranging from $65-95 per person, you will be permitted a round of golf. The package includes greens fees, golf clubs, and a cart rental.

Tennis:
The largest tennis facility is also at **Mullet Bay Resort**. There are 16 courts available at a charge of $7 per person and racket rentals for $4/hour.

Horseback Riding:
One of the newest additions to St. Maarten is ***Bayside Riding Club**. Take one of the horses for a gallop along a mile of sandy beach, then guide the horse for a swim through the water. The stable is located to the right of Orient Bay, and the guides take riders on natural dirt paths to a private beach, not along congested roads. The stable also uses a neoprene saddle which is much more comfortable than regular leather saddles. Be sure to bring your bathing suit for the water, and a hat for the sun. Beach rides are scheduled at 9AM and 2PM, $45 per person with a free refreshment on the beach. For reservations call (011-599) 5-873385. Advanced reservations are preferred, but they are willing to make arrangements to help cruise passengers.

Windsurfing:
Baie l' Embouchure is one of the best places to spend the day windsurfing. Hourly rentals at **Tropical Wave** are $20, and $45 for a half-day. Lessons are also available for $45 (board rental included). **Lagoon Cruises & Watersports** at Mullet Bay also has windsurfers available for $15/hour.

Parasailing:
Lagoon Cruises & Watersports at Mullet Bay offers the best in parasailing. A 10-minute flight costs $30 per person. Take a flight over the lagoon, then relax and enjoy a day at Mullet Bay Beach.

Water-skiing:
Lagoon Cruises & Watersports also has boats for water-skiing. Rates are $20/15 minutes, $40/30 minutes, and $75/hour. Ask about special packages for more than one person. The **Marina**

Waterfront at the Pelican Resort also offers water-skiing for $35/30 minutes, and lessons for $35 per person.

Jet Skis/Wave Runners:

The **Marina Waterfront** at the Pelican Resort offers a variety of jet skis and wave runners to choose from. Rates for wave runners are $25/30 minutes single rider, $30/30 minutes double rider. Super jet skis are available for $25/30 minutes. Next to the Pelican Resort at Kim Sha Beach, **Westport Watersports** offers powerful jet skis for $25/30 minutes single rider, and $30/30 minutes double rider. The operation also has wave runners for $40/hour single rider and $50/hour double rider.

Scuba Diving:

Leeward Islands Divers offers the best in scuba trips around St. Maarten. One-tank dives are $35, and they offer equipment rental for $10. Single tank dives leave at 9 AM, returning at 1 PM. Specialty dive trips to St. Barths leave at 9 AM, return at 3 PM, and include two tank dives for $90. The group also offers snorkeling trips for $30. All scuba equipment is available for rent, and transportation from the pier area is possible with prior notice. Call for reservations and more information (011-599) 5-42262.

Pelican Resort has a qualified dive center with daily single and double tank dives. Rates are $45 for a guided one-tank dive, and $90 for a two-tank reef or wreck dive. The dive center also offers equipment for rent. Call ahead for reservations (011-599) 5-42503, and ask about specialty dives to the outer island, Saba.

Diving in Anguilla is available at **Tamariain Watersports Ltd.**, at Sandy Ground. A five-star PADI international training center, with a complete line of scuba equipment, they have scuba rentals at $45-$60 per diver. Take the ferry across the sea from Marigot to explore some of the most beautiful uncharted, undisturbed, and untouched coral reefs in the northern Caribbean. Dive packages are available upon request. Telephone number for prior contact, (809) 497-2020. (Also see Self-Guided Tours.)

One-Day Itinerary

To thoroughly enjoy St. Maarten, rent a car by 9 AM so you will have a full day to explore the island. Schedule six to seven hours for a driving tour around the island including various stops at beaches, shopping areas, and exclusive resorts. Follow the itinerary for a self-guided island tour, and do not worry about getting lost–there are plenty of road signs and friendly locals who will assist you if needed. Take your time and enjoy the heavenly beaches, the delicious food in Marigot, and the duty-free shopping in Philipsburg.

What to Bring:
Be sure to bring a towel and wear your bathing suit if you plan to swim or sunbathe at the beaches, as most of the secluded beaches have no changing facilities. Also bring suntan lotion and water to protect against painful sunburn and dehydration.

Directions:
Refer to the island map for numbers corresponding with the suggested sites described. If you were able to rent a car in Philipsburg, begin your tour at number 1. If you rented a car at Juliana Airport, begin your tour at number 2.

1. To leave Philipsburg, take the Walter Nisbeth Road, or Long Wall Road to the left towards the left-side of the island, keeping the town and ocean at your back. The Walter Nisbeth Road circles the Great Salt Pond and parallels Long Wall Road exiting Philipsburg. Both roads merge to bring you to Bush Road, where you take a left up and over Cole Bay Hill. Bush Road follows a coastal route for 5-10 minutes until it comes to another intersecting road, Welfare Road. Here you take a left towards Juliana Airport. (This route will take you past a series of spectacular views. If you take the right, the road will lead you directly to Marigot within about 15 minutes.) Keep following Welfare Road. You might want to stop along the road near Simpson Bay Lagoon at Plaza de Lago for souvenir shopping.

2. After paralleling the airport, Welfare Road enters Maho Bay Resort. By keeping to the right, you will enter **Mullet Bay**, one of the most luxurious resorts on the island, complete with shopping plazas, casino, tennis courts, and an 18-hole golf course. Take a few minutes to explore the grounds, the French shops and boutiques, and perhaps a stop at the long stretch of beach near the rear entrance of the resort. Stay to the right through the first 'Y' in the road, then continue along the golf course to the second 'Y'. Here a sharp left through a guarded gate will take you to Mullet Bay beach, and a right leads straight to Lagoon Watersports. You can exit the resort by staying to the left through the rear entrance, past a few more hotels until you cross over onto the French side, as indicated by road signs written in French.

3. In approximately 10 minutes, past Cupecoy Beach, you should find a sign for **Baie Longue**. Take the secondary road on your left for your adventure to Baie Longue, one of the most beautiful beaches on the island. Follow the dirt road until you pass the entrance of La Samanna, one of St. Martin's exclusive resorts. Follow the road to the right of La Samanna but begin to watch for a chain-link-fenced parking area, approximately 100 yards on the left-hand side of the road. There are many private homes along the road, but drive slowly and you will be sure to locate the entrance.

Leave your car and hike down the pathway to the beach. (Do not leave valuables in the car.) Baie Longue is a mile-long beach perfect for sunbathing and privacy. There are underlying rocks along the shore in the water, so be very careful when swimming. If you are a sun worshiper, you may wish to stay here awhile to soak up the vibrant rays, but limit your time to no longer than an hour if you want to see the rest of the island on schedule. Upon leaving, head back to the main road, then make a left to get back on track.

4. Follow the main road for a few miles past private estates, and other smaller beaches. You are about 15 minutes from Marigot, so take your time and enjoy the scenery which makes St. Martin unique. The main road will direct you into the French capital, **Marigot**, and a left on Rue de la République will take you straight down to the harbor where you can park in a lot on the left.

Unless you are planning to visit Martinique or Guadeloupe, Marigot may be the closest you come to visiting France in the Caribbean, so enjoy the town's foreign atmosphere. Be sure to take time to walk through the stores along the waterfront, and when you are ready for lunch, ask for directions to **Marina Port la Royale**. There are numerous restaurants featuring exquisite French food, but try a crepe, any kind will do, for a truly French delicacy.

At this point, Marigot is only 20-30 minutes from Philipsburg. If you continue along the eastern coast to Philipsburg, it will take approximately 60-90 minutes non-stop. To stay on schedule, spend 1 1/2 hours in Marigot for shopping, sightseeing, and lunch.

5. Make your way out of Marigot via Rue de Hollande leading past the main harbor to the right. The easiest way to know that you are heading in the right direction is to watch for the signs to Grand Case and Cul-de-Sac. Continue along this winding road for 20 minutes until you reach an open meadowland area, and locate the sign for Grand Case. Make a left onto the narrow street until it ends, then turn right on the main street. There is a dirt parking area on the right where you can leave your car.

Take a stroll back along the surface road toward the beach and lavish restaurants. **Grand Case** is known as the "Restaurant Capital of the Caribbean" and hosts some of the most expensive restaurants in all the islands. From Grand Case you can see the silhouette of Anguilla, an outer island which offers some of the best coral reef diving in the Caribbean.

Spend up to 30 minutes viewing the sites of Grand Case, then drive back along the road past the restaurants (do not turn down the one-way road you came in on) to the end of the restaurant strip and make a left onto the main road.

6. The next few locations on the route feature topless beaches, spectacular coastal views, and some hide-a-ways only found on St. Maarten. Continue on the main road past the French airport, Aerodrome de l' Esperance for about 10 minutes, until you reach a fork in the road. Toward the left is **Cul-de-Sac**, a pleasant detour to some of the undeveloped land on the island. If you are ahead of schedule and would like to take a side-trip, travel down the road, make a left on Rue de l'Anse Marcel, then a quick right onto a dirt road that leads down to the coastline. (Cul-de-Sac is 45 minutes from Philipsburg.)

Continuing on the main road will take you through the most rural part of the island, leading to another beach resort. If you brought your camera be sure to stop at a lookout spot just past a large electrical tower on the right-hand side of the road. There is an observation platform which overlooks **Orient Bay** and one of the most dramatic coastlines in the Caribbean.

Just a few yards down the road, a sign on the left-hand side of the road will direct you to Club Orient Hotel and Baie Orientale, the most popular "clothing optional" beach on the island. The beach has facilities for renting snorkeling gear, windsurfers, and wave runners, two eating locations, and shopping tents full of bathing suits and T-shirts. Note that to the right of the parking area is the "nude beach." If you wish to avoid the "au naturel" sunbathing, stay on the beach to the left-side of the shopping tents. If you did not spend much time at Baie Longue and are ahead of schedule, you may wish to stay at Baie Orientale for swimming and sunbathing. (Baie Orientale is 30 minutes from Philipsburg)

7. Returning to the main road, turn left. You have now crossed back over to the Dutch side's farming area, so be watchful for goats, sheep, and cows crossing the road. Follow the paved road for 15 minutes. Stay on the road to the right until you see a sign for **Oyster Pond** and **Dawn Beach** on the left-hand side of the road. Make a sharp left, another right, and finally a left up a steep dirt road clearly marked for Dawn Beach and Oyster Pond. (Do not worry–it is an easy transition.) In another 15 minutes you will have to stop for a view when you reach the top of the hill overlooking the Atlantic coastline. From this vantage point you can view St. Barthelemy, an outer French island, and Dawn Beach–one of the best bodysurfing and snorkeling spots on the island.

Slowly make your way down the steep road until you reach the hotels below. Visitors are allowed to drive through the Dawn Beach Hotel in order to reach the beach. If you have time on your schedule, do some snorkeling, swimming or walk down the beach to visit the Oyster Pond Hotel.

8. When you have made it back up the steep winding road, and have reached the main road, make a left onto the main road for the descent back into Philipsburg. As you travel down the winding road, you will have an opportunity to view Philipsburg, the Great Salt Pond, and your cruise ship. When you reach the edge of the Great Salt Pond, you can turn either left or right to get back into Philipsburg. A left will take you back to A.C. Wathey pier, and a right will lead you into downtown Philipsburg, or to Bush Road and the airport.

If you have time before your ship sails, be sure to walk through downtown Philipsburg and do some last minute souvenir shopping. At the completion of this excursion, you should have spent between six and seven hours touring the entire island, with stops for lunch, sunbathing, swimming, and viewing the variety of hotels and coastal sites of St. Maarten.

Antigua

A Beach for Every Day of the Year

Island Description:
Ruins of windmills and wandering Sicilian donkeys dot the rolling landscape, free of urban clutter. Antigua (pronounced an-tee-guh) is a rural island formed of coral and limestone with few inhabitants. Although wide and straight, the roads are gutted with potholes, which the taxi drivers happily dodge while passengers may feel they have been on "Mr. Toad's wild ride." The island's highest point is Boggy Peak, 1,360 feet above sea level. But, as a coral island, Antigua's claim to fame is 365 white sand beaches.

During his second voyage to the New World, Columbus bestowed the name of Santa Maria de la Antigua on the largest of the Leeward islands, 108 square miles. Antigua contained no gold or natural spring water, but it did have ferocious Carib Indians, so the Spanish did not attempt to colonize.

The first successful settlement was established by a group of English who came from nearby St. Kitts in 1632. Although the Caribs waged attacks to eject the British, the settlers held their ground and began to cultivate cash crops such as tobacco, indigo, and ginger. In 1674 Sir Christopher Codrington came from Barbados and established the first successful sugar plantation, called Betty's Hope after his daughter. (Betty's Hope, with its unique twin windmills has recently been established as a non-profit trust, and is open Tuesday-Saturday 9 AM to 5 PM.)

Codrington's success encouraged others to begin sugar production, and over 150 sugar mills were built on Antigua's flat landscape, manned by slave labor. Although slavery was abolished in 1834, sugar remained the principal source of Antigua's income until the twentieth century when tourism took its place. With miles of open countryside, agriculture is a large part of the economy. (Antigua's black pineapple is famous for its sweetness.)

Barbuda, Antigua's sister island is 27 miles northeast of Antigua, about 20 minutes by air. Barbuda is known for its pink sand beaches and the Frigate Bird Sanctuary, but the island remains difficult to reach for a one-day excursion.

Island People:
The only "town" on Antigua is St. John's, the capital, while every other populated area is considered a "village." With a distinct sense of pride, locals will point out their own village and name their relatives living in other villages. The villages are small, filled with tin-roofed wooden chattel houses on raised foundations as a protection against flooding. Chattel houses, which can be moved from place to place as the owner moves, were the original type of dwellings occupied by slaves.

The island's population hovers around 75,000, which keeps the island rural and uncrowded. Antiguans have a friendly, peaceful nature, untouched by the hustle and bustle of urban chaos. Taxi drivers are trained to describe local plants, flowers and historical sites, and enjoy becoming tour guides for their passengers.

The most important event on Antigua is Carnival, to commemorate the emancipation of slaves. Carnival is celebrated for ten days, beginning at the end of July and ending with two days of nonstop parades, music, and dancing on the first Monday and Tuesday of August. The festivities include beauty pageants, a Calypso King contest, and a steel band competition. Carnival Monday features a costume contest with elaborate outfits full of sequins, feathers, beads, and glitter paraded across stage during a spirited competition. Carnival Tuesday, the "Last Lap," is the last day for street dancing or "jamming" which begins early in the morning and continues well past midnight.

Island Foods:
- **Breadfruit:** Brought to the Caribbean from the South Pacific by Captain Bligh to feed to the slaves, breadfruit is a staple in the island diet. An oblong green vegetable, grown on local trees, it is cooked as a vegetable or made into bread, pie and pudding.
- **Cassava:** A starchy vegetable, the cassava was a staple of the Arawak and Carib Indians. Cassava is a root, which can be ground into a meal to make bread. The juice is often spiced with sugar, cinnamon, and cloves to make cassareep, an ingredient used in West Indian dishes.
- **Christophine:** A large squash with pale green flesh, which can be eaten raw or cooked as a side dish vegetable.

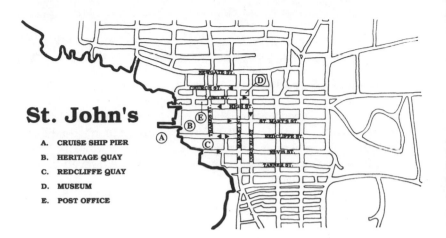

St. John's

A. CRUISE SHIP PIER
B. HERITAGE QUAY
C. REDCLIFFE QUAY
D. MUSEUM
E. POST OFFICE

Antigua

1. ST. JOHN'S
2. NELSON'S DOCKYARD
3. HAWKSBILL BEACH RESORT and GALLEY BAY

A. RUNAWAY BEACH CLUB
B. HALCYON COVE / DICKINSON BAY
C. RAMADA RENAISSANCE

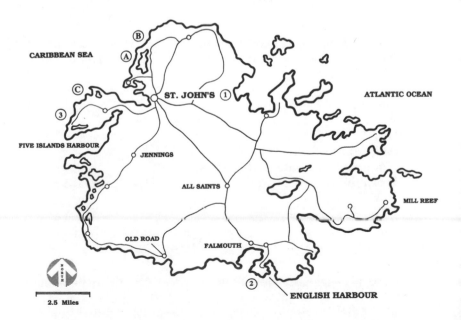

- **Dasheen:** Plants which supply the West Indian diet with edible spinach-like leaves, and tubers similar to potatoes. Soup made from dasheen is very tasty.
- **Fungee:** A pudding made with cornmeal and okra, and served as a side dish to flying fish or pepperpot stew.
- **Guava:** A tropical fruit about two inches long with a pinkish flesh that can be steamed, eaten raw or used to make a delicious drink.
- **Mango:** A yellowish-orange fruit commonly served at breakfast or for dessert.
- **Maubi:** A slightly fermented iced drink made from the bark of a tree mixed with ginger and sugar.
- **Pawpaw:** Commonly known outside the Caribbean as papaya, the fruit can attain weights of up to 10 pounds. It makes a delicious breakfast fruit.
- **Plantain:** The islands produce 13 varieties of banana, and plantain is the largest, less sweet, and has a starchy texture. It is used in casseroles, as a side dish, or fried in oil.
- **Roti:** A curried dish made from almost any kind of meat, mixed with vegetables and spices, wrapped in a light dough before cooking.
- **Sorrel:** A small annual plant whose red leaves are used to make a Christmas beverage.

Holidays:
When cruise ships are in port on Sundays and scheduled holidays, some shops in Heritage Quay and Redcliffe Quay will remain open for passengers.

January: 1st–New Years.
April: 1st–Good Friday; 3rd–Easter.
July: 28th–Carnival starts.
August: 2nd–Carnival ends.
November: 1st–Independence Day.
December: 24th–Christmas; 25th–Boxing Day; 31st–Old Year's Day.

The Pier

Cruise passengers arriving in Antigua dock directly in the island's capital of St. John's at a specially designed pier. Passengers can walk from the cruise ship straight into the modern duty-free shopping center, Heritage Quay (pronounced key) which contains a casino, a hotel, a pizza parlor, a car rental agency and a wide variety of shops. Visitors can also venture around the town of St. John's without the need of a taxi.

Pier Phones:
Exiting the ship, two credit card phones are located on the right, outside the Heritage Hotel. Further inside the shopping mall a bank of phones are located on the left. Antigua has a modern telephone system, Cable and Wireless, that can handle a credit card call, a Phonecard call, or collect call to any desired location. Antigua is the first Caribbean island to offer passengers a Phonecard system. For more information, see the Introduction Chapter, Pier Phones. The AT&T number for U.S.A. Direct Service is #1.

Museums & Historical Sites

The Museum of Antigua and Barbuda:
Located on the corner of Market and Long Streets, the Museum of Antigua and Barbuda occupies the Old Court House, built in 1750 of stone quarried from Antigua's northeastern coast. Opened in 1985, the museum visually displays the story of Antigua from its geological birth, through political independence, to the present day. It was designed with children in mind, with displays that encourage visitors to touch and experience first hand.

Special exhibits include a "wattle and daub" house model, pottery, steel pans, touchable artifacts, and utilitarian objects. One of the most prized possessions of the museum, exhibited by the front entrance, is the cricket bat used by island native Vivi Richards, the famous captain of the West Indies cricket team. Admission to the museum is free, but donations are encouraged. The museum is open Monday through Thursday 8:30 AM to 4 PM, Friday until 3 PM, and Saturday 10 AM to 2 PM. A museum gift shop contains books, postcards, and local handicrafts for the frequent visitor.

Nelson's Dockyard National Park: (Also see "One-Day" Itinerary)
The most unusual historical landmark on Antigua is Nelson's Dockyard, at English Harbour, one of the five most protected natural bays in the world. The British Royal Navy recognized the value of the bay and established the headquarters for its entire Caribbean fleet in the harbor. During the 150 years of use, the British built an astounding complex of naval facilities and fortifications.

Horatio Nelson was the military commander in the Caribbean from 1784 to 1787. Unbending when it came to following the naval rulebook, Nelson earned the animosity of the locals. Regulations stated that ONLY the goods produced on British colonies could be carried as cargo on British ships. Island merchants, who earned their livelihood by importing and exporting goods from all over the West Indies, were severely hampered by Nelson's strict adherence to regulations. The situation got so bad that Nelson feared for his life, and refused to sleep on land while in port. Nelson's tenure was short, and he never lived in the Admiral's House on the park's grounds, actually built in 1855. Nelson's later fame in the battle of Trafalgar made him a hero.

Today the Dockyard is the best preserved example of a British naval yard in the Caribbean. Many restored structures are currently used for yachting businesses similar to those originally occupying the buildings. English Harbour is renowned as the host of the Antigua Sailing Week at the end of every April, with more than 120 racing yachts competing in the regatta.

In Town

Currency:
Legal tender in Antigua is the Eastern Caribbean (E.C.) dollar which is tied to the U.S. dollar at approximately $2.70 E.C. to $1.00 U.S. The U.S. dollar, credit cards, and traveler's checks are accepted virtually everywhere, although exchange rates are better at banks than with local merchants.

A variety of banks are located near Heritage Quay on High Street. Banking hours are Monday-Thursday 8 AM to 1 PM and Friday 8 AM to 4 PM, while some banks close for lunch on Fridays. An automated teller machine is at the airport, and the Bank of Antigua and Swiss American Bank, Ltd. have branches at Nelson's Dockyard.

Postage:
As an independent country, Antigua issues its own postage. The Post Office on High Street in St. John's is a short walk to the left of the cruise port. The cost to mail a postcard is 30 cents E.C., or 12 cents U.S. (Remember U.S. postage is not accepted.) For passengers interested in collecting Antiguan stamps, the post office has a

Philatelic bureau inside the building to the left, offering a wonderful assortment of collectable stamps.

Shopping

Shops near the cruise port are open from 9 AM to 5 PM Monday-Saturday and on Sunday if a cruise ship is in port. The only duty-free shopping is offered in Heritage Quay and Redcliffe Quay. Carry your ship's boarding pass and picture identification to guarantee duty-free pricing.

Heritage Quay

Heritage Quay is one of the two duty-free shopping areas containing the popular stores Little Switzerland, Gucci, Benetton, and Colombian Emeralds. (See Introduction Chapter, Shopping)

Street Level Shops

SHIPWRECK SHOP offers island T-shirts, dolls, sun products, newspapers, and books about the islands.

NORMAS features gifts from around the world, and island-made plates, figurines, and ceramic house fronts made to resemble local houses.

RICHIE RICH is the only store offering Persian rugs, as well as West Indian cloth, jewelry, souvenirs, and household items.

Shops Upstairs

***CRAFT EMPOREUM carries merchandise that is 99% Caribbean-made including dolls, original art, handmade jewelry, candles with shells in the wax, locally made house front plaques, and hand painted plaques made from salvaged oil drums. The owners and shop personnel are also craftsmen, and will proudly point out their own work.

ISLAND ARTS contains a wide array of paintings, pottery, prints, and wood carvings presented in a pleasing atmosphere.

THE LAND SHOP is a manufacturer's outlet store featuring quality leather handbags, wallets, luggage, and accessories–all designed in Land's trademark colors, crafted from hand-cut cowhide with a five-year guarantee.

Redcliffe Quay

As you reach the end of Heritage Quay shopping area, turn right on Thames Street and walk one block to Redcliffe Street, the entrance to Redcliffe Quay. This area was once a slave compound, but a project beginning in the 1980's transformed the ruins into a unique shopping and dining area, retaining the original architecture and old world ambience. Shops are located on Redcliffe Street and in the interior courtyard, which can be entered through an alleyway off the street.

Shops on Redcliffe Street

DALILA offers handicrafts made in the Caribbean as well as a variety of colorful tropical clothing.

BEACH STUFF has a large selection of swim wear, T-shirts, sunglasses, hats, snorkeling equipment, and beach shoes. Almost anything needed for the beach is available at this shop.

***ISLAND WOMAN has exquisite designer dresses made out of filmy layers of fine batik fabrics. Swimwear, handbags, hats, sandals, and accessories are available.

***THE GOLDSMITTY features jewelry designs by owner Hans Smith, who was born in Holland, has been living in Antigua since 1965. Smith uses gemstones, pearls and gold to capture the shimmering beauty of coral reefs, frothy surf, and delicate spider webs in the most elegant pieces of jewelry on the island. All the jewelry is made on the premises.

POTPOURRI has the finest quality exotic fish and bird sculptures. They look remarkably real. The shop also carries unique jewelry and other island art.

TOY SHOP has toys for every age of child imported from England. The store also carries beach games, local baskets, souvenirs, and confections.

***GIFTS AND BASKETS (on the right of the interior plaza) has the best quality handmade merchandise, all made in Antigua, including special baskets, delicious jams, potpourri, chairs, original paintings, dolls, and souvenirs. For the stamp collector, a variety of stamps is also available.

POTTERY SHOP has a fine collection of hand-painted locally made figurines and pottery.

Shopping On The Island

LORD NELSON'S DOCKYARD has a gift shop that contains a fine selection of local handicrafts and nautical items. Also available at the entrance of the park is the Market Square with locals selling T-shirts, beaded jewelry, belts, and handicraft items.

TOURIST ATTRACTIONS around the island have friendly ladies who sell beaded necklaces (which they string themselves). Their necklaces and bracelets make excellent gifts, at very reasonable prices. Do not be put off by these persistent women; their trade is their livelihood, and a friendly bargaining session will leave you with fun memories.

Transportation, Excursions

Taxis:
Directly in front of the pier area, island taxis await cruise passengers in vehicles ranging from minivans to small cars. Most taxis are available for trips to the beaches, or an island tour to Nelson's Dockyard. Rates are for the whole taxi, seating one-five persons. You may try to bargain for a round-trip ride, but most drivers stay within the established rate guidelines.

Taxi Chart:

Destination	Cost*
Nelson's Dockyard	$16.00
Hawksbill Beach Resort	$12.00
Ramada Renaissance	$10.00
Halcyon Cove	$6.00
Runaway Beach	$6.00
Cedar Valley Golf Club	$6.00
Galley Bay	$12.00

All rates are for the whole taxi, with one to four persons.

Rental Cars:
Driving is on the left in Antigua, but the wide roads make driving easier for American drivers. However, the roads are in poor condition which makes driving a bit uncomfortable. Visitors must acquire a temporary Antiguan driver's permit for $12, available at the rental agencies. Minimum age to rent a car is 21, and a major credit card is required for rentals. Rates vary between $40 and $50 for air-conditioned four-door cars and jeeps. Gasoline is not included, and a Collision Damage Waiver is available for $10.

Rental Agencies: The area code for Antigua is (809), and is considered a long distance call from the United States.

    Budget 462-3009/462-3051/462-3007/toll free 1-800-648-4985
    Hertz 462-4114/462-4115
    Dollar Rent A Car 462-0362/462-0123/toll free 1-800-800-4000
    St. John's Car Rentals 462-0594/462-4600

Self-Guided Tour

Antigua has one of the most beautifully restored historical sites in all of the Caribbean. **Nelson's Dockyard National Park** has been permanently set aside for the protection of the natural environment, and for preservation of its extraordinary historic buildings. Entering the Dockyard is like stepping back into a time when sailors were exploring the seas, and English Harbour was a used as the headquarters for the British Royal Navy. A scenic 20-minute drive will bring you to the main entrance of the Dockyard, where you can explore the grounds and experience the lifestyle of the deck hands and officers centuries ago.

Organized Tours & Activities

All prices are quoted in U.S. dollars

1. *Jolly Roger* is one of the best party cruise boats in the Caribbean, with day cruises scheduled on Mondays, Tuesdays, and Wednesdays 9:30 AM-12:30 PM. The five-hour cruise can be arranged through the Ramada Renaissance tour desk (809) 462-3733 for $50 per person, or by calling the Jolly Roger directly, (809) 462-2064. The trip includes a barbecue lunch, dancing on the deck, walking the plank, and having a swing on the pirate rope.

2. An island tour down to Nelson's Dockyard, Shirley Heights, and the Dow's Hill Interpretation Center is available through the tour desk at the Ramada Renaissance. Tours leave at 10 AM and return at 1:30 PM for $17.50 per person. Contact the hotel directly to sign up for the tour by calling (809) 462-3733, or have a taxi driver take you to the Ramada after arriving in port.

3. The *Kokomo Cat* offers a variety of catamaran cruises throughout the week, leaving from the Ramada Renaissance at 9 AM returning at 5 PM.

- On Monday, Tuesday, Thursday, and Saturday a cruise around Antigua's majestic coastline is offered for $75 per person.
- An outer island trip to Bird Island National Park is available on Wednesdays for $60 per person.
- A special "Triple Destination" cruise offered on Sundays includes a beach-pickup cruise to Green Island for lunch and snorkeling, a sail down to English Harbour and Nelson's Dockyard for sightseeing, and finally a stop at Shirley Heights to enjoy the Antiguan sunset. The return trip to the Ramada is provided by taxi, for an all-inclusive price of $85 per person.

All cruises include a Caribbean buffet lunch, open bar, and snorkeling gear for the scheduled two hours of snorkeling on each cruise. Reservations for the *Kokomo Cat* are recommended. Call (809) 462-SAIL (7245) or 460-3550, or contacting the tour desk at the Ramada, (809) 462-3733. Do not miss the opportunity to sail the clear blue waters with one of Antigua's best catamaran cruises.

4. Sailing trips through Halcyon Watersports can be arranged by calling (809) 462-0256/0258 ext.217. Half-day trips, 9 AM-1 PM, are $35 per person, and full-day trips, 9 AM-4:30/5 PM, are $60 per person.

- *Quick Getaway* is a 40-foot sloop available for both half-day and full-day sailing trips, as well as snorkeling trips arranged with prior notice.
- *Tom Cat* is a 27-foot catamaran that offers open bar and snacks for half-day or full-day trips around the coastline of Antigua.
- *Tony's Glass Bottom Boat* is an unique sailing excursion with daily trips leaving daily at 2 PM. Take a ride around the coral coastline of Dickenson Bay to view the underwater sealife without getting wet. The cost is $20 per person, and the boat may fill up quickly.

5. A special two-hour snorkeling trip and glass bottom boat ride aboard the *Splish Splash* to Sandy Island leaves at 1:45 PM every day from the Ramada Renaissance's beach. Snorkeling equipment and drinks are included for $20 per person. Advance booking is recommended. Call (809) 461-0383 or the tour desk at the Ramada (809) 462-3733.

Antigua Beach Chart:

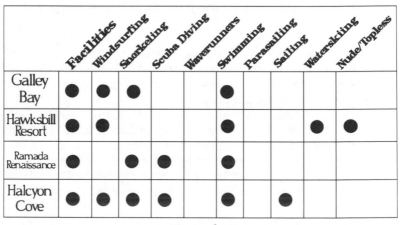

	Facilities	Windsurfing	Snorkeling	Scuba Diving	Waverunners	Swimming	Parasailing	Sailing	Waterskiing	Nude/Topless
Galley Bay	●	●	●			●				
Hawksbill Resort	●	●				●			●	●
Ramada Renaissance	●		●	●		●				
Halcyon Cove	●	●	●	●		●		●		

Beaches

The author's favorite beaches on Antigua are at Galley Bay and Hawksbill Beach Resort. Both resorts offer a beach-side restaurant and bar for daily visitors, and are 15-20 minutes from the pier area.

1. Galley Bay has a selection of picturesque thatched-roof "Gauguin Cottages" that offer a "primitive" hotel room for the most adventurous traveler. The wide stretch of beach is ideal for relaxing in the Caribbean sun, the pounding waves, and rocky coast to the right create perfect conditions for windsurfing and snorkeling. Good swimmers can locate a sunken wreck just off the beach, an interesting site for snorkeling. Snorkeling equipment is available for rent, $15/hour, as well as windsurfers from the office on the beach, but most visitors just enjoy resting in the sun.

The beach-side restaurant serves delicious island dishes, as well as continental cuisine. Cruisers can use the facilities if they frequent the beach bar, or dine in the restaurant for lunch. Galley Bay can offer some peace and quiet, or a day enjoying the watersport activities for island visitors.

2. Hawksbill Beach Resort is the perfect place for passengers who may wish to enjoy time on a beach offering a little privacy. There are four cove areas to choose from, and the beach farthest to the left is reserved for those wishing to sunbathe in the nude. Each beach-lined cove is a short walk from the main resort building, and allows visitors to find their own private space.

The resort is spread out on a large piece of property with rooms and cottages set right along the beach. An old sugar mill situated in the middle of the property is still being used today as a hotel gift shop and may be the closest some passengers get to seeing a piece of Antigua's past. Those interested in watersports can inquire at the social desk next to the beach-side restaurant.

3. The **Ramada Renaissance Royal Antiguan** has a private cove perfect for spending the entire day at the beach. A 15-minute taxi takes visitors to the main entrance of the hotel, and a short walk through the grounds leads to the beach. The hotel has a restaurant, rest room facilities, and a watersports office right on the beach. The beach office has chairs and watersports equipment for visitors to rent. The **Aquanaut Diving Centre** next to the beach offers daily dive trips and scuba equipment for rent.

4. Halcyon Cove on Dickenson Bay has the best beach for water-sports and beach activities, but be aware the beach is quite popular and may be crowded on bright sunny days. A 15-minute taxi ride takes passengers to the resort, which has a restaurant, beach-side bar, and watersports center for all visitors. **Dive Antigua** has an office set up at the far right of the beach for daily dive trips, and **Halcyon Watersports** offers paddleboats ($10/hour) and windsurfing. Beach chairs are reserved for the hotel guests, but passengers can usually find a place along the mile-long stretch of white sandy beach.

Island Sports & Activities
All rates quoted in U.S. dollars

Golf:
Just three miles from St. John's is the 18-hole golf course designed by Ralph Aldridge. Daily green fees are $25 (18 holes) and $25 for cart rentals (18 holes). Green fees are $20 (9 holes), and an additional $13 for cart rentals (9 holes). Clubs are also available for $10 per day. The 10-minute taxi ride will cost only $6 for the whole taxi.

Tennis:
Courts are available at the **Ramada Renaissance** only 15 minutes from the cruise pier. A tennis pro is available for lessons (which run approximately $15 per hour) and equipment rentals. Contact the guest service desk at the Ramada to arrange court times: (809) 462-3733.

Horseback Riding:
Beach and mountain horseback rides are available from **Reliable Stables** through the Ramada Renaissance. Morning rides start at 9 AM and afternoon rides begin at 2 PM. The beach ride is 1 1/2 hours, with a cost of $30 per person; mountain rides are one hour and cost $20 per person. Advance reservations are recommended. Call either the Ramada guest service desk, (809) 462-3733, or Reliable Stables (809) 461-4086.

Bicycles:
A safe and easy way to see the rolling hills of Antigua is on a mountain bike. **Sun Cycles** rents bikes for $10 a day. Call (809) 461-0324 to make prior arrangements. The quiet scenic roads that make Antigua so beautiful are much easier to travel on by mountain bike than by car or taxi! However, riders should remember to get an island map from Sun Cycles and only bring along necessary items.

Windsurfing:
Halcyon Watersports offers a windsurfing school where they guarantee visitors will be windsurfing in two hours. Students learn about the equipment, practice on a land simulator, then perform the fundamentals of windsurfing in the water. Lessons are given from 10 AM to 2 PM for $40 per person. Advance bookings are required through the hotel's guest service desk, the water sports center (809) 462-0256, or 462-0383 (an answering machine). Basic windsurfing rentals are also available for $10/hour. Dickenson Bay is a great location for both beginners and advanced windsurfers.

Galley Bay, not usually crowded with tourists has high winds in its crescent-shaped bay, excellent conditions for windsurfing. Rentals are $25/30 minutes through the rental group on the beach.

Hawksbill Beach Resort next to Galley Bay also offers windsurfing for $20/30 minutes through the social area located near the restaurant on the beach. Both beaches are quiet and secluded, which make conditions perfect for beginners.

Water-skiing:
Hawksbill Beach Resort is one of the most glorious beaches on the island. They have water-skiing for $11/hour. Visitors can arrange for the activity with the social desk near the restaurant.

Scuba Diving:
For the dive experience of your life, take a trip with John Birk of **Dive Antigua**. John carries a large writing slate which he uses throughout the dive to explain sealife or point out curious creatures and he is by far the most prolific dive master with a slate you will ever encounter. Dive Antigua is at the Halcyon Cove Hotel but will make arrangements to pick up passengers at various locations. A single-tank dive costs $40 per person, and the two-tank dive is $60 per person, leaving at 9:30 AM and returning at 2 PM. The price includes tanks, weights, mask, fins, and snorkels; divers can also rent a regulator and BC jacket for $15. First-time divers can arrange for a Resort Scuba Course for $75 per person, including a lecture, pool session, and one open-water dive on the reef. All equipment is supplied, but passengers must arrange for the session before they arrive on the island. Dive Antigua takes divers to unmarked dive locations especially suited for viewing Antigua's sealife. Be sure to watch for 10-pound lobsters and the occasional nurse shark resting under the coral reefs. Contact Dive Antigua, (809) 462-DIVE (3483), or Halcyon Cove (809) 462-0256/0257 ext. 217 to arrange for the ultimate dive adventure.

Aquanaut Diving Centre, located on the beach at the Ramada Renaissance has a variety of diving trips for all levels of divers. Single-tank dives are $40 per person, and two-tank dives are $60 per person, with dives leaving at 9:30 AM from the Ramada's Beach. Snorkelers are also welcome on the dives, if space is available, for $20 per person. Equipment rentals are extra and cost $10 for regulators, $10 for BC jackets, or $15 for the combination. Contact Aquanaut in advance to reserve a dive by calling the dive shop through the Ramada Renaissance (809) 462-3733, or contact the owner Robert Billau on his private number (809) 461-8641. Ramada's beach is a perfect location for before and after the dive, offering every amenities.

Another popular location on the island, **Runaway Beach**, also has a qualified dive operation. **Dive Runaway** offers daily boat dives in the morning, leaving at 9:30 AM, returning in time for lunch at 12:00 PM, and an afternoon dive leaving at 1:30 PM, returning around 4:30 PM. A single tank dive costs $40 per person, a two-tank dive is $60 per person, and a Scubapro BC with Air II octopus and regulator is available for $15. Dives leave from the Runaway Beach Club, but with prior notice the dive boat can arrange to pick up passengers near the St. John's pier area. Contact Dive Runaway at (809) 462-2626 to make reservations for the daily dive, or have a taxi take you to the beach in time for the boat's departure.

One-Day Itinerary

Although Antigua claims to have 365 beaches, two of the best beaches have been selected for the "one-day" itinerary. Allow between six and seven hours for touring the island, visiting Nelson's Dockyard, and relaxing in the warm Caribbean sun. Rather than battling the rough roads on Antigua, plan to hire a taxi for the trip to English Harbour and the surrounding historical sites. You can either make arrangements for a round-trip journey with one driver or take multiple taxis from each location.

The following list gives the driving times to the sites, and the approximate cost for single trips with a taxi driver. The total taxi fare for the cab (1-4 persons) is $53.

Nelson's Dockyard and sites	20 minutes	$25
Hawksbill Beach Resort/Galley Bay	25 minutes	$16
St. John's	15 minutes	$12

What to Bring:
Bring along a camera to capture one of the best panoramic views of English Harbour and Nelson's Dockyard from Shirley Heights, which is the most photographed site on Antigua. Wear or bring a bathing suit for the day spent on one of Antigua's white sandy beaches and swimming in the blue crystalline waters. Plan to have lunch at Hawksbill Beach Resort or Galley Bay and, if asked politely, the hotel will usually allow passengers to borrow a towel for the beach rather than bringing one from the ship.

Directions:
Refer to the island map and a map from Nelson's Dockyard for numbers corresponding with the suggested sites described.

1. Begin your journey from St. John's at 9 AM in order to have plenty of time to explore the island. You can hire a taxi outside the cruise pier area to get to **Nelson's Dockyard** at English Harbour.

2. Upon entering the main entrance, you can acquire a map of the Dockyard and spend $1 per person for a guide to take you around the grounds. A Dockyard guide can explain the history and preservation efforts of the National Park. Spend up to two hours wandering around Nelson's Dockyard viewing one of the best examples of working history that could be imagined.

- Pass through the **Market Place**, with vendors offering island crafts and T-shirts, to the Engineer's Office which has been transformed into the **Admiral's Inn Hotel and Restaurant**. Take a walk through the lobby, which resembles an English pub, and visualize how the whole building might have looked when it was used as a Pitch and Tar storage area. Outside the building is a walkway leading to the remnants of the Boat House. The giant stone pillars that once held up the Boat House are an amazing example of the craftsmanship of past builders. Notice the man-made trough where the ships would sail into the building to have work done on their masts. Perhaps one day the Dockyard will reconstruct the full Boat House.
- Walk along the main street towards the **Admiral's House** found on the right. Built in 1855, the house was originally constructed as a residence for the Naval Officer in charge and the Storekeeper. Admiral Nelson never occupied the house, nor any other commanding admiral, but the ground floor museum houses interesting yachting mementos and naval relics once used during Nelson's command. Take a walk through the museum to see the display of yachting trophies won by local teams in the yearly sailing regatta. A gift shop to the left of the building has a superb collection of souvenirs of the Dockyard and surrounding sites on Antigua.
- Next to the Admiral's House is the large **Copper and Lumber Store**, a magnificent example of Georgian architecture, which has been converted into a hotel and restaurant. Be sure to notice the two large circular cisterns outside the building– built over 200 years ago and still holding water for the Dockyard today. Very little restoration has been needed on these structures because they were so expertly constructed by the English.
- On the right side of the Copper and Lumber Store is the **Officer's Quarters** which has two levels for visitors to explore. The upper level contains a Tea Shop Restaurant and Limey's Bar,

the Lord Nelson's Gallery, Art Centre, and Dockyard Photo Shop. The galleries contain a wide assortment of paintings and prints from local artists which make excellent gifts. The lower level of the building houses the Customs and Immigration office, as well as the Port Authority office where modern sailors entering English Harbour report for clearance.

- One of the last but most intriguing sites in the Dockyard is the **Capstan House**. Capstans were devices used to turn the ships on their side so repair work on the bottom of the boats could be done. Only the capstans themselves have been restored, but you can still imagine the amount of work required to turn one of the large sailing ships onto its side. From this vantage point, you can see the next stop on the itinerary, the Clarence House, situated across the harbor up on the hill.

- Upon leaving the Dockyard, have the taxi drive to the **Clarence House**, and listen to the guide of the house explain the rooms and the history of past occupants. Spend about 20 minutes on the hill, and be sure to take a picture back towards Nelson's Dockyard and surrounding harbor. Do leave a tip for the guide to encourage his future efforts.

- The next stop is the new **Dow's Hill Interpretation Center** offering a multi-media presentation of the history of Antigua and the British occupation of English Harbour. The 30-minute presentation is definitely worth viewing.

- The final historical site is **Shirley Heights**, where the most magnificent view of the entire Nelson's Dockyard National Park and English Harbour can be seen. From here you can take a beautiful panoramic photograph. The current structure was once used as a signal station. Message flags were flown to forewarn the Dockyard of approaching ships. The Old Lookout Building has been restored and contains a small restaurant and bar, perfect for a refreshing drink. Outside on the patio, there is always a group of sweet (but persistent) ladies selling hand-strung beaded necklaces for very low prices.

The taxi ride to Shirley Heights passes old structures once used by British troops, but now the site of weekly musical gatherings for locals and visitors to the island. The views of the Antiguan coastline and English Harbour are spectacular and make the trip from St. John's worthwhile.

3. When you are ready to head for the beach, you will need to decide whether you want privacy and relaxation or watersports and activities. **Hawksbill Beach Resort** has four beaches for visitors to choose from and you can usually find a peaceful spot. **Galley Bay** is a wide sandy beach with activities for sports enthusiasts and ocean lovers. Either trip will take approximately 20-25 minutes from the English Harbour area and, while crossing the countryside, be on the lookout for Sicilian donkeys which inhabit most of the island. (Also see Beaches for detailed descriptions of the two beaches.)

4. Spend up to three hours for lunch and relaxing on the beach–which should make the time approximately 4 PM. A 15-minute taxi ride back to St. John's will allow you an hour or more for shopping in Redcliffe Quay or Heritage Quay before the cruise ship departs. (Also see Shopping.)

St. Kitts

ATLANTIC OCEAN

Golden Rock Airport

The White House

Royal St. Kitts Golf Club

CARIBBEAN SEA

5

BASSETERRE

6

Frigate Bay

South Peninsula

South Friars Bay

Turtle Beach

1. ROMNEY MANOR &
   CARIBELLE BATIK FACTORY
2. BRIMSTONE HILL FORTRESS
3. BLACK ROCKS
4. RAWLINS PLANTATION
5. CONAREE BEACH
6. PELICAN MALL

NORTH

0   MILES   3

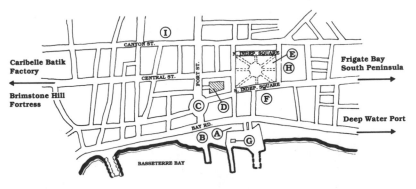

CANTON ST.

Caribelle Batik
Factory

N. INDEP. SQUARE

E

H

Frigate Bay
South Peninsula

CENTRAL ST.

FORT ST.

Brimstone Hill
Fortress

S. INDEP. SQUARE

F

C

D

Deep Water Port

BAY RD.

B A

G

BASSETERRE BAY

Basseterre

A. PELICAN MALL
   & TOURIST BUREAU
B. POST OFFICE
C. THE CIRCUS
D. TDC MALL

E. INDEPENDENCE SQUARE
F. GEORGIAN HOUSE
G. FERRY TICKET OFFICE
H. CATHOLIC CHURCH
I. ST. GEORGE'S ANGLICAN CHURCH

St. Kitts & Nevis

The Sugar Plantations of the Caribbean

Island Description:
St. Kitts was known as Liamuiga, the fertile isle, to the Caribs before Columbus dubbed it St. Christopher. The French, British, Dutch and Spanish were all aware of St. Christopher but none braved the fierce Caribs to settle there until Sir Thomas Warner arrived in 1623 with a small group of English settlers. He claimed the island for the British who shortened the name to St. Kitts.

Not long afterwards the French established a settlement at Basseterre, south of the British settlement near Old Road. The two cultures peacefully shared the island for a time in the same manner as the Dutch and French occupy St. Maarten today. However, the Carib Indians were unwilling to share their territory, and attacked the British settlement, murdering many of the settlers.

Sir Thomas Warner escaped to recruit British and French troops, who banded together and mounted an attack to drive the Caribs from their stronghold in the hills. As a result, the picturesque island became the scene of one of the bloodiest battles in Caribbean history. An estimated 2000 Caribs were slaughtered, causing the river to flow with blood for days. The site of the massacre was named Bloody Point and island tour guides speak of the incident with a sense of remorse.

Having no common enemy to unite against, the British and French were not content to share St. Kitts for long. As early as 1690 the French captured Fort Charles to the north, and the British mounted the first cannon on the promontory above Fort Charles, in an effort to recapture the fortress. The site later became known as Brimstone Hill, "The Gibraltar of the Caribbean," with its massive fortifications and unparalleled views of surrounding islands.

The British began the construction of Brimstone Hill, but the French breached the bastion in 1782. The British were heavily outnumbered when 8,000 French soldiers attacked 1,000 British who were manning the partially completed fortress. The British fought valiantly and were able to hold out for over a month before surrendering. As a sign of respect the French allowed the British soldiers and their commanders to march out of the fortress with all the honors of war, then return home to England. A year later the Treaty of Versailles returned St. Kitts to the British who were able to retain control of the island.

Today restoration of the Brimstone Hill Fortress encompasses five bastions spread over 37 acres. It is the most complete fortress in the Caribbean, built out of dark volcanic stone, and topped by the colossal Citadel of Fort George on the topmost peak. Brimstone Hill is the most interesting fortress in the islands, and well worth a visit. (See One-Day Itinerary.)

The French left a legacy on both St. Kitts and Nevis in the form of the green vervet monkey. The animals were imported by the French as pets and were turned loose when the adult monkeys became feral and too hard to handle. When the French left the islands, the monkeys remained and adapted quite well to island living, foraging for food in the dense rain forest and raiding plantation gardens. The breed thrived, and islanders joke that there are more monkeys living on the island than there are people. The black-faced shy creatures are about the size of a large dog, with white chest and a long tail used mainly for balance. They avoid contact with humans, but can often be sighted in the rain forest and on the road leading to the South Peninsula. Green monkeys have now lived on the islands for so long that they have evolved differently from their African cousins.

Shaped like a turkey drumstick, St. Kitts has a volcano at the northern end of the island (fat end of the drumstick), surrounded by lush rain forest. The fertile lowlands in the central region are home to the island's small population and Basseterre, the capital. The South Peninsula is relatively undeveloped, although a newly paved road provides access to future resorts. Its sister island, Nevis, is just two miles away from the southernmost tip of St. Kitts' peninsula, and has its own volcano and tropical atmosphere.

Nevis

Ask any local where Nevis got its name, and they will probably begin to laugh. The joke on Nevis is that when Columbus saw the wispy white clouds perpetually clinging to the volcano he claimed it looked like snow. Columbus then named the island Las Nieves,

Atlantic meets Caribbean Sea off St. Kitts

meaning snow, perhaps because he had run out of Saint's names, or felt homesick for his own snowcapped mountains in the Pyrenees. When the British occupied the island, they shortened the name to Nevis (pronounced nee-vus).

Almost circular in shape with its volcano in the center, Nevis looks like a cone from a distance and is more lush and tropical than St. Kitts. Lying nearly two miles apart, both islands share the same basic history. The popular American patriot, Alexander Hamilton was born on Nevis and Lord Horatio Nelson, the hero of the battle of Trafalgar, met and married his wife Frances Nisbet on Nevis. Museums have been established to commemorate both events and are a worthwhile tourist attraction. (See Museums and Historic Sites, and Organized Tours.)

Nevisians are quick to point out that Nevis is a much nicer place to live than St. Kitts although the reverse is also claimed by Kittitians. The small agricultural island has a character of its own, almost old-world in nature. Old plantation houses built from quarried volcanic stone have been converted into romantic guest houses and the coral reef surrounding the island creates intriguing white sand beaches, an oddity on volcanic islands.

The capital, Charlestown, is crowded only when the daily ferry arrives from St. Kitts, and on Saturday mornings when farmers bring their goods to sell in the open-air produce market. Sea island cotton (used in Caribelle batiks) is grown on Nevis, while ginger is used to make ginger beer and exported as a spice.

The Island People:
An agricultural island, St. Kitts is one of the few Caribbean countries still growing sugar cane. Relatively untainted by tourism, the island possesses a picturesque charm. A drive through the countryside reveals acres of green flowing sugar cane fields, small farms with immaculate flower gardens, and quaint Victorian cottages set against a backdrop of verdant green forests rising to meet the angular, rocky face of a mist-covered mountain.

Kittitians are proud of their English heritage. Their capital city, Basseterre, may retain a French name, but "the Circus" in the center of town with its tall green Victorian clocktower is very British. Independence Square, surrounded by stately Georgian-style homes, was once a thriving slave market and the lines dividing the white section from the black still are visible, though unused today.

Trafalgar Falls, Dominica

Nevis

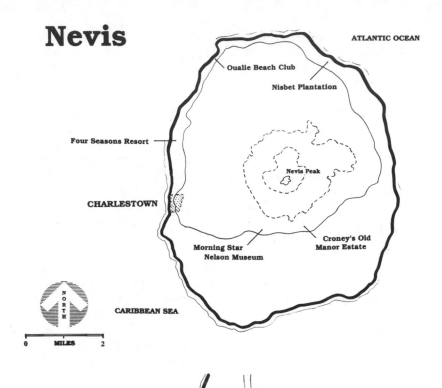

ATLANTIC OCEAN

Oualie Beach Club

Nisbet Plantation

Four Seasons Resort

Nevis Peak

CHARLESTOWN

Morning Star
Nelson Museum

Croney's Old
Manor Estate

NORTH

CARIBBEAN SEA

0   MILES   2

Charlestown

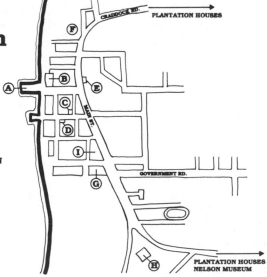

CRADDOCK RD.

PLANTATION HOUSES

MAIN ST.

GOVERNMENT RD.

PLANTATION HOUSES
NELSON MUSEUM

A. FERRY PIER

B. TAXI STATION

C. TOURIST BUREAU

D. PHILATELIC BUREAU

E. POST OFFICE

F. ALEXANDER HAMILTON
   MUSEUM

G. COURT HOUSE
   & LIBRARY

H. BATH HOTEL

I. MEMORIAL SQUARE

During Carnival, Independence Square becomes the center of festivities, with parades, calypso music, and street dancing. The highlight of Carnival is to watch the "clown dancers" snapping their "whips" overhead. The male dancers dress in costumes of colorful cloth which dangle in long strips, like the raggedy garments their slave ancestors used to wear. The whips, made from long strips of palm fronds, symbolize the emancipation of the slaves, now free to brandish their whips in a mocking pantomime of their old slave masters.

Learning from the mistakes of other islands, St. Kitts is approaching the development of tourism cautiously. Their first major undertaking was to construct a duty-free shopping mall at the ferry pier near the center of Basseterre. The Pelican Mall is an attractive structure blending English and Caribbean architecture. The next phase of construction will be to create a cruise ship docking facility connected with the mall, and to relocate the visiting cruise ships from their current docking facility in the Deep Water Port, which was originally built for commercial vessels. The cruise ship pier will probably be completed by the time you read this.

A few plantation houses on St. Kitts and Nevis have been renovated and opened to the public as hotels and restaurants. These stately dwellings are surrounded by sugar cane fields and recreate an era of grace and elegance. Take lunch at the White House, sip a cocktail at Rawlins Plantation, or simply shop at Romney Manor, and you will experience a tranquil West Indian setting. (See Self-Guided Tours and One-Day Itinerary.)

Island Proverbs:
"Don't worry be happy," is the best known island proverb. The West Indies slang, sometimes called Creole or Patois, includes unique sayings which help to understand the people and their special way of viewing the world. The following are just a few:

* "No badduh me." (Leave me alone.)
* "What ever in de old goat is in de kiddie." (Children often grow up like their parents.)
* "When de hog dance, rain's a coming." (Look for omens to foretell specific things.)

Holidays:
The ever increasing number of passenger ships frequenting St. Kitts are important to the island's economy. Docking schedules are

made public so everyone is aware of the arrival of their special daily guests. Businesses make an effort to stay open during peak hours and taxis are always on duty.

January: 1st–New Year's Day
April: Good Friday; Easter
May: 1st Monday–Labor Day; Witt Monday
June: 2nd Saturday–Queens Birthday
September: 19th–Independence Day–Carnival
December: 25th–Christmas; 26th–Boxing Day; 31st–Old Year's Day

The Pier

Until a permanent cruise ship pier is built at the new Pelican Mall, ships either anchor in the Deep Water Port and tender their passengers into the ferry pier at Pelican Mall, or dock at the commercial concrete pier facility. Few amenities are available on the commercial pier, and the distance to town is 2 1/2 miles. Cruise ships with 200 or fewer passengers such as Windstar, Club Med, and Renaissance Cruise Lines, normally anchor at Deep Water Port long enough for passengers to disembark for island tours and shopping. A few hours later, these ships may leave the pier area to sail down the coastline and anchor in a bay just off South Friars Beach. There they will await the return of their passengers. Taxi drivers are familiar with the ship's schedule and know where to return passengers after their adventures on St. Kitts. If you choose not to explore the island you can wait until the ship docks in the bay, then spend the day at the beach. (See Beaches.) Only a few smaller cruise lines schedule a stop at South Friars Beach, so ask your ship's personnel whether your ship makes the location change.

Pier Phones:
At the commercial Deep Water Port, a bank of phones is located dockside for passengers to use for local or long distance calls. Closer to town, the Pelican Mall also has phones for visitors to use. The AT&T Direct long distance service can be reached by calling 1-800-872-2881 from St. Kitts when using an AT&T credit card. An international operator assists in making collect calls, but the cost may be more expensive than other islands.

Arts & Crafts On The Pier:
Local islanders are well aware of ships due in port, and vendors line up alongside the dock displaying their goods for incoming tourists. Some shops in town also carry locally made coral jewelry, hand-made clothing, and souvenirs, but the dock area is probably the best place to view and purchase local handicrafts.

In Town

Currency:
The Eastern Caribbean dollar, tied to the U.S. dollar at approximately $2.70 E.C. to $1.00 U.S., is widely used in St. Kitts. Taxi drivers and tour operators often quote their rates in U.S. dollars, so be sure to ask if a price is quoted in E.C. or U.S.! Most merchants price merchandise in E.C., but gladly figure the exchange rate and accept U.S. currency, traveler's checks, and credit cards.

You may get a better exchange rate at a bank or through your credit card company than with local merchants. If the cruise ship visits several islands using E.C. currency, it may be prudent to cash some traveler's checks at a bank to secure the better rate. Banks in Basseterre are located in the Pelican Mall and TDC Mall off Fort Street leading away from the Circus. Bank hours are Monday-Friday 8 AM to 12 PM, and 3 to 5 PM on Fridays only.

Postage:
Postal facilities are at the Pelican Mall, and the St. Kitts' Post Office is next door to the Mall in downtown Basseterre. St. Kitts and Nevis both produce stamps bearing their own island's name and the rate to send an airmail postcard from either island is 50 cents E.C., or about 20 cents U.S. A great selection of St. Kitts collector issues are available at the Philatelic Bureau in the Pelican Mall (see Shopping, Pelican Mall). Also visit the Philatelic Bureau on Nevis which is to the right of the ferry station, near the open-air market square.

Museums & Historical Sites

St. Kitts:
Brimstone Hill is the finest restored fort found in the Caribbean. The entry charge is $5.00 and the site is open 9:30 AM-5:30 PM daily. Eight sites are currently restored within the 37 acres of five

bastions. You will notice cannons turned vertically on end lining the narrow drive to the fort, and set along the fort walls inside the massive entry gate.

A map is available at the entrance identifying the sites with numbers that correspond with markers in the historic area. A climb up the long stairway to the Citadel is rewarded by unsurpassed views of the steep slopes, Sandy Point, and the island of St. Eustastius in the distance. A small museum is at the top of the fort containing pre-Columbian artifacts, and a variety of British, French, and American Garrison displays are located in the old barracks rooms. A 25-minute drive to the Brimstone Hill Fortress National Park is an excellent site to visit, and is included on all taxi island tours. (See One-Day Itinerary.)

Nevis:
Alexander Hamilton, who drafted the U.S. Constitution and served as the U.S. Secretary of the Treasury, was born on Nevis. Hamilton's likeness appears on the U.S. $10 bill, but because Nevis was his place of birth, he was prohibited from running for the U.S. Presidency. Nevisians are proud of their link with the United States, and maintain Hamilton's birthplace as a landmark and the site of the **Nevis Historical Museum**. The museum is open Monday-Friday 8 AM to 4PM and Saturday 10 AM to 12 PM, with no charge for admission. (See Self-Guided Tours.)

The **Morning Star Nelson Museum** is an air-conditioned building containing Nelson memorabilia, clothing worn by Nelson and his wife, personal portraits, and historical displays. The museum is open Monday-Saturday 9:30 AM-1:00 PM with a charge of $2 for adults, and 75 cents for children. (Also see Self-Guided Tours.)

Historical Walking Tour

A guided historic walking tour of Basseterre, St. Kitts is available from the Georgian House at 10:30 AM Tuesday through Saturday with a four-person minimum. The cost is $15 without lunch or $35 including a gourmet lunch. The walk starts at Pelican Mall and ends at the historic Georgian House, where participants sip a complimentary beverage under a mango tree in a beautifully manicured walled garden.

The **Georgian House**, one of the oldest habitable buildings in St. Kitts, is on Independence Square in Basseterre. It is owned by

Roger Doche, a wonderful chef and personable individual, who runs an elegant gourmet restaurant and takes pride in his adopted island home. Roger personally leads the historic walking tour, and maintains an immaculate garden which he enjoys showing to guests. Call (809) 465-4049 or 3944 in advance for reservations or for an afternoon lunch.

Shopping

Stores are open from 8 AM to 4 PM, but some shops close during the noon hour for lunch. The shops are closed on Sundays, unless cruise ships are scheduled to arrive.

Around The Circus

ISLAND HOPPER carries West Indian crafts, presented in a pleasant atmosphere. The shop contains a selection of Caribelle Batiks (ask to see the batik process samples). If visitors cannot get out to see the Caribelle factory, the Island Hopper is the next best choice. The prices are exactly the same as at the factory, and the quality of the finished pieces has attracted repeat customers over their long history of production. The wall hangings with several overlays of color are intricate and take a great deal of time to produce, all by hand. The clothing is very comfortable, especially in the humid Caribbean climate.

PALMS ARCADE features locally designed, handmade clothing and accessories as well as a variety of island-made merchandise and souvenirs.

***OBJECT ART is an on-site jewelry factory with a showroom featuring black coral and conch shell sculptures, jewelry, and leather masks that rival any wall art in designer boutiques. The examples of local fine art are available at very reasonable prices. This factory/shop is located in the TDC Mall just off Fort Street, a half-block from the Circus.

RAMS DUTY-FREE is a one-stop shopping center just off the Circus on Liverpool Row. Rams carries Waterford crystal, Wedgewood china, Hummel figurines, Swarovski crystal, watches, jewelry, souvenirs, and offers great prices on island design T-shirts.

Pelican Mall

This is a new mall which offers duty-free prices comparable to those in larger shopping ports, but without the swarms of people. St. Kitts is new to the duty-free business, but sells perfumes, jewelry, porcelain and crystal at duty-free prices. Your browsing and buying will support their efforts.

PHILATELIC BUREAU contains a wide selection of attractive stamps for the collector, all bearing the name of St. Kitts. This is a relatively new stamp-producing country, and these beautiful editions would make a great gift for any collector. Stamps bearing the Nevis name are available only on Nevis.

LITTLE SWITZERLAND (See Introduction Chapter, Shopping.)

LINEN SHOP has a wide assortment of garments and products with prices comparable to those found on St. Thomas and St. Maarten and it is also a great place to find silver jewelry.

RAMS DUTY-FREE is a smaller shop than the one off the Circus, but offers the same great prices on duty-free items.

WINDJAMMER (upstairs) is a factory outlet store for tropical sports wear in vibrant colors. The quality of the clothing is excellent, and the line is not available in all duty-free shopping ports. The factory is located on St. Lucia, but great prices are offered on St. Kitts as well. Be sure to visit this outlet store!

TOURIST INFORMATION CENTER has a very helpful and friendly staff supplying free information, directions to banks, phones, or the post office, and island maps and brochures for daily visitors

SKANCRAFT (upstairs) is the government sponsored shop featuring island handicrafts. Batik paintings, tie-dyed clothes, embroidery, coconut shell designs, straw baskets, and homemade jams and jellies are among the many items in the store. The store is staffed by the craftspeople themselves, so tourists can talk to the creators and gain a better appreciation for their work. Excellent souvenirs are available at reasonable prices.

Shopping on the Island

***CARIBELLE BATIK** is housed in a historic 17th-century sugar plantation house, Romney Manor (see One-Day Itinerary), with five acres of gardens, and the largest tree on the island–a 350-year-old Saman tree. The work rooms where artists create vibrantly colored batik on sea island cotton are open to the public. A free tour and explanation of the batik process helps shoppers understand the quality and value of the merchandise available for sale in the adjoining showroom. Batik prices are based on the number of colors in the cloth, where each permanently dyed color represents a separate waxing and dying cycle. Sea Island cotton, grown on Nevis, feels almost like fine silk. The factory is open Monday-Friday 8:30 AM-4 PM (closed weekends and public holidays).

ROSE CAMERON'S GALLERY is located in a historic structure on Independence Square and gathers the best work of local artists, including the "Dancing Clown" paintings by Rose Cameron. These colorful characters whirl, and whip through her paintings to capture the spirit of Carnival. Rose Cameron's clown paintings are also displayed in the Tourist Information Center at the Pelican Mall (though not for sale), where you can see her work before visiting the gallery.

Transportation, Excursions

Taxis:
The taxi station at Deep Water Port has a long line of taxis awaiting the arrival of cruise passengers, often lining up the night before the ship arrives. You can take taxis into downtown Basseterre for shopping, out on the island for a sightseeing tour, or to one of the many beach-side resorts for fun in the sun. Taxi fares are regulated by a taxi association, and priced for the whole taxi, one to four persons. Some taxi fares out on the island are priced for a round-trip, so be sure to ask the driver for clarification. Prices are often quoted in U.S. dollars, but confirm the price before entering the taxi. The majority of drivers make enthusiastic tour guides, so take advantage of their friendly attitude for a wonderful day on the island.

Taxi Chart:

Destination	Cost
Romney Manor/Caribelle Batik	$15.00 rt
Brimstone Hill Fortress	$27.00 rt
Rawlins Plantation	$25.00 rt
The White House	$6.00 ow
Basseterre	$4.00 ow
Royal St. Kitts Golf Club	$4.00 ow
Frigate Bay	$5.00 ow
Conaree Beach	$5.00 ow
South Friars Bay	$5.00 ow
Ocean Terrace Inn	$4.00 ow
Turtle Bay Beach	$7.50 ow

The taxi rates are regulated as either a round-trip fare in the same taxi, or as a one-way passage.

Rental Cars:
Cars are available for rent in downtown Basseterre. Driving is on the left on St. Kitts and Nevis, so don't drive unless you can manage the English-style turnarounds and have no difficulty staying to the left side of the road. The unpaved island roads can be narrow and not clearly marked for tourists exploring on their own. The continuous road that encircles the entire island makes directions easy, but the total trip takes about six hours, time that few passengers may wish to spend.

Before renting a car, you must acquire a temporary driver's license at either the police or the fire station in Basseterre. The cost for a temporary license is $12, and most rental agencies can assist you in acquiring the license. A Collision Damage Waiver is highly recommended and costs $5-$10 from the rental agency. The minimum age for renting a car is 25 and a credit card is required to cover the deductible Collision Damage Waiver. Rates vary between $30 and $50, not including gasoline, for automatics and cars with air-conditioning. The cool island breezes on St. Kitts make air-conditioning an unnecessary expense. Jeeps are fun to rent and usually run $40 for the day, not including gasoline.

Rental Agencies: The area code for St. Kitts and Nevis is (809), a long distance phone call from the United States.

Sunshine Car Rental 465-2193, in the U.S. 1-800-621-1270
Delisle W. Alwyn Rentals 465-8449
Caines Rent-A-Car 465-2366

Self-Guided Tours

All prices are quoted in U.S. dollars

When St. Kitts was a flourishing sugar cane producing island, sugar plantations dotted the entire landscape. Today visitors to the island can still enjoy visiting several restored Great Houses and old Windmill ruins. Two of the most beautifully restored and maintained plantation houses are The White House, and Rawlins Plantation.

1. The White House is set in the foothills overlooking Basseterre and hosts one of the most exquisite restaurants on the island. Built in the early 1800's, the property and current Great House have undergone extensive renovations to recapture the plantation's former glory. The swimming pool and flower gardens are fabulous, and the view towards Basseterre is breathtaking. If you don't want to venture far from the ship or downtown, The White House is a good place to enjoy a gourmet lunch and the charming atmosphere of an old plantation. A 15-minute taxi ride can get you here for lunch, but you should call ahead first. Contact Janice Barber (809) 465-8162.

2. If you are venturing out on the island for a scenic tour, the best stop for lunch is also one of the oldest sugar cane estates on St. Kitts. **The Rawlins Plantation** has weathered hurricane Hugo and numerous renovations to become the immaculate and beautiful estate property it is today. The dining room was constructed over the ruins of the old boiling house, and its chimney is still in remarkable condition. One of the ten guest rooms occupies an old sugar mill, beautifully remodelled to create an interesting and special experience for visiting clientele. The property is perfectly manicured, and the buffet lunch served daily is tantalizing. Before leaving on the island tour, you or your taxi driver should contact the plantation to reserve space for an afternoon lunch. The West Indian buffet features typical island delicacies and a sampling of fresh produce from the gardens of the Rawlins Plantation. It is a feast not to be missed! Contact Paul or Claire Rawson at (809) 465-6221 to reserve space for the lunch and a guided tour around the facilities. It will take 45-minutes to reach the plantation, but the drive and views are spectacular.

3. Caribelle Batik Factory and **Brimstone Hill** (see One-Day Itinerary).

4. If you are interested in an outer island excursion, a trip to the sister island Nevis is definitely worthwhile. Behind the Pelican Mall in Basseterre is the ferry reception desk where you can purchase tickets and receive a current ferry schedule. Tickets are $4 one-way per person. The current ferry schedule to Nevis is as follows. (Be sure to check with the ferry reception desk for any changes to the schedule.)

Departs:	Arrives:
Monday:	
8:00 AM Basseterre	8:45 AM Charlestown
3:00 PM Charlestown	3:45 PM Basseterre
Tuesday:	
2:00 PM Basseterre	2:45 PM Charlestown
6:00 PM Charlestown	6:45 PM Basseterre
Wednesday:	
7:00 AM Basseterre	7:45 AM Charlestown
8:00 AM Charlestown	8:45 AM Basseterre
4:00 PM Basseterre	4:45 PM Charlestown
6:00 PM Charlestown	6:45 PM Basseterre
Thursday: no service	
Friday:	
8:30 AM Basseterre	9:15 AM Charlestown
3:00 PM Charlestown	3:45 PM Basseterre
Saturday:	
8:30 AM Basseterre	9:15 AM Charlestown
2:00 PM Charlestown	2:45 PM Basseterre
Sunday: no service	

After arriving in Charlestown, take a walk around the small town starting to the left on Main Street. Two blocks down on the left is a small museum of Nevis historical memorabilia and the location where Alexander Hamilton was born. The museum opens its gates at 10 AM and charges no entrance fee. After viewing the museum and Charlestown, hire a taxi for an island tour, which takes about 3 1/2 hours and costs $45 for one-four persons. Also see the Nevis map for sites that should not be missed, including the following:

- **The Bath Hotel & Spring House**. Just outside Charlestown lies this, the oldest hotel in the Caribbean. The hotel is unique in that it sits over a fault line which has a hot spring running beneath the property. The spring has been used for hot baths for over 200 years, and visitors today can relax in the stimulating water for a nominal charge.

- **Morning Star Horatio Nelson's Museum.** The Morning Star was a sugar plantation and the site of a 1706 battle between the British and the French. When Britain's most famous admiral Lord Nelson used Nevis as a base of operations, he fell in love and married a local islander, Frances Nisbet, in 1787. The present museum has a wonderful personal collection of Lord Nelson's and Frances Nisbet's memorabilia. The museum is open Monday through Saturday 9 AM-1 PM, with an admission charge of $2 for adults and 75 cents for children.
- **Croney's Old Manor Estate.** One of the loveliest restored sugar plantations on Nevis has preserved many sugar producing items and historical buildings for visitors to appreciate. There is a perfect view of the Nevis volcano from the charming grounds. If you can only visit one plantation, it should be the Old Manor.
- **Nisbet Plantation** is a more modern plantation with one of the most gorgeous and artistic gardens in the whole Caribbean. A walk through the rows of Royal Palm trees leads to a mile-long stretch of white coral sand beach that cannot be matched anywhere else. You are welcome to view the property but you should advise the front desk personnel of your presence. The Nisbet Plantation is one of the most magnificently maintained plantations on Nevis.
- **Oualie Beach Club.** If you get an early start on the island, you should plan to have lunch at this enchanting beach-side resort. Oualie Beach has a row of quaint cottages set along the beach with a wonderful view of the big island of St. Kitts. The private suites and cottages are specially designed to be distinctive to Nevis and they do not resemble a typical resort found anywhere else.
- For lunch in Charlestown, try **Eddy's Restaurant & Bar** opposite the Memorial Square. Eddy's prepares exquisite local island dishes and tropical drinks. Relax on the veranda of a 19th-century Great House overlooking the 18th-century streets of Charlestown. From here, passengers are only a block away from the ferry pier back to Basseterre.

Organized Tours & Activities

All prices are quoted in U.S. dollars

The following tours can be arranged through island hotels, who make special arrangements to accommodate cruise passengers if contacted prior to your arrival on St. Kitts. Most sailing trips and island excursions begin at 9 AM and return by 5 PM. For space availability and current times, please contact the tour group directly.

1. Both **Sunshine Travel & Tours** (809) 465-2193 (or toll-free 1-800-621-1270) and **Tropical Tours** (809) 465-4167/4039/9649 offer the following group of tours:

- **Guided Island Tour.** Consists of a drive along the coastline through sugar cane fields to the Black Rocks, the Brimstone Hill Fortress & Museum, and Romney Manor's Caribelle Batik Factory. The entire tour lasts three-four hours for $12 per person.
- **Queen City/Sister Island Tour;** takes passengers on the ferry over to Nevis for a day of exploring the Nelson Museum, Alexander Hamilton birthplace, the Old Bath House, and historical sites around the island. The tour is an all day adventure, 6-7 hours for a cost of $40 per person.
- **Volcano Crater Tour.** A rainforest hike for the very fit adventurer to the extinct Volcano Crater Lake. Hikers have the opportunity to view shy green monkeys, exotic birds, and fragrant orchids. The tour is six to seven hours and $35 per person.
- **Rain Forest Safari** is an expertly guided hike for all ages through the unspoiled rainforest of St. Kitts. The tour is four-five hours long and costs $30 per person.

2. Tropical Tours also offers a sailing trip aboard the *Celica III*, a full-day catamaran trip which includes a visit to Nevis for a beach barbecue and snorkeling. Transportation, open bar, and snorkeling equipment are all included in the price of $35 per person. The crew aboard the *Celica III* makes sure everyone has a great time swimming, dancing, snorkeling, or walking the plank. For more information call (809) 465-4167/4039/9649.

3. Sail on St. Kitts' only glass bottom catamaran, the *Tropical Dreamer* for $40 per person. The price includes a fabulous beach barbecue, an open bar, and snorkeling with sea turtles and colorful marine life. The sail to Nevis allows passengers to rest and relax, or dance the day away on the spacious deck. For daily sailing times contact (809) 465-8224.

4. The local taxi association has **Island Tours** leaving from Deep Water Port to the Brimstone Hill Fortress, Romney Manor and Caribelle Batik Factory at $30 per person. There is an additional $5 entrance fee to the Fortress, and the mini-tour lasts three hours. A complete island tour, including the Fortress and Batik Factory, takes five hours and costs $48 per person. If you have time for the longer tour, it is worthwhile. But the mini-tour is just as interesting and allows you the opportunity to spend time at one of the beaches or wandering around Basseterre. The taxi drivers on St. Kitts are among the most pleasant and informative in the islands.

St. Kitts Beach Chart:

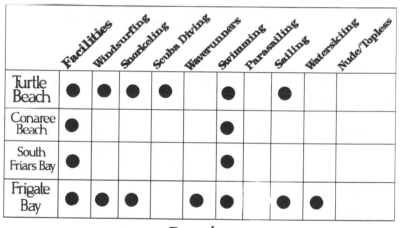

	Facilities	Windsurfing	Snorkeling	Scuba Diving	Waverunners	Swimming	Parasailing	Sailing	Waterskiing	Nude/Topless
Turtle Beach	●	●	●	●		●		●		
Conaree Beach	●					●				
South Friars Bay	●					●				
Frigate Bay	●	●	●		●	●		●	●	

Beaches

1. The South Peninsula is an undeveloped area of St. Kitts inhabited by hundreds of shy Green Vervet Monkeys. On the edge closest to the sister island of Nevis lies a special beach area known as **Turtle Beach**. If you prefer to spend the whole day at a beach this is a good choice, with its beach-side restaurant, bar, private stretch of sand, and a protected tropical reef perfect for snorkeling or scuba diving. Visitors can also rent windsurfers, kyacks, and bicycles for exploring the peninsula. You may well fall in love with the island given the chance to relax on the beach, observe the island's unique monkey population, and view all the colorful tropical fish inhabiting the local waters.

The beach has a volleyball court for athletes, shade trees for those requiring sun protection, and on Sundays it hosts an exceptional lunch buffet with a steel band between 12:30 and 3 PM. Turtle Beach is 20-30 minutes from the Deep Water Port and costs $31 for one-four persons round-trip. The trip out to the beach along the Atlantic Ocean is breathtaking and, while at the beach, you may feel as though you have the entire place to yourself.

2. A long, wide white sandy beach often uninhabited by people is **Conaree Beach**. You can hire a taxi to take you to the Sun 'n Sand Beach Village and a stroll through the grounds will lead straight to the beach. The beach is situated on the Atlantic side of Frigate Bay, with pounding waves that are both dramatic and powerful. Swimmers should stay close to the shore, but you can have an adventurous time playing in the waves. The beach is large enough for all cruise passengers and allows everyone to have a private piece of paradise. Be sure to wander through the Sun 'n Sand complex, complete with a restaurant, grocery store, and small gift shop, which is definitely one of St. Kitts' loveliest beach-side resorts. Taxi drivers are always available at the hotel and the ride is 15 minutes from downtown.

3. Twenty minutes from town on the South Peninsula lies **South Friars Bay**, a popular destination of some cruise ships like the Windstar and Club Med. South Friars Bay is located down a long road away from all other hotels, which allows passengers the freedom and privacy for enjoying the day on a Caribbean beach. Watersports are available when cruise ships are in port, and a $25 taxi for one to four persons brings you to the beach from Deep Water Port.

4. The Caribbean-side of Frigate Bay is home to **Timothy Beach Resort** and **RG Watersports**. Passengers can take a 15-minute taxi ride to the beach and have some fun in the sun. The **Coconut Cafe** at the Timothy Beach Resort offers lunch and facilities for daily cruise passengers. Down the beach is the **Anchorage Restaurant**, with appetizing island food as well as American dishes. RG Watersports, to the right of Timothy Beach Resort, has jet skis, beach chairs, snorkeling equipment, water-skiing and windsurfers for rent. The equipment is in average condition, but the rates are reasonable.

Island Sports & Activities

All rates are quoted in U.S. dollars

Golf:
Only 15 minutes from Basseterre is a lush 18-hole championship golf course. Designed by five-time British Open Champion Peter Thomson, the course borders both the Atlantic and Caribbean beaches. **The Royal St. Kitts Golf Club** has greens fees of $20 (9 holes), or $30 (18 holes). Cart rentals are $25 (9 holes), and $30 (18 holes). Clubs are also available for $10 (9 holes) and $15 (18 holes). Advance booking for tee times is recommended during the peak season, January-March. Call (809) 465-833 or 5776. A toll-free number is available in Chicago at 1-800-582-6208, and a local number in New York–(212) 535-1234–can also be used for reservations.

Horseback Riding:
Horseback rides through the rain forest or on the beach are available for all levels of riders. The rain forest ride with Tropical Tours is three-four hours long, while the beach ride with Sunshine Travel & Tours is one hour. Both rides cost $35 per person. It is strongly recommended that you contact one of the two operators before arriving because rides are often reserved for hotel guests on the island. Call Tropical Tours (809) 465-4167/4039/9649, and Sunshine Travel & Tours (809) 465-2193, toll-free 1-800-621-1270.

Windsurfing:
A quiet but exciting area to windsurf is out on the South Peninsula at Turtle Beach. Rentals are $10/hour and a fine selection of boards and sails are available. On the Caribbean side of the island, rentals are available from RG Watersports for $10/hour with a $10 deposit. Frigate Bay is only 15 minutes from the pier and has calmer seas that make learning much easier.

Jet Skis:
RG Watersports at Frigate Bay offers jet ski rentals at $35 for 30 minutes, and $60 for 90 minutes. The open bay on the Caribbean side of the island has wonderful conditions for learning, or playing in the surf.

Scuba Diving:
Pro Divers on Turtle Beach offer daily dives off the beach's protected coral reef. Specially trained dive instructors take extra precautions to protect the natural beauty of the underwater world on

St. Kitts. A single-tank dive is $40 per person; a double-tank dive is $60 per person, including all equipment. To help capture the feeling of the dive, underwater cameras with film and strobe are available for $20, and an underwater video system is also available for only $30 per dive.

For first-time divers, Pro Divers offer an Introductory Resort Course for $75 per person. The 3 1/2-hour course includes lessons, a boat trip, two shallow-water dives, equipment, and soft drinks. For those only interested in snorkeling, Pro Divers also offer half-day snorkel trips, 3 1/2 hours long, to three different sites, with equipment and drinks included for a cost of $25 per person. For large groups, boat charters to Nevis are available for $25 per person (minimum six persons) and full-day charters including snorkeling stops for $30 per person (minimum six persons).

For bookings and inquiries call (809) 465-3223 or 2754. Passengers can also make advanced reservations by calling the Ocean Terrace Inn's toll-free number, 1-800-524-0512, and asking about the Turtle Beach dive operator Pro Divers.

Kenneth's Dive Centre located on the waterfront in Basseterre offers a variety of dive packages for the daily visitor. Single-tank dives are $40 per person, and two tank dives are $60 per person. A resort course for non-certified divers is available for $60 per person including a pool session, and a shallow water or wreck dive. Kenneth Samuel takes certified divers to shipwrecks, black coral reefs, and other undisturbed coral reefs around St. Kitts for the dive experience of a lifetime. For advance reservations contact (809) 465-2670 or 7043.

One-Day Itinerary

One very special feature St. Kitts offers visitors is its friendly and informative locals. That most definitely includes the taxi drivers. To arrange passage with one driver, speak with a few of the drivers to find one willing to give a site-specific island tour. The cost of the taxi for a full day should be $100-$125 for one-four persons, which may be more expensive than other islands, but well worth the money! To assist in planning the island tour with the taxi driver, the sites and times recommended for each location are listed below. The total trip from Deep Water Port to Conaree Beach should take 5 1/2 hours.

Romney Manor & Caribelle Batik Factory	30 minutes
Brimstone Hill Fortress	1 hour
Black Rocks	30 minutes
Rawlins Plantation	1 hour 30 minutes
Sun 'n Sand Hotel/Conaree Beach	2 hours

What to Bring:
Of all items to bring, a camera with lots of film is a necessity. St. Kitts is a most impressive looking island with its rolling fields of sugar cane and dramatic coastlines. Bring along a bathing suit for the time spent at the beach. Lunch should be pre-arranged at Rawlins Plantation by having the taxi driver call, or by contacting Paul or Claire Rawson yourself at (809) 465-6221.

Directions:
Refer to the island map for numbers corresponding with the suggested sites described.

1. Begin your adventure from the Deep Water Port at 9 AM after hiring a taxi driver for the day. The driver will begin the tour through the capital of Basseterre, then travel up the coast to Romney Manor, home to the Caribelle Batik Factory. While driving to the factory, have the driver point out the unusual Indian petroglyph rocks sitting in a yard along the road.

Visitors to the factory will get the unique chance to see the actual process of producing high quality batik designs. First a design is sketched onto a piece of white cotton, then with great care molten wax is applied by a pen-like tool that pours out the wax, on the areas not to be colored by the first dye. Wherever wax is placed, the color will not be absorbed. Next the fabric is colored either by painting or dipping into the dye. For every color on the batik design, a separate waxing and dying process has to be performed. A wide selection of prints, light fabric clothes, and other dyed items are available for purchase from the store inside the factory.

2. The next stop on the coastline is **The Brimstone Hill Fortress National Park**. An entrance fee of $5 for adults and $2.50 for children will allow you to explore "The Gibraltar of the West Indies." Of all the forts and historical ruins in the Caribbean, The Brimstone Hill Fortress is the best and most complete example of British and French fort architecture open to the public. The entire grounds can be explored within an hour, but a visit to the Fortress would not be complete without a hike up the steep stairs to the top of Fort George. Excellent views of the surrounding countryside and the outer island St. Eustastius make a photographers dream come alive atop the walls of the fort. The **Fort George Museum** at the top of the stairs displays British, French, American, and Pre-Columbian artifacts in old barracks rooms. Built in the mid 1600's, this is definite highlight of St. Kitts.

3. A tour of the coastline would not be complete without a stop at the dramatic **Black Rocks**. These volcanic rocks along the coastline are jagged and sharp crevasses which create large sprays of water when the rough Atlantic waves crash against the massive rocks. The waves create great shots for video camcorders and photographers.

4. With prior arrangements, lunch at **Rawlins Plantation** is the next stop for the day. The gourmet West Indian buffet lunch contains an assortment of local dishes, including fresh fruit and produce grown on the property. The price for lunch is approximately $15-$20 per person, and highly recommended for any tourist visiting St. Kitts. Take a stroll through the manicured gardens, and view the remains of the sugar mill–once the center of activity on the plantation. Spend up to 90 minutes here, then proceed down the coast back through Basseterre.

5. Those searching for a wide stretch of coral white sand should head to **Conaree Beach**. Have the taxi driver stop at the entrance of the Sun 'n Sand Beach Village, then walk through the grounds to the beach. Pounding Atlantic waves hit the crescent-shaped cove of Frigate Bay in row after row–dramatic to watch and excellent for playing in the surf. Even good swimmers should stay close to the shore here. The long beach is also perfect for relaxing in the sun, with enough sand for everyone.

6. Upon arrival at the beach, passengers can either arrange for the driver to return in a few hours or dismiss him. After time at the beach, a taxi is easy to acquire from the hotel for the drive back into town, to the ship, or to Pelican Mall for some last minute souvenir shopping. At the conclusion of the tour, passengers should have spent between five and six hours of sightseeing.

Dominica

The Caribbean's "Nature Island"

Island Description:

It was on a Sunday that Columbus sailed past Dominica (pronounced domee-neeka), so the island was named after that day of the week. Iit is said that, to describe the island when Columbus returned to Spain, he crumpled a piece of stiff paper and placed it on a table, telling his audience that Dominica was an island of jagged peaks rising from the sea–an apt description for an island composed of towering mountains, deep river gorges, cascading waterfalls, and boiling lakes.

Formed by the eruptions of several volcanoes, at least two-thirds of Dominica's land area is covered by forest or other natural vegetation, with thousands of acres under the protection of national parks established by Dominica's farsighted government. The mountainous terrain is dissected by deep valleys and steep gorges, with some 365 streams and rivers, a hiker's paradise and a gardener's dream. Almost anything will grow in the rich volcanic soil–watered by almost 350 inches of water falling in the rain forest each year.

Dominica's inaccessible territory produced a turbulent history for the island, which changed ownership between the English and French many times. Both armies found it difficult to wage a successful land campaign, as the steep cliffs prevented conventional invasions, forcing an army to trudge through miles of extreme terrain to wage a "sneak attack" on their enemies. The two armies were known to pass within a mile of each other without meeting, and the forces of nature could defeat both armies before a battle was actually waged.

The dense jungle also proved beneficial to those who wished to hide from the dominating armed forces. Rebel slaves called Maroons, ran away from their masters disappearing into the tropical forest. Their resistance against slavery took the form of raiding estates and burning crops. The Maroons were defeated in 1815 in the Maroon War, but their influence was an element in the collapse of the economics of slavery.

Today, agriculture is the primary source of income for the majority of island inhabitants. Bananas are the largest export crop grown, and can be seen in large groves on the steepest of mountains. The banana plant is unique because it produces one bunch of bananas, and then it must be cut down to allow another plant to sprout from its roots. Blue bags which can be seen covering the stalks protect the bananas from insects and filter the sun's rays to improve growth. Another large source of income is the coconut, which is grown on the island, then made into hand soap, shampoos, and lotions in a local factory. Another small factory packages guava, passion fruit, and hot sauce from plants grown by locals.

The Island People:
Dominican culture is the closest to true native Caribbean life found in the islands, untainted by tourism. The island did not have paved roads until 1970 when a new road system was engineered to link the villages that were once completely isolated from each other.

Until the roads were built, men undertook the arduous land journey to the "big town" of Roseau rarely and only for business. A villager could be recognized by his distinctive looks, his family name and his accent, all linked to a village type. Children from the countryside who were sent to school in Roseau at great expense and sacrifice to their families were looked on as backward by their town-bred schoolmates. When paved roads linked the island and made travel easier, inter-village marriages became more common and the island began the process of melding into a modern society. The villages are slowly becoming a part of the whole country of Dominica, though individual village pride and identity are still displayed in community festivals and yearly religious events.

Today tourism has not infringed upon the island lifestyle to any large degree, and you will find few enterprises existing strictly for your pleasure. The government has shown its commitment to protecting the natural environment, and is developing tourism slowly. World economic factors may change attitudes as European trade agreements threaten to eliminate British price protections, which have traditionally favored Caribbean agriculture. Dominica may be forced to play the tourism game, but the island as a whole will continue efforts to protect its fragile environment.

Island Proverbs:
The following West Indian proverbs provide food for thought:

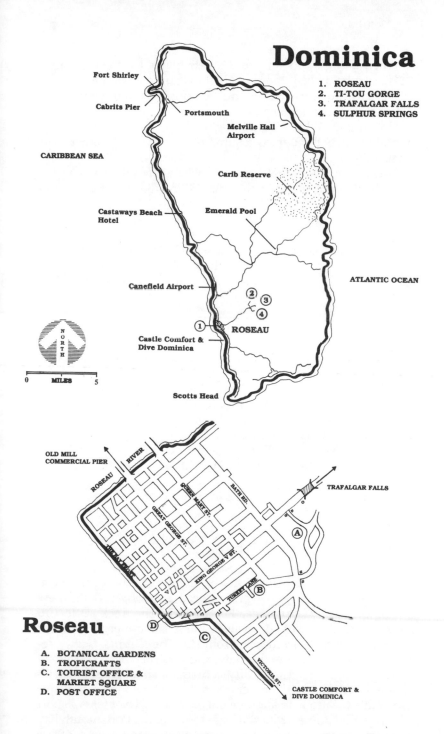

Dominica

1. ROSEAU
2. TI-TOU GORGE
3. TRAFALGAR FALLS
4. SULPHUR SPRINGS

Fort Shirley

Cabrits Pier

Portsmouth

Melville Hall Airport

CARIBBEAN SEA

Carib Reserve

Castaways Beach Hotel

Emerald Pool

Canefield Airport

ATLANTIC OCEAN

② ③
④
①　ROSEAU

Castle Comfort & Dive Dominica

NORTH

0　MILES　5

Scotts Head

Roseau

OLD MILL COMMERCIAL PIER

RIVER

ROSEAU

QUEEN MARY ST.

GREAT GEORGE ST.

BATH RD.

TRAFALGAR FALLS

Ⓐ

KING GEORGE V ST.

TURKEY LANE

Ⓑ

Ⓓ

Ⓒ

VICTORIA ST.

CASTLE COMFORT & DIVE DOMINICA

A. BOTANICAL GARDENS
B. TROPICRAFTS
C. TOURIST OFFICE & MARKET SQUARE
D. POST OFFICE

- "When a dog sucks an egg, he gets blamed fer everything." (Those who do bad things are blamed automatically.)
- "What hurt de turkey don't hurt de duck." (What bothers one doesn't bother another.)
- "How it go?" (What's happening?)
- "Make sure better den cock sure." (Know the truth rather than assuming.)
- "Home drum beats first." (See to your own family first.)
- "De truth come out when the spirit go in." (Alcohol loosens the tongue.)

Holidays:
As tourism has not become a major industry on Dominica, be prepared for shops to close on public holidays. However, taxis, tour guides, and dockside vendors are available whenever a cruise ship is in port.

January: 1st–New Year's Day; 2nd–Merchant's Holiday (shops close)

February: Carnival (Monday-Tuesday preceding Ash Wednesday)

April: 1st–Good Friday; 4th–Easter Monday

May: 2nd–May Day; 23rd–Whit Monday (Pentecost)

July: Domfesta (festival of the arts)

August: 1st Monday–August Monday

October: 20th–Heritage Day; 25th–Jorne Creole

November: 3rd–Independence Day; 4th-Community Service Day

December: 25th–Christmas; 26th–Boxing Day

The Pier

There are two docking locations on Dominica, the commercial docking area near Roseau (pronounced rose-oh) and the new docking center at Cabrits near Portsmouth. The dock at Roseau receives the majority of cruise ships but is a commercial docking area with minimal facilities for tourists. The Cabrits facility receives quite a few ships at this date, and was specifically designed for the tourist trade. The facility contains a small museum with displays of artifacts and local crafts, public telephones, a souvenir shop, and a theatre with audiovisual programs. The pier is a short walk from Fort Shirley which affords views of the Portsmouth Bay and gives visitors a sense of the colonial military importance of this location. The larger cruise ships dock at the port in Roseau, so the remainder of the chapter will use Roseau as a starting point for all tours and excursions.

Pier Phones:
Two public telephones are available at the commercial pier in Roseau for passengers, and the larger hotels near downtown Roseau may also allow visitors to use their phones for overseas calls. The modern docking facility at the Cabrits pier has a bank of public telephones for the express use of cruise ship passengers. Check with the tourist information desk to purchase island Phone Cards, or call 1-800-872-2881 to connect with the AT&T Direct service.

Arts & Crafts on the Pier:
When ships dock in Roseau, the local craftspeople literally set up shop at the pier. Intricately woven Carib baskets, carvings, walking canes covered with weaving, local jams, jellies, and dolls in authentic island costume can all be found at the ship's dock. The Cabrits tourist center has a souvenir gift shop stocked with the same type of island-made merchandise.

In Town

Currency:
The Eastern Caribbean dollar (E.C.) is the official currency of Dominica, tied to the U.S. dollar at approximately $2.70 E.C. to $1.00 U.S. Tour guides and taxis accept U.S. currency, but it is wise to use E.C. currency for making purchases in town and on the Carib Reserve. Be sure to carry bills in smaller denominations as it is difficult to receive change for larger bills in the rural areas. Credit cards and traveler's checks are widely accepted by merchants in Roseau.

Banks in Roseau are located on Hillsborough Street and across from the post office, open Monday-Friday 8 AM to 1 PM, and Fridays 3 to 5 PM. Passengers can also cash their traveler's checks and receive a better exchange rate for E.C. currency.

Postage:
Some of the most beautiful stamps in the islands are sold at the main post office in Roseau, located along the waterfront at the corner of Bay Street and King George V Street. Go to the ocean side

of the building and walk upstairs to find the entrance. Make your way through the construction now underway to improve the entire waterfront area and you will reach the Post Office. A special window is provided outside the office for the Philatelic Bureau, and many of the stamps available for purchase are displayed inside on the wall. Dominica produces beautiful stamps showing fish, humming birds, and historical events that will appeal to collectors. The rate to send an airmail postcard is 55 cents E.C., or approximately 20 cents U.S.

Museums & Historical Sites

The Old Sugar Mill Cultural Center:
A short ride from the cruise ship port in Roseau are the remains of a water-driven sugar cane mill with large wheels, some 20 feet in diameter, on display for visitors. The Old Mill was one of the largest and longest running mills on the island and it operates today as a cultural center and museum. Before leaving for the Old Mill, ask the taxi driver if the facility is open, since it may be closed for renovation.

Many of the old photographs taken by Andrew Green, a millionaire who bought the estate in 1908, are on display at the museum. Mr. Green reorganized the mill operations with steam crushers and electricity to produce a citrate of lime. Visitors can obtain an overview of the island's history, geography, and folklore from artifacts and displays in the museum. Be sure to walk up the hill to the right of the Old Mill to visit the Old Mill Woodcrafters. They are using the former overseer's house as a woodworking shop and showroom. Watch the artists at work carving superb pieces, then shop in the second story showroom filled with elegant finished pieces.

The Carib Reserve:
The dense forests and impassable terrain saved the race of Caribs from extinction on Dominica. When Europeans began settlements in the north at Cabrits and in the south at Roseau, the Caribs withdrew into the dense forest waging a guerilla war against any foolish enough to follow. Unhappy slaves often disappeared into the forest in much the same way, living off the land, raiding estates, and eluding their white masters. Today the Carib Reserve has been formally granted to approximately 3,000 Carib descendants. The Carib Indians engage in agriculture, fishing, and their

native crafts of carving canoes and weaving intricate straw goods.

The reserve is more like a township or province occupied by a particular ethnic race than a typical reservation for Indians. The property is owned by the entire tribe, and the Caribs have the right to build houses and raise crops on almost any part of the land they choose. When you are drive through the reserve, the distinctive physical characteristics distinguishing the Caribs from their West Indian neighbors are evident. Like many American Indian tribes, the Caribs have broader facial features, straighter dark hair, and skin more olive in color than black. The Caribs are shy, but their natural curiosity may cause them to stare at white tourists with the same wonder that causes the tourists to stare at them.

Be sure to stop at the small roadside craft shops, where delicately woven baskets, carved snakes that look almost real, canes covered in woven matting, and carved gourds are displayed for sale. The shy shop owner may be hesitant to tell you the price, and in many cases you may have to force them to sell you something. (See Shopping on the Island.)

Fort Shirley:
Dominica was the last island in the Caribbean to be colonized, and the forbidding topography limited the number of choice sites for construction. Fort Shirley, once the most important military outpost on the island, is a short walk from the new Cabrits cruise ship port in Portsmouth. The remaining structure is an excellent example of 18th-century British military defense systems and offers a wonderful view down into the harbor.

Shopping

Roseau

It is necessary to take a taxi into Roseau from the port area, so have the driver stop at the Botanical Gardens, near the cages of the Sisserou parrot exhibit. The exhibit features the elusive and nearly extinct Sisserou parrot, the national bird of Dominica, along with two colorful but endangered Amazon parrots. The Sisserou parrots are quite striking, with purple chest feathers accented by a multitude of green and blue feathers. The parrot exhibit was established to increase awareness by locals and visitors of the plight of the endangered birds. Too many parrots have been captured, smuggled out, and sold to collectors abroad, while the remaining birds have vanished deep into their own forests.

After viewing the parrot exhibit, wander through the gardens to see the colorful flowers and lush vegetation up close. When leaving, walk downhill on the main road leading out of the Botanical Gardens towards the ocean. Cross Bath Road and follow Queen Mary Street about one block. On the corner of Queen Mary Street and Turkey Lane (to the left) is Tropicrafts.

TROPICRAFTS, located near the Botanical Gardens, is the best place to find an assortment of locally made merchandise. The prices are reasonable, the quality exceptional, and the variety of products is nicely displayed. The store carries Carib Indian baskets, coconut soaps, guava jam, passion fruit concentrate, original artwork, books about the island and the Caribbean, and wood carvings. Local women may be observed weaving large grass floor mats, and they enjoy meeting visitors who stop in to admire their craft. The shop is well organized, and accepts credit cards and traveler's checks.

Turn left after exiting Tropicrafts, walk down Queen Mary Street one block, and turn left on King George V Street. Walk downhill towards the water and you will find yourself in the midst of a true West Indian town. Do not expect all the glitz and glamor of a duty-free shopping mall designed to appeal to tourists. Roseau was built over the years to handle the daily business of an agricultural island and to serve as its capital. Take time to walk the narrow streets of the town and see how business on a small scale is conducted. Visit the curio shops, bakeries and restaurants, and notice the buildings constructed with second story verandas, a reflection of the French influence on the island.

The Tourist Information Office is near the Post Office in the Old Market Square and has island information for daily tourists. The square has been maintained to reflect the past and houses interesting small open-air shops where tourists can browse and purchase souvenirs or postcards.

Shopping Outside Roseau

THE OLD MILL WOODCRAFTERS is to the right of the Old Sugar Mill Cultural Center and offers wooden sculptures made on-site by local artists. (See Historical Sites, Old Mill.)

CARIB INDIAN RESERVE SHOPS, 30 minutes from the town of Roseau, is in the Carib Reserve. Here you can visit a small strip of local shops run by the shy Carib Indians, offering a selection of woven baskets, hand-made items, and carved canes. You may need to ask the prices of merchandise that interests you, as the owners do not like to intrude. The prices for items are quoted in E.C. and you should carry small denominations of currency. Be sure to ask about the "wife leaders," a special instrument used by the ancient Caribs in raids to steal Arawak women, who were valued for their height. The unique tool is sure to be a conversation starter (or stopper) at home.

Transportation, Excursions

Taxis:
Passengers arriving at the commercial port on Dominica will find a great number of taxis waiting on the pier, and a few outside the commercial gates. Taxis are available to take passengers on island tours, or to desired locations for established taxi fares regulated by the local taxi association. One important factor visitors to Dominica should realize is that the drivers of taxis or tour vans rely heavily upon their fares. They will not try to cheat daily visitors, but will do their best to show them their spectacular island. The locals around the island are among the friendliest and most honest of all the Caribbean islands. Upon completion of an island tour or excursion, it is customary to tip the driver.

Taxi Chart:

Destination	Cost
Castle Comfort/Dive Dominica	$4.00
Emerald Pool	$22.00
Portsmouth	$43.00
Roseau	$2.00
Trafalgar Falls	$10.00

All rates are for the whole taxi, one to four persons.

Rental Cars:
Driving is on the left in Dominica, and only the truly brave should attempt driving. Of all the Caribbean islands, Dominica has some of the best conditioned roads, but the roads are also the narrowest and the steepest you will encounter. The local tour guides and taxi drivers know the "ins and outs" around the island, drive cau-

tiously, and are the safest and most reliable transportation on the island. You should only consider renting a car or four-wheel jeep if you feel confident driving on the left-side of the road, have the patience to drive slowly around sharp corners, honk when approaching blind curves, and remain very alert!

Most agencies offer a free pick up and return to the port, a Collision Damage Waiver at the rate of $6 per day, and require a credit card to cover the $400 for damage or loss to the vehicle. Visitors must also acquire a temporary driver's permit for $10 and must be over the age of 25 to rent a car. Rentals start at $35 and prior arrangement is not necessary.

Rental Agencies: The area code for Dominica is 809, a long distance phone call from the United States.

> **Budget Rent-A-Car** 449-2080
> **S.T.L. Rent-A-Car** 448-2340/4525/3425
> **Pierro Rental & Nature Safari** 448-2292
> **Wide Range Car Rentals** 448-2198/4099

Organized Tours & Activities

All tour prices are quoted in U.S. dollars

Before venturing out on the island, you must realize that Dominica is a very rural and unspoiled island that does not have attractions specifically designed for weekly tourists. Dominica's natural landscape and rainforest allows visitors to appreciate how Caribbean islands once appeared to British and French explorers. The island may not appeal to everyone, but after walking through the rain forest, or climbing over rocks to reach a breathtaking waterfall, the experience will bring out the adventurer hidden within. Go out on the island with an open mind, and you will probably be quite impressed with what you discover.

Ken's Hinterland Adventure Tours & Taxi Service provides the most interesting and informational tours on the island. The tours listed below are approximately five hours long, but with prior reservations the guides can customize a tour to the ship's particular schedule. The cost for the tours is $20 per person, based on one to four people, and are conducted in an air-conditioned, comfortable minivan with a local island guide. Ken's Tours are only available by reservation, so call before arriving in Dominica to be assured the greatest adventure on the "Nature Island" of the Caribbean.

1. Tour #1 is a trip to **Emerald Pool** and a drive through the **Carib Indian Reserve**. Emerald Pool is one of the first areas to be developed as a tourist attraction and features a 20-foot waterfall cascading into a shimmering pool below. The water is cool and refreshing; most visitors feel compelled to jump in and splash around. A special bonus provided with Ken's tours is a knowledgeable guide who will point out particular trees and vegetation unique to the Caribbean and Dominica along the pathways and roads.

The second part of the tour takes passengers through the only specially designated reserve in the Caribbean where original descendants of the Carib Indians still live and prosper on their own land. A stop at the craft stores in the reserve allows visitors the opportunity to purchase handmade straw and wooden souvenirs directly from the Carib Indians. The prices are unbelievably reasonable and the quality of baskets and crafts will impress visitors. Be sure to carry small amounts of U.S. or E.C. currency to avoid the hassle of making change. You will notice that the faces of the Carib Indians greatly resemble those of the American Indians who once dominated the U.S. The Indians have a close-knit society and continue to live in a tribe as their ancestors once did. The Carib Reserve also gives you an opportunity to see the rocky eastern coastline and the lush vegetation along the inland roads.

The tour guide will make stops along the roadside to point out the wide variety of bananas, passion fruit, cocoa trees, and allow you to taste different fruits. The total tour will leave you with the feeling that you have seen the natural side of Dominica with all its culture and beauty.

2. Tour #2 takes a drive along the west coast to the smaller cruise port area and the second major town on Dominica–**Portsmouth**. The tour first stops at the mouth of the Indian River for a boat trip into the tropical jungle. A boatman will take you on an adventure which creates the sensation of floating up the exotic Amazon river in South America. Fortunately on this river trip you will not have to worry about alligators or poisonous water snakes; simply sit back and enjoy the peace and tranquility of the rainforest. The boat ride costs an additional $8 U.S. or $20 E.C. and if you enjoy your time afloat a tip to the guide will be appreciated.

The second stop is at the **Cabrits Pier**, the alternate pier area currently receiving fewer ships than the pier in Roseau. The pier terminal has been specially designed for cruise passengers and has a collection of island artifacts on display for passing visitors. A short walk from the pier there is a trail leading to **Fort Shirley**, an excellent example of the massive fortresses that once protected the island from invaders. Wander through the ruins and imagine how the populated fort may have looked in the 18th century.

Tour #2 is easier, without as much walking, but with plenty of sightseeing and the unique experience of traveling up the tranquil Indian River. The drive along the west coast is dramatic, with views of high cliffs, crashing waves, and small fishing villages.

3. For a truly exhilarating experience, travelers to Dominica have a new tour option for exploring the rain forest. **Rain Forest Helicopter Tours** has established a new helicopter tour business that will intrigue the daily cruise passenger visiting the tropical island. A 10-15 minute ride takes you over the jagged peaks of the rain forest to view the steep mountains, lush valleys, and the Emerald Pool waterfall from the air. With music and a guide explaining the island's history, you get a complete island tour in 1/8 of the time it would take in a taxi. Weather conditions do not limit the flights and you will stay warm and dry while flying through the rain clouds hovering over the island. Cruise travelers arriving in Roseau are driven to a take-off point near Emerald Pool, while those arriving at the Cabrits Pier are picked up by the helicopter to begin their flight around the island. Helicopter tours are limited to one to four persons, at a cost of $50 per person. Contact Rain Forest Helicopter Tours by phone (809) 448-7623 or by fax (809) 448-2053.

4. The local taxi association also provides **Island Tours** at a cost of $17 per hour for one to four persons. These taxis are available at the pier, where you can arrange the price and inquire as to what sites will be covered by the tour. A two-to-three-hour tour to the Botanical Gardens, the lookout point over Roseau, and up to Trafalgar Falls should cost $10 per person. An island tour including a trip to the Emerald Pool, the Botanical Gardens, and the lookout point overlooking Roseau should cost $20 per person, and take three to four hours. Trips along the west coast to Portsmouth and the Indian River take four-five hours and cost $35 per person.

Cascade aux Ecrevisses waterfall, Guadeloupe

Beaches

Dominica is a volcanic island with dark to silvery grey beaches which are not as pleasant as coral islands for beachcoming. Dominica's specialty is its lush tropical rain forest, but if you are intent on going to a beach, the **Castaways Beach Hotel** is the closest beach to Roseau. A 30-minute drive along the west coast will bring you to the only beach-side resort on the island. The hotel has a restaurant and bar for visitors and you are welcome to use the facilities. However, because Dominica receives over 300 inches of rain per year, you may encounter an occasional rain shower during the day. The hotel also offers windsurfing, snorkeling, and diving. Call (809) 449-6244 to arrange for these activities in advance.

Ocean Sports

Rates are quoted in U.S. dollars

Scuba Diving:
Scuba diving reached new levels on Dominica when Derek and Ginette Perryman began **Dive Dominica**. The Perrymans have the most organized, professional, and friendly dive operation you will find in the Caribbean. Dive Dominica's underwater guides and dive instructors are highly qualified and the quality of their dives can't be matched anywhere on the island. Located 15 minutes from Roseau at Castle Comfort, they can make special arrangements with cruise passengers. Boat dives include tanks and weights; the rates are $40 for a one-tank dive and $70 for a two-tank dive. Snorkeling rentals include mask, fins, snorkel, and safety vest for $25 per person. If you want to learn how to dive, you can arrange for a "resort course" which includes all equipment, a short lecture, and two dives for the combined cost of $130 per person. A buoyancy vest and auto inflator are available for $8, regulators for $8, and a dive computer for $10.

Certified divers have a variety of locations to choose from, depending upon weather and water conditions. The hot bubbling reef at Champagne, the thriving sealife at The Pinnacle, and the swim through holes at Soufriere Pinnacle are among the best diving spots along the southern coastline. Spotted drum fish are abundant, as are bottom-dwelling snake eels, so keep your eyes open for them. Even snorkelers will enjoy every minute in the water; there is a great deal to see.

Relais du Moulin Hotel's windmill, Guadeloupe

Contact Dive Dominica before your ship arrives in port to ensure space availability on their daily boat departures. Derek and Ginette Perryman can be reached at (809) 448-2188, or by fax at (809) 448-6088.

If your ship is arriving at the Cabrits Pier in Portsmouth, Larry Bryant of **Windward Island Divers** offers dive packages for all levels of divers. With prior reservations, they can arrange to meet passengers at the pier terminal and provide transportation to and from the dive boat. A single-tank dive costs $35 per person without rental gear or $45 per person including all dive equipment. The dive boats leave at 9 AM and return at 2 PM for a half-day of diving the northern coastline of Dominica. Windward Island Divers can be contacted at (809) 445-4295, or fax them at (809) 445-5104.

One-Day Itinerary

Dominica offers the unique opportunity to visit a perfectly preserved rain forest island. In order to truly appreciate the island's natural beauty, you have to get out and hike the island. **Ken's Hinterland Adventure Tours** has a magnificent tour to Trafalgar Falls, Ti-Tou Gorge, and the Sulphur Springs geared for the "one-day sight-seer." The only deterrent is the possibility of bad weather. If there has been excessive rain before you arrive, the waterflow in Ti-Tou Gorge and at Trafalgar Falls may make access impossible, so rely on the judgment of your guide. The sites are amazing for those who make the effort, and this particular tour is designed for the nature lover who wants to explore. Be prepared to get wet and have the best day of your entire cruise.

The cost of the tour is $20 per person and must be reserved prior to arrival on the island. Ken's Tours can arrange to pick up passengers at the docking pier and you will spend up to five hours visiting the most breathtaking sites on the island. To make arrangements for the tour contact Ken George Dill at (809) 448-4850 or (809) 448-3517 (after hours).

What To Bring:
As you might expect, while hiking in the rain forest you are likely to encounter rain, so bring along a light rain jacket or clothes that dry quickly. Rather than carrying an umbrella, wear a baseball hat or a hat with a wide brim to allow the rain to run off. Also wear comfortable walking shoes or old tennis shoes with good traction for climbing over slippery rocks. Sandals with a strap around the

ankle and thick gripping soles are also excellent for walking through the river streams and climbing rocks. Finally, wear a bathing suit beneath your clothes and bring a towel for drying off after the swim up Ti-Tou Gorge and a dip in the hot springs at Trafalgar Falls. Bring a camera only if it is water-resistent and will not be damaged by the water in the rivers. Do not bring valuables (which would be left in the tour van). Just bring yourself and a sense of adventure.

Directions:
Refer to the island map for numbers corresponding with the suggested sites described.

1. If you contact Ken's Tours before arriving in Dominica, the tour van will be waiting near the pier for your arrival.

2. The tour itinerary is very flexible so, depending upon the conditions of the weather, the first stop is **Ti-Tou Gorge.** Located 20 minutes into the tropical rain forest above Roseau, Ti-Tou Gorge is one of the most fascinating places in the Caribbean. As its name, (meaning "little throat hole") implies, the gorge allows visitors to swim up the narrow "throat" of the mountain, and marvel at the twisted rock formations carved out by the power of the river. It is best for hikers to keep their shoes on during the swim because unseen rocks on the river bottom can be quite sharp on bare feet. After a short swim through a narrow slit in the mountain, you will be enchanted by the sculpted beauty of the gray canyon walls and will feel like an explorer forging a new path. At the end of the swim, the gorge opens into a misty cavern with a thundering waterfall that maintains a constant current of fresh water, which also makes for a fun and easy swim back out of the gorge.

3. The next stop is **Trafalgar Falls**, the most magnificent falls on Dominica. There are actually two waterfalls at Trafalgar, which you can view from the lookout point at the end of the 15-minute hike into the lush forest. The fall on the right is not easy to hike to, and is best viewed as a backdrop for pictures. The taller of the two falls, located to the left, is the most popular on the island. Cascading 200 feet down a rocky cliff face, the water gathers into small pools and pockets at the base. A stream of hot spring water trickles down the left side near the bottom, distinguished by bright orange streaks covering the rocks. The orange substance is not moss, but a chemical reaction from the hot water bringing out the color of iron-ore composites in the volcanic rock. The hot water flowing down over the rocks makes a great place to sit back, relax, and enjoy a hot shower. The thundering falls and hot springs are truly an unforgettable experience.

Trafalgar Falls are 20-25 minutes from Ti-Tou Gorge, and entail a 15-minute walk from the parking area to the viewing spot below the falls. For those in fairly good shape, or people who feel they can manage the climb up to the base of the falls, the fun really begins there. The tour guide leads and assists you up and over rocks for 10 minutes to the pools at the base of the fall. Upon reaching the falls, visitors often want to jump onto the rocks to find their pocket of hot spring water. The guide will point out the cold and the hot areas of the fall, as well as the safest way of climbing the rocks to reach your own private area. Once you have found your spot, allow the hot spring water to flow over your neck and back for a natural massage. Be careful on the hike down, but you should feel refreshed and rejuvenated.

4. A natural wonder unique to volcanic islands are the **Sulphur Springs**, which are pools that release hot gases directly from the bowels of the earth. The Sulphur Springs are a bubbling mass of black molten rock heated to temperatures will above the boiling point. Only 15 minutes from Trafalgar, the Springs are an easy walk from the road. Unless you are planning a trip to St. Lucia to visit its "drive-in volcano," the Sulphur Springs on Dominica may be the closest you get to seeing a volcano outlet. You may want to hold your breath while viewing the spring, but the hot pulsating bubbles splashing out of the ground are sure to impress even the well-traveled sightseer.

5. The drive along the steep winding roads of Dominica will give you the impression you have entered a tropical jungle deep in South America. The fabulous views of jagged mountains dropping straight down to the coastline, and the dense vegetation of the rain forest shrouded in mist, will intrigue you The trip should take approximately five hours, and the tour guide will return you directly to the pier terminal. Ken's guides are the most informative and the friendliest guides on the island; they will work hard to deserve an extra tip at the end of the day.

The French West Indies

Guadeloupe & Martinique

Island Description:
A visit to either Guadeloupe or Martinique is literally a visit to a region of France. Both islands are Overseas Departments of France. In 1974 the islands were given the further status of "Region" with full representation in the French Parliament in Paris.

After their discovery by Columbus, Spanish treasure hunters were successfully repelled by the indigenous Carib Indians and did not settle on either island. The first settlements were established in 1635 by the French, who fought the Caribs and drove them to neighboring islands. Cash crops introduced to the islands thrived in the rich volcanic soil, and the slave system enhanced the profitability of sugar cane and banana production.

The French and English battled over control of the islands until 1763, the year that France relinquished all rights to Canada in exchange for the French West Indies. The tug-of-war continued until 1815 when the Treaty of Paris designated both islands as French.

The British still claim ownership of the Rocher du Diamant/Diamond Rock, a small rock-island rising 600 feet from the sea just off the west coast of Martinique. The British used the rock as a "sloop of war" in 1804, and manned it for 17 months against all odds. Legend says the wily French invaded the rock, first with barrels of rum as bait and then with regiments to cast out the British. Since then, the site has been jokingly called "H.M.S. Diamond Rock," but it looks more like a green egg floating on the surface than a once-valuable military landmark.

The abolishment of slavery in the French West Indies occurred in 1848, largely through the efforts of Victor Schoelcher, who later donated 5,000 books and a strange looking house which became a library in Martinique. After the slave system ended, indentured Indians from Calcutta and Pondicherry were imported to replace the low level laborers, and many stayed when their contracts had ended.

Guadeloupe and Martinique are both volcanic islands, with recent volcanic activity. The town of St. Pierre in Martinique was completely destroyed by an eruption of the Mount Pelee volcano in 1902, but today the volcano appears harmless. Guadeloupe's volcano, La Soufriere is considered dormant but fumaroles emitting wisps of sulfurous vapor can be seen from miles away. Museums have been established on both islands to explain volcanology, and to visually demonstrate the catastrophic effects of an eruption.

The rain forests, natural by-products of volcanoes, are currently protected by the French Government in a Parc Naturel Regional/Natural Regional Park on each island. The parks are a part of the "Green Tourism" program which protects beautiful sites, landscapes, architectural and rural activities, and provides facilities for visitors to enjoy.

Island People:
The islands of the French West Indies are actually "France with a difference." As with most islands in the Caribbean, the people are a blend of ethnic strains from Africa, Europe, South America, and India. The mother country may be France, but the islands are 4,000 miles away and are influenced by an island atmosphere which adds spice to the French way of living.

Over three centuries, the disparate cultures have merged to create a new social structure and new customs. Traditions like Carnival are similar to those on other Caribbean islands, but savory cuisine and cosmopolitan attitudes are exclusively French, contributing to a distinctive island culture.

Language:
French is the official language and Creole is the common slang which is understood by West Indians in general. If you are not comfortable with French you may want to confine your shopping to the larger cities and stick with the larger hotels where English is spoken more frequently. Cruisers who plan to venture out on the islands should carry a French phrasebook to avoid awkward situations.

Currency:
The French franc is the official currency of the French West Indies, but U.S. dollars are accepted almost everywhere. The exchange rate is 5 francs (FF) for $1.00 U.S. dollar although the value of the franc fluctuates from week to week. It is a good idea to check the current exchange rate at the Tourist Information Center on the cruise ship pier, but when shopping or renting a car, use a credit card to obtain the best exchange rate. Banks are open from 8 AM to noon and from 2 to 4 PM weekdays. Some banks in Guadeloupe are open on Saturdays from 8 AM to 12:45 PM, and banks in Martinique open as early as 7:15 AM, but are not open on Saturdays.

Postage:
The islands of the French West Indies use the same postage as France, with no special island issues which might interest stamp collectors. Post offices in Guadeloupe and Martinique are crowded, confusing, and very difficult to utilize. They conduct many types of business at the post office, so very long lines are not uncommon. By all means buy stamps on the ship or in small shops rather than attempting to go to the post office. Local "cafes-tabacs," newsstands, and some souvenir shops also sell stamps. The postage rate to mail a postcard is currently 3.40 FF or about 70 cents U.S. When looking for postcards, do not be surprised to see "topless" picture postcards displayed openly on the racks near shops, as the French do not consider nudity immodest.

Guadeloupe

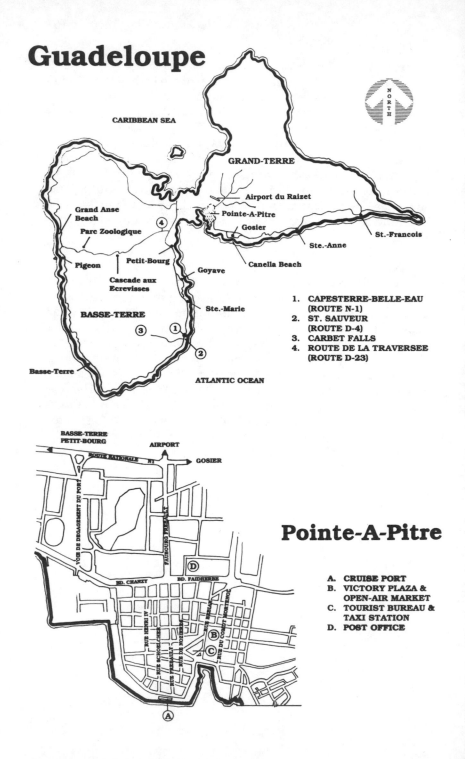

NORTH

CARIBBEAN SEA

GRAND-TERRE

Airport du Raizet

Grand Anse Beach

Parc Zoologique

Pointe-A-Pitre

Gosier

St.-Francois

Pigeon

Petit-Bourg

Ste.-Anne

Goyave

Canella Beach

Cascade aux Ecrevisses

BASSE-TERRE

Ste.-Marie

Basse-Terre

ATLANTIC OCEAN

1. CAPESTERRE-BELLE-EAU (ROUTE N-1)
2. ST. SAUVEUR (ROUTE D-4)
3. CARBET FALLS
4. ROUTE DE LA TRAVERSEE (ROUTE D-23)

Pointe-A-Pitre

BASSE-TERRE PETIT-BOURG

AIRPORT

ROUTE NATIONALE N1

GOSIER

VOIE DE DEGAGEMENT DU PORT

FAUBOURG FREBAULT

BD. CHANZY

BD. FAIDHERBE

RUE HENRI IV

RUE SCHOELCHER

RUE FREBAULT

RUE DE NOZIERES

RUE BEBIAN

RUE DU COMMDT MORTENOL

A. CRUISE PORT
B. VICTORY PLAZA & OPEN-AIR MARKET
C. TOURIST BUREAU & TAXI STATION
D. POST OFFICE

Guadeloupe

Land Of Beautiful Waters

Island Description And People:
The Indian name for Guadeloupe was "Karukera," meaning island of the Beautiful Waters, and a visit to one of their beaches will give you the same impression. Guadeloupe is actually two islands separated by a very narrow saltwater river, the Salee River, but connected by a bridge. Grande-Terre, where most of the large hotels are situated, is a large flat land mass with white sandy beaches. Basse-Terre is mountainous and contains the Parc National rain forest and the Soufriere volcano. Together the two halves look like a big green butterfly.

This is basically an agricultural island, growing bananas as its main crop, as well as sugar cane, fruits, spices, and flowers for export to France. Rum distilleries are still operating and are important to the economy, while tourism is becoming more vital each year.

Holidays:
The French are always sure to close their businesses on national holidays, and sometimes half a day before the scheduled holiday. Taxis and tours are available when a cruise ship is scheduled to arrive in port, but shopping might be scarce during a holiday period. During Carnival, all business comes to a halt for five days, but the festivities make a visit at Carnival time highly desirable.

January: 1st–New Years Day; 6th–Three Kings Day or Epiphany.
February: 12th through 16th–five days of carnival when all business comes to a halt; 15th–Mardi Gras, height of carnival, with parades and street dancing; 16th–Ash Wednesday.
April: 3rd–Easter Sunday; 4th–Easter Monday.
May: 2nd–Labor Day; 8th–VE Day; 27th–Slavery Abolition Day; 12th–Ascension Thursday; 23rd–Pentecost Monday.
July: 14th–Bastille Day; 21st–Schoelcher Day.
August: 15th–Assumption Day
November: 1st–All Saints Day (all cemetery tombstones are illuminated with candles); 11th–Armistice Day (fireworks).

December: 24th–Christmas Eve (dancing and revelry); 25th—Christmas Day; 28th Young Saints Day (costume parade); 31st New Year's Eve celebrations.

The Pier

The St. John Perse is a new complex where cruise ships dock in the heart of the downtown Pointe-A-Pitre commercial center. The French West Indies-style complex was built specifically for cruise passengers, combining traditional colonial architecture with a modern French design in a style like no other port in the Caribbean. Passengers can walk off the ship and straight into the duty-free shopping plaza or to town.

The new complex at the dock is only two years old, and just beginning to attract interesting shops. A currency exchange center with ATM credit card machines, a newsstand, and small boutiques are already open, but plans include a car rental agency, laundromat, and a long distance calling station. The Tourist Information Center is located just past the crowd of taxi drivers to the right near Victory Plaza. Brochures and information are available in French and English from a staff of English-speaking personnel.

Pier Phones:
Until a calling station opens at the pier, public telephones near the pier will be scarce. When exiting the ship there is one phone to the right near a restaurant, and another phone to the left at the end of the dock building. Ask at the Tourist Information Center for new phone locations and where to purchase "Telecartes," a prepaid discount phone card which can be used in special booths marked "Telecom." Telecartes can be purchased from outlets marked "Telecart en Vente Ici."

Making a telephone call from Guadeloupe is almost as difficult as placing a call from Paris, and similar in cost. When making a long distance call, dial 0 to reach an operator and let the recording in French run until a real operator comes on line. It may take an operator a very long time to answer, and there is no guarantee the operator will speak English. The best plan would be to wait a day and make your call from another island.

In Town

Shopping

The best buys on Guadeloupe are on luxury items made in France, including perfumes, china, crystal, champagne and wine. A discount of 20% is usually given to tourists who pay for their purchase with traveler's checks or major credit cards. Paying by credit card is a good idea as credit card companies secure a better exchange rate for their customers, but be sure the credit card slip is marked with FF or FRS to establish the correct currency type.

The French invented the concept of "chic boutiques" and define the meaning in elegant small shops filled with merchandise from worldwide sources and local artisans. The boutiques often appeal to the shopper seeking unusual and elegant merchandise. Shops are open weekdays from 9 AM to 1 PM, closed from 1 to 3 PM and reopen from 3 to 6 PM. Most shops are also open Saturday mornings and are closed Sundays and holidays. Personnel in the pier shops make an honest effort to speak English and assist passengers with their shopping.

Shops at St. John Perse

L'ARTIST PARFUMEUR is a boutique selling perfumes, silk shirts, jewelry, post cards and souvenirs.

MACABOU features island souvenirs, coral jewelry, and trinkets to fit every price range. The jewelry made from the spines of sea urchins is particularly attractive.

SIGNATURE–JEAN LOUIS PADEL is a designer jewelry store featuring the designs of Jean Louis Padel. The store also carries fine porcelain figurines, and crystal from France in an attractive modern setting.

COCAUUELLE features typical island souvenirs, and handicrafts. The stamp collector should ask to see the variety of "hard to find" older issue island stamps available only in this shop. The local post office is intimidating and the stamps available are plain issues, so the true collector should shop at Cocauuelle.

***COU DE SOLEIL** is the author's pick for the best store in the pier complex. Their locally designed and handcrafted coral and shell jewelry will delight the most sophisticated buyer. The displays are pleasing to the eye as well as to the pocket book. Be sure to climb the interior circular staircase to the second level where exotic specimens of coral, fish, and rock sculptures are displayed for sale. (Another outlet of this fine shop is located near the hotel strip in Gosier.)

BIJOUX AFRICAINS, meaning African jewelry, lives up to the name. This shop on the second level of the pier complex offers African-style jewelry designed by the owner, Suzanne Moulin, who warmly greets tourists. She also displays unique African boxes, and sculptures.

Shopping in Town

Just across the street from the St. John Perse complex are two shops offering Haitian wood carvings, and painted boxes, but no local crafts. The three narrow streets leading away from the pier complex contain duty-free stores with 20% discounts on perfumes, French fashions, crystal, and china if you pay with traveler's checks. It takes a hardy shopper to confront the traffic-choked commercial district, and those who do should plan their shopping from the cruise ship's list of recommended stores. If you dislike city congestion, shop in the St. John Perse complex, then take a taxi out of the city. Boutiques in the smaller beach towns are a much better choice for leisurely shopping.

The open-air market where locals buy fresh fruits, vegetables, and spices can be reached by walking along the waterfront heading right to Victory Plaza (starting with your back to the ship). Caribbean-style open-air bazaars are lively and offer the tourist a glimpse into the French West Indian culture.

Transportation, Excursions

Taxis:
Cruise ships docking at the St. John Perse in Pointe-A-Pitre will find taxis waiting to transport passengers on island tours and on trips to outer island attractions. Taxis either use meters in francs, or negotiate fares regulated by the government based on the whole taxi, which seats one to four people. The vehicles used on Guade-

loupe range from Mercedes-Benz cars to minivans, and the drivers take great pride in them. This is reflected in higher taxi rates compared to other islands.

On the French islands most taxi drivers do not speak fluent English, but they try to speak a few words for basic communication. Negotiating a taxi fare with drivers may be more difficult due to the language barrier, but be sure to establish a rate in francs or U.S. dollars before entering the taxi. Use a notepad to write down the number, and show it to the driver while negotiating to be sure the taxi price you have established is understood by both parties. A half-day island tour costs $85 U.S. for one to four persons.

Taxi Chart:

Destination	Cost
Airport	$6-8.00
Ste.-Anne	$20-25.00
St.-Francois	$30-35.00
Gosier	$10-15.00
Carbet Falls	$40-50.00
Pigeon Island	$20-25.00

All rates are for the whole taxi, one to four persons.

Rental Cars:
Driving on Guadeloupe is on the right which is easier for Americans. The roads and highways are clearly marked and they can be driven with the assistance of an island map.

You can rent a car at the airport by taking a taxi or call an agency prior to arrival and arrange to have a car waiting at the port area. When calling Guadeloupe, ask for someone who speaks English before trying to make arrangements. Most of the agencies at the airport have clerks who speak English and can easily assist passengers. A taxi to the airport will cost approximately $6, and prices for a daily rental range between $50 and $65. A valid driver's license is needed to rent a car and agencies usually require a credit card to cover the damage deposit. When you pay for the car, be sure the agency writes the total amount on the credit card slip in francs with a FF or FRS.

French motorists drive very fast, so drive defensively. Follow the road signs and be sure to get a map from the rental agency to avoid getting lost. Do not pull off the road in the rain forest unless there is a cleared parking area with gravel. Grassy areas are always soft and muddy; unknowing tourists can easily get stuck.

Rental Agencies: For a call to Guadeloupe, dial (011), the international access code, (590), the country code, then the local phone number as follows:

Avis 82-33-47/90-46-46
Budget 82-95-58
Hertz 82-00-14/82-88-44
Thrifty 91-55-66

Self-Guided Tours

All prices are quoted in U.S. dollars

1. Touring the Basse-Terre region of Guadeloupe gives visitors the opportunity to explore the **National Park**. The park is a lush rain forest with sites off of the Route de la Traversee like **Cascade aux Ecrevisses/Crayfish Falls**, and the **Parc Zoologique et Botanique/Zoological Park**. The 30-foot waterfall is an easy five-minute walk from the turn-off and the cool refreshing pool is ideal for a dip. The Zoological Park is an interesting botanical garden and zoo with mongooses, iguanas, and the island's own variety of raccoon. At the end of the route is **Ilets Pigeon/Pigeon Island**, where Jacques Cousteau has established a scuba diving preserve, with daily boat trips for divers and snorkelers. The total trip from Pointe-A-Pitre to Pigeon Island, with stops at the falls and zoo, takes between 90 minutes and two hours. The round-trip taxi fare should cost $50-$70 for one to four people.

2. Another trip to the southern section of Basse-Terre guides visitors to **Chutes du Carbet/Carbet Falls**. One hour from Pointe-A-Pitre, there are three hikes through the rain forest to extraordinary cascading waterfalls. The route to the falls passes through small seaside towns, a drive lined with flamboyant trees, and a section with tall royal palms. The scenic drive is beautiful, but the Carbet Falls are spectacular.

The lower waterfall is a 30-minute walk, and is the easiest hike for cruise passengers. The Premiere fall takes 2 1/2 hours to hike and is only recommended for those in good physical condition with six to seven hours to spend on the island. Another hike to the Grand Etang and La Soufriere volcano is an arduous three hours. It is a long venture not recommended for cruise passengers. All three hikes take visitors through shaded pathways, allowing them to experience the rain forest first hand. The waterfalls make excellent places to photograph and offer picturesque locations for an afternoon picnic. There are food vendors at the beginning of the trail to the falls with plenty of refreshments. Guadeloupe's most spectacular attraction is by far the Carbet Falls. The 3-hour round-trip costs approximately $80-95 by taxi, 1-4 people, but a rented car allows more flexibility.

Guadeloupe Beach Chart:

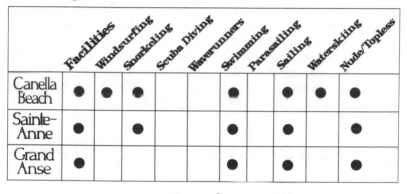

	Facilities	Windsurfing	Snorkeling	Scuba Diving	Waverunners	Swimming	Parasailing	Sailing	Waterskiing	Nude/Topless
Canella Beach	●	●	●			●		●	●	●
Sainte-Anne	●		●			●		●		●
Grand Anse	●					●		●		●

Beaches

A note for parents bringing children to the beach: Guadeloupe discourages complete nudity on the beach but, as in France, topless sunbathing is quite common.

1. The white sandy **Canella Beach**, located in Gosier along the southern edge of Grande-Terre, is ideal for cruise passengers. Taxi drivers can take you to one of the beachside hotels–a 15-minute drive from the pier. Canella Beach is lined with hotels where you can spend the afternoon and enjoy the watersport activities available on the beach. The hotels have restaurants for lunch and the nearby marina also contains shops and smaller tourist restaurants.

2. Further along the southern edge of Grande-Terre is the small town of **Sainte-Anne**, with a public beach stretching along the coastline. A 30-minute drive from Pointe-A-Pitre, the beach at Sainte-Anne is great for snorkeling or sailing Sunfish boats ($30-$40 per hour). The **Relais du Moulin**, located off the road between Gosier and Sainte-Anne, is a picturesque stop for visitors. The turn-off to the hotel is clearly marked with a billboard, and the old sugar windmill used as their reception area is visible from the road. The beautiful property is covered in multicolored bougainvilea vines, and the windmill is ideal for photographs. The hotel is an interesting side-trip on the way to the beach and has a wonderful restaurant for an afternoon lunch, but the personnel do not speak English. You can take a taxi direct to Sainte-Anne and back, but a better plan would be to make it part of a three-to-four-hour island taxi tour.

3. Located on the western coast of Basse-Terre is the most popular and beautiful beach on the island, **Grand Anse**. A 45-minute drive across the Route de la Traversée, a right turn at the end of the road intersection, and another 10 minutes along the coastline (N2) brings you to the turn-off on the left. A sign to Grand Anse leads you to this wide and very long stretch of sand–always alive with people picnicking, sunbathing, or enjoying the watersports available. Cruise passengers should include a stop at Grand Anse only if they are on an island tour, or renting a car for a day exploring Guadeloupe. A round-trip taxi ride to Grand Anse may cost up to $50 for one to four people, allowing one-two hours at the beach. Rates can be negotiated, but a rented car may be the best option.

Island & Ocean Sports

All rates are quoted in U.S. dollars

Golf:
Located 45 minutes from the port is a 18-hole golf course in the Saint-Francois region on Grande-Terre. The course was designed by Robert Trent Jones and offers a pro-shop, lockers, bar, restaurant, and an English speaking golf pro. The green fees are $45 and a taxi ride will take approximately 40 minutes to reach Saint-Francois. The course is quite far from Pointe-A-Pitre, so passengers should combine a trip to Saint-Francois with an island tour, or plan to spend time at the nearby beaches.

Tennis:
There are two tennis clubs near the port area at the **Marina Club** and the **Centre Lamby-Lambert** in Gosier. A 15-minute taxi ride can take passengers to either club, and court fees range between $15-20 an hour.

Ocean Sports

Unless passengers speak French, renting ocean sport equipment may be difficult. The hotels along the beach in Gosier have water-sports available for their guests, and often have personnel who speak some English. The following suggested ocean sports can be found along Canella Beach in Gosier.

Windsurfing:
Rates range between $12 and $14 an hour from many operators along the beach.

Waterskiing:
Rates begin at $20 for 15 minutes of waterskiing; rates can be negotiated lower for three or more people.

Sailing:
Hobie Cats are available for $40 an hour, Sunfish for $14 an hour, and pedalboats for $10 an hour.

Snorkeling:
Excellent reefs are located off the beach in Gosier, at the St. Francois reef, and Ilet du Gosier. Equipment is available for $15 per set, and hourly rates can be arranged through the hotels.

Scuba Diving:
The best scuba diving on Guadeloupe can be found off Pigeon Island, at the Jacques Cousteau Underwater Reserve. **Chez Guy et Christian** has a diving operation on Pigeon beach, but unless you speak French, it is highly recommended that you contact the group prior to arrival to arrange for an English speaking dive instructor. Chez Guy has a few members who speak English, and certified divers not using a dive computer should have an English speaking guide. The rate for a one-tank dive is $30 and the dive boat leaves at 9 AM, returning at 12:30 PM. The reserve is well protected and has striking coral reefs, enormous barrel sponges, and large schools of jacks. The underwater sites cannot be matched anywhere on the island, and it is worth the special effort needed to arrange a successful dive. Contact (011-590) 98-82-43 and use a French phrasebook for making arrangements.

One-Day Itinerary

Guadeloupe may prove difficult for those who do not speak fluent French, but exploring the wonders of nature requires no language skills. Guadeloupe's National Park contains spectacular waterfalls, and the drive down the coast to the Carbet Falls is quite picturesque. To begin the adventure, you should rent a car, which will give you the freedom to experience Basse-Terre on your own. The itinerary will take between four and five hours.

What to Bring:
Hiking shoes, or shoes with a gripping sole, are important for the trek to the waterfall. Secondly, a packed lunch and bottled water is vital because only snacks and pastries are available from the vendors at the beginning of the trail to Carbet Falls. Occasional rain showers are common to the rain forest, so bring a hat and light jacket to repel the raindrops, and if interested in taking a dip at the base of the fall, wear a bathing suit. Other than these few items, bring your spirit for adventure and a camera to capture the spectacular sites of the day.

Directions:
Refer to the island map for numbers corresponding with the suggested sites described.

1. Start as early as possible by reserving a rental car ahead of arrival, or by taking a taxi to the airport to make arrangements. Leave Pointe-A-Pitre by the main highway N-1, Route Nacional heading west towards Basse-Terre. Watch for signs to Petit-Bourg continuing on N-1. The road passes through Goyave to the town of **Sainte-Marie** where Columbus once landed and with a statue commemorating his visit. On the road towards Capesterre-Belle-Eau you pass through the "**Allée des Flamboyants**," a lane of overhanging flamboyant trees covered with bright red flowers which bloom from mid-June through September. Upon reaching the town of Capesterre-Belle-Eau, you will encounter the famous "**Allée Dumanoir**," a road lined with century-old royal palms.

2. After 45 minutes of driving, shortly after the row of palms, look for St. Sauveur and a sign to the right for **Chutes du Carbet**. Road D-4 will direct you through a large banana plantation on a narrow road which dead-ends at the trail to the falls. Follow the appropriate signs for 15 minutes, drive cautiously watching for other drivers, and honk when approaching blind curves. Once you have reached the end of the road, you can park along the road and begin the hike up to one of the falls.

3. Carbet Falls has three hiking trails to tiered waterfalls, and one to the Grand Etang and La Soufriere volcano. Cruise passengers should plan to hike to the first waterfall, a 65-foot cascade that is most impressive for photographs. The 30-minute hike through the tropical rain forest on a well traveled path, leads along the creek bed past giant ferns, palms, and flowering bushes on the way to the great fall. There is another smaller waterfall to the left of the Carbet Fall, where locals are often seen climbing with ropes. The base of the fall is ideal for a picnic lunch in the tranquility of the rain forest. Spend up to an hour exploring the grounds around the waterfall, then begin the journey back down the trail.

4. Another 30-minute walk back from the falls, a 15-minute drive back to the main highway, and 45-minutes to Pointe-A-Pitre will return you to the port. If you have more time to spend on the island, consider taking the Route de la Traversée for more sightee-ing (see Self-Guided Tours). The total trip, counting stops, should take between four and five hours. Guadeloupe's best attraction is its natural beauty, which can only be appreciated by getting out to explore the island.

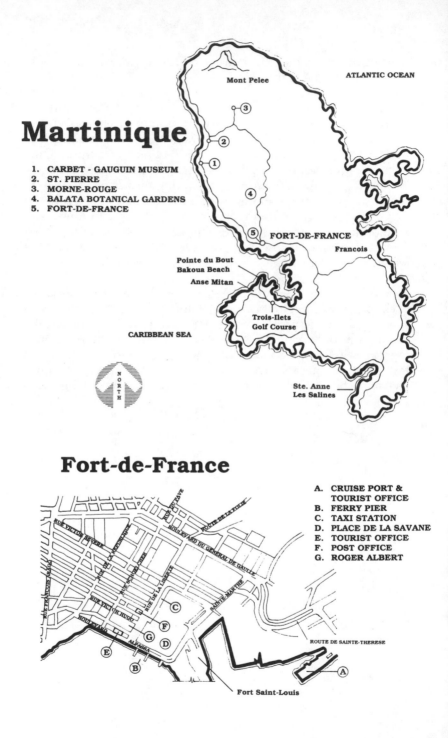

Martinique

1. CARBET - GAUGUIN MUSEUM
2. ST. PIERRE
3. MORNE-ROUGE
4. BALATA BOTANICAL GARDENS
5. FORT-DE-FRANCE

Mont Pelee

ATLANTIC OCEAN

FORT-DE-FRANCE

Francois

Pointe du Bout
Bakoua Beach
Anse Mitan

Trois-Ilets
Golf Course

CARIBBEAN SEA

Ste. Anne
Les Salines

Fort-de-France

A. CRUISE PORT &
   TOURIST OFFICE
B. FERRY PIER
C. TAXI STATION
D. PLACE DE LA SAVANE
E. TOURIST OFFICE
F. POST OFFICE
G. ROGER ALBERT

ROUTE DE SAINTE-THERESE

Fort Saint-Louis

Martinique

Isle Of Flowers

Island Description & People:
The Carib Indians called Martinique "Madinina," meaning Isle of
Flowers, and the French endeavor to protect the lush atmosphere.
Martinique is the larger of the two French islands, elongated in
shape with two large natural harbors on the calm Caribbean Sea.
The largest port at Fort-de-France, the capital, is continually filled
with yachts, sailboats, and visiting cruise liners. The other harbor
and the most beautiful beaches are at the southernmost point on
the island near Sainte-Anne.

The volcano and rain forest are at the northern end of the island
near Saint-Pierre, while the center of the island consists of several
mountain masses linked by hills called "mornes." The mountains
make the roads steep and winding, but they are lined with lush
tropical foliage, which makes the drive most enjoyable. The coastline, perfect for fishing and boating in the calm Caribbean waters,
has been Martinique's main asset. Saint-Pierre was known as the
"Paris of the West Indies," until it was destroyed in a volcanic
eruption, but today the village is just as beautiful as it ever was.

Two particular sites unique to Martinique are the birthplace of
Napoleon's wife, Josephine, and the site where the French painter,
Gauguin, lived on the island for five months in 1887. A special
museum commemorating each historical figure has been established for tourists (see Museums).

Holidays:
The French take national holidays seriously and close their businesses, sometimes half a day before the scheduled holiday. Taxis
and tours are always available when cruise ships are in port, but
shopping can become difficult on national holidays.

January: 1st–New Years Day; 6th–Three Kings Day or Epiphany.
February: 12th through 16th–five days of carnival when all
business comes to a halt; 15th–Mardi Gras (height of carnival,
with parades and street dancing); 16th–Ash Wednesday.

April: 3rd–Easter Sunday; 4th–Easter Monday; 18th to 25th–Aqua Festival Du Robert, a festival of the sea.

May: 2nd–Labor Day; 22nd–Slavery Abolition Day; 12th–Ascension Thursday; 23rd–Pentecost Monday; in St. Pierre all month long a program of theatre, dance, music and art commemorating the history of the city.

July: 14th–Bastille Day; 9th to 21st–Festival of Fort-de-France, a program of theater, dance, music and art commemorating the history of the city.

August: 15th–Assumption Day.

November: 1st–All Saints Day (all cemetery tombstones illuminated with candles); 11th–Armistice Day (fireworks); Semi-Marathon, a 22-km race; International Guitar Festival during the last part of the month.

December: 24th–Christmas Eve (dancing and revelry); 25th–Christmas Day; 28th–Young Saints Day (costume parade); 31st–New Year's Eve celebrations.

The Pier

The cruise ship terminal, located in the commercial district, is a 15- to 20-minute walk from Fort-de-France. If you want to walk into town, stay to the left upon leaving the pier area until you arrive at the Place de la Savane Park. The park contains a few historical statues and an open-air market across from the main downtown shopping area. The facilities at the pier include a Tourist Information Office, a telephone, a shady area for awaiting taxis, and a fine duty-free shop where you can purchase French perfume, champagne, wine, and other products.

Pier Phones:

As on Guadeloupe, making a long distance call from Martinique is difficult, frustrating, and should be avoided unless absolutely necessary. Only one phone is available at the pier. When trying to reach an operator, dial 0, then let the recording run for many minutes until a real operator comes on line. A "Telecarte" makes long distance calls easier and less expensive, but a one-minute call to the U.S. still costs 11.5 FF, about $2.30 U.S. The prepaid phone card can be used only in special booths marked "Telecom." Telecartes can be purchased from outlets marked "Telecart en Vente Ici." Ask the Tourism Office at the port for the nearest places to buy and use a Telecartes.

Shopping At The Pier:
La Maison Creole is located near the cruise terminal and carries top brand names in perfume, writing instruments, silk, leather goods, fancy jewelry, gold crafts, wine, champagne, and tobacco at duty-free prices. The staff is well-trained, friendly, and speaks English. Regulations require delivery of purchases at La Maison Creole directly to the ship before departure. You can then pick up your goods from the ship's purser or cruise director.

In Town

Museums

The **Martinique Departmental Museum**, located opposite La Savane park, is an archeological museum with exhibits portraying the Arawak culture and the Carib Indian's relationship to the history of Martinique. The museum is open weekdays from 9 AM to 1 PM, then from 2-5 PM, and 9 AM to 12 PM on Saturdays.

The **Gauguin Museum** is a small museum honoring the French painter who spent five months on the island in 1887. It contains Gauguin's personal documents, letters, and reproductions of his paintings, displayed in the heart of the landscape Gauguin loved. Located in Carbet on the route to St. Pierre, the museum is open daily from 10 AM to 5:30 PM. Admission is $2.

The **Vulcanological Museum** in St. Pierre is on the site of a former battery overlooking the sea. The museum recalls the tragic eruption of Mont Pelée in 1902. Only one person in the entire town survived the disaster. Photographs, oxidized glass, distorted musical instruments from the town's theater, and other items recovered from the ashes are on display. The museum was founded by the American vulcanologist Frank Perret in 1932 and is open daily from 9 AM to 12:30 PM and 3 to 5 PM.

La Pagerie Museum in the Trois-Ilets district is located on the spot where the Empress Josephine was born in 1763. Before she married Napoleon and ruled as the empress of France from 1804 to 1809, Josephine was married to Alexandre de Beauharnais. There was no love lost between them, as Alexandre had actually wanted to marry one of Josephine's more attractive sisters. The museum is a small exhibit of Josephine's mementos, including her childhood bed, paintings, and a passionate love letter from Napoleon. The collection was compiled by Dr. Robert Rose-Rosette and is displayed in the former kitchen of the estate, which lies in ruins–having been destroyed by a hurricane. Visitors may wander through the grounds containing the ruins of an old sugar-mill and thousands of colorful flowers. The museum is open Tuesday through Sunday from 9 AM to 5 PM.

Shopping

Fort-de-France has a reputation for being a miniature Paris in the heart of the Caribbean. Imported French fashions, perfumes, champagne, wine, crystal, and china are the best buys on the island. The **Roger Albert** store at 7 Rue Victor Hugo, across from the La Savane park is the best place to buy perfume, Lalique crystal, and French designer merchandise such as Cartier, Lacoste, Yves Saint Laurent, and Dupont. You will save 20% if you make your purchase with traveler's checks or a credit card. The staff at Roger Albert are friendly, speak English, and have been specially trained to provide service.

The best clothing shops can be found on the streets leading away from the La Savane park, on Rue Victor Hugo, Rue Moreau de Jones, Rue Antoine Siger, and Rue Lamartine. Jewelers are located primarily between Rue Isambert and Rue Lamartine. Look for their unique gold "knot necklaces" and "slave chains."

Local craftsmen create exotic coral and shell jewelry, bamboo objects, and basketry which can be purchased in an open air market across from Roger Albert in the La Savane park. Madras cloth, silk batik scarfs, enameled jewelry boxes, pottery from Poterie de Trois-Ilets, and baskets from Morne-des-Esses are local specialties which can be found in the boutiques.

Gourmets may wish to stop in at a local Supermarché, where French delicacies such as tinned paté, canned quail, or bottled foie gras may seem a true bargain. Be sure that any agricultural or food products are packaged in sealed containers, or customs may not allow them to be transported into the U.S.

French Restaurants and Sidewalk Cafes

A visit to the French West Indies would not be complete without sampling true French cuisine. The following restaurants offer superb French pastries, baguettes, or an assortment of mouth-watering crepes:

- **Le Lafayette**–Rue de la Liberté
- **Le Desnambuc**–Rue de la Liberté
- **La Creperie**–4 Rue Garnier Pages (corner of Rue de la République)

Transportation, Excursions

Taxis:
Passengers disembarking at the pier in Fort-de-France will find a great number of taxis and drivers waiting to take you out on the island. Some drivers use minivans, but the minivans seen around town operate as "Collective" taxis for island locals. The taxis are not metered, but trips around the island are regulated by the taxi association, and you may have difficulty negotiating fares due to the language barrier. All fares are based on the entire car, seating one to four people, but before entering a taxi determine if the rate is in francs, or U.S. dollars. Outer island excursions often take three or more hours. To keep the cost per person down it is wise to share the ride with three or more people .

Taxi Chart:

Destination	Cost
Fort-de-France	$8.00
Pointe du Bout	$35-40.00
Trois Ilets	$30-35.00
Ste. Anne	$50-60.00
St. Pierre	$45-50.00
Balata Gardens	$15-20.00

All rates are for the whole taxi from the port area, one to four persons.

Rental Cars:
Driving on Martinique is on the right, which is much more comfortable for American drivers. The roads outside of Fort-de-France are easy, but motorists on Martinique drive very fast. Drive defensively, take your time, and enjoy a pleasant day on the island.

Cars are available for rent in downtown Fort-de-France at agency offices near Roger Albert and the ferry terminal. You can either walk or take a taxi into town. A valid driver's license is necessary, and the minimum age to rent a car is 21. Agencies are open weekdays 8 AM to 12:30 PM and they reopen from 2:30 to 5:30 PM. Most agencies are closed on Sundays, but are open 8 AM to noon or 1 PM on Saturdays. Rates range between $60 and $80 for daily rentals, and advance reservations are recommended. During the high season, rental cars are in short supply and can be very difficult for cruise passengers to obtain on the day of arrival. Few agencies have English-speaking personnel, so use a phrasebook when arranging for a car. It is best to use a credit card for the rental, but make sure the agency writes FF or FRS for the amount in francs. Get hold of a map for exploring the island, and drive defensively, always alert to other motorists.

Rental Agencies: To call Martinique, dial (011), the international access code, (509), the country code, then the local number as follows:

Avis 70-11-60/70-63-11/73-73-20
Budget 63-69-00/70-22-75
Hertz 60-64-64
Europcar 73-33-13
Inter-Rent/Dollar 60-00-77/50-01-02

Self-Guided Tours

All prices are quoted in U.S. dollars

1. Just outside Fort-de-France, on the road to Morne-Rouge, is the **Jardin de Balata/Balata Botanical Gardens**. Martinique is named the "Isle of Flowers" and the garden displays every type of tropical vegetation, including many flowering plants and trees, with colorful hummingbirds darting around the park. There is a self-guided nature walk along the shaded pathways, and the old Creole house on the grounds offers a glimpse into the island's French colonial past. It is a great escape from the congested city streets of Fort-de-France. Admission is $6 for adults and $2 for children. The garden is open daily from 9 AM to 5 PM. A 20-25-minute taxi ride along the winding roads will bring you to the gardens.

2. Another way to escape from Fort-de-France is by taking a ferry across the marina to **Pointe du Bout**. The ferry boats leave from

Alfassa Boulevard next to the Place de la Savane, the park near the Roger Albert store. Passengers can walk 15 minutes from the pier to the ferry area, or take a five-minute taxi ride. Ferries cost $4 per person for a round-trip, and leave Fort-de-France and Pointe du Bout at the following times:

Fort-de-France:		Pointe du Bout:	
6:30 AM	12:15 PM	6:10 AM	12:05 PM
7:30	12:45	6:45	12:45
8:00	1:15	7:15	1:45
8:30	2:30	8:00	2:30
9:00	3:00	8:30	3:30
10:00		9:00	4:00
11:00		9:30	4:30
11:45		10:30	5:00
		11:30	5:30

Once in Pointe du Bout, you can hire a taxi to the Trois-Ilets area– home to three unique museums. **La Pagerie Museum** is the birth- place of Empress Josephine, and has mementos from her home and family. **The Shell Museum** has an interesting shell collection de- signed to represent island life, and the **Maison de la Canne/Sugar Cane Museum** explores the distillation process of sugar cane used to produce rum products. You can also spend time at **Bakoua Beach/the Meridien Hotel**, the only beach near the port area. Sandwich shops near the ferry dock serve great baguettes for lunch, and there are a few boutiques for shopping.

Organized Tours & Activities

The majority of tour operators in Martinique do not speak fluent English, so you may not fully enjoy an organized tour. If you do want to take a tour, you would do well to see the island with a taxi driver who speaks English. Taxi drivers offer a full seven-hour island tour for $214 U.S., or a two-to-three-hour island tour for $80. Both are based on one to four people in the tour, and prices may be negotiated.

Beaches

1. The only beach close to the pier area is across the harbor at **Pointe du Bout**. The small beach near the Meridien Hotel is called **Bakoua Beach**, and passengers are allowed to use the beach area, but not the hotel facilities. Watersport rentals are available from the hotel, and there are sandwich shops near the beach for lunch. One word of caution for parents–the French do not allow nude sunbathing, but topless sunbathing is quite common. You can take the ferry to Pointe du Bout, and walk 10 minutes to the right down to the beach. It is not spectacular, but it's a place to enjoy the sun.

2. The best beach on Martinique is an hour's drive from Fort-de-France to the southernmost point on the island. The region of Sainte-Anne is home to **Les Salines**, the longest stretch of white sand on the island. The Caribbean cove is ideal for bodysurfing, snorkeling, and swimming. There are shady benches available for picnic lunches and rest room facilities that are a unique experience in themselves. Les Salines is certainly worth the drive, but you should combine the trip with an island tour to make the most of your time and money.

Martinique Beach Chart:

	Facilities	Windsurfing	Snorkeling	Scuba Diving	Waverunners	Swimming	Parasailing	Sailing	Waterskiing	Nude/Topless
Pointe du Bout	●	●	●	●		●		●		●
Les Salines	●		●			●				●

Island & Ocean Sports

All rates are quoted in U.S. dollars

Golf:
Across the harbor from Fort-de-France is the 18-hole golf course at Trois-Ilets. The course, designed by Robert Trent Jones, is one mile from the Pointe du Bout ferry dock, or accessible via a 20-25-minute taxi ride from the cruise ship pier. The **Golf de l'Imperatrice Josephine** has an English speaking golf pro, a pro shop, bar and restaurant. Special green fee rates can be arranged for cruise passengers if you contact (011-596) 68-32-81. If you are interested in playing one of the most beautifully designed courses in the Caribbean, contact the golf club in advance or immediately upon arrival.

Tennis:
There are three tennis courts at the Golf de l'Imperatrice Josephine golf course, the Meridien Hotel has two courts, and the two courts at Le Bakoua are available by reservation. All three locations are across the harbor from Fort-de-France in Pointe du Bout, and the courts are usually reserved for hotel guests. However, cruise passengers can make special arrangements with the hotel or golf course to play an hour or more of tennis. Rates vary, but range between $15 and $25 per hour.

Ocean Sports

The beachfront hotels on Bakoua Beach at Pointe du Bout have watersports available, but most operators do not speak English. The language barrier may make renting equipment difficult for cruise passengers, but the following activities are available for sport enthusiasts.

Windsurfing:
Rates range between $12 and $20 an hour, and 30-minute lessons are offered for $12-$16.

Snorkeling:
The coastline around Pointe du Bout and nearby Anse Mitan have excellent reefs for snorkeling. Snorkeling gear is often limited, but rates range between $10 and $15 per hour. A separate ferry from Fort-de-France takes visitors straight to Anse Mitan, or certain ferries to Pointe du Bout also make a second stop at Anse Mitan. Ask the ferry attendant for the proper ferry if you are interested in going directly to Anse Mitan.

Scuba Diving:
A diving group called **Bathy's Club** at the Meridien Hotel, and another group who operate from their boat, the *Planete Bleue*, are both located in Pointe du Bout. The two dive groups offer single-tank dive packages for approximately $45, and Bathy's Club can be contacted prior to arrival by calling (011-509) 66-00-00. If you do not have their own dive computer, it is wise to ask for an English-speaking dive instructor. If the dive operations on Martinique do not have an English speaking instructor, plan to dive on another island.

One-Day Itinerary

Martinique is fortunate to have a unique historical site. Mont Pelée is a volcano at the northern end of the island that erupted and destroyed the coastal town of Saint-Pierre in 1902. The town has since been rebuilt, but an area of ruins has been preserved. Visitors can view remnants from the eruption in the Vulcanological Museum in Saint-Pierre, and the volcano itself can be explored if you have three hours for the hike.

The drive to Saint-Pierre takes 45 minutes to an hour, and the total itinerary lasts six to seven hours. The best way to explore the island is by renting a car. Be sure to acquire a road map.

What to Bring:
If you are planning to spend the whole day on the island, bring small U.S. bills or francs to pay for lunch and entrance fees to the museums. Also bring a camera to capture the beauty of Martinique's northern countryside.

Directions:
Refer to the island map for numbers corresponding with the suggested sites described.

1. Begin the island adventure by renting a car at 9 AM to get an early start on the day. With the assistance of a map, and directions from the rental agency, take the road out of Fort-de-France heading **north**. Soon you will see signs for Schoelcher, Case-Pilote, Bellefontaine, and Morne-Vert–small fishing villages with magnificent coastal views. In approximately 30 minutes from Fort-de-France, you will enter Le Carbet and should begin looking for the sign to the **Gauguin Museum**, located on the right-hand side of the road.

A narrow dirt road takes you to the entrance of the museum which commemorates the one time inhabitant of Le Carbet. The Gauguin Memorial Art Center was erected to honor the famous French painter, and has a collection of personal letters, and photographic reproductions of works from Gauguin's "Martinique period." The museum also houses a collection of traditional island costumes, headdresses, and artwork made by Martinique artists. The entrance fee is $2 and it is worth a 30-minute stop on the journey to Saint-Pierre.

2. Upon leaving the Gauguin Museum, turn right for a 15-minute drive to **Saint-Pierre**, once known as the "Paris of the West Indies." As you enter the town, the roads become one-way. Follow the signs to the **Vulcanological Museum**. The museum is open between 9 AM and 12:30 PM, then it reopens between 3 and 5 PM. Plan to arrive at the museum no later than 11 AM, and allow 30-45 minutes for viewing the photos, distorted musical instruments, a cracked liberty bell, and other items that survived the volcanic eruption.

When the Mont Pelée volcano erupted in 1902, the devastating heat and suffocating ashes killed almost everyone living in the coastal town of St. Pierre. The only survivor was a prisoner who was buried in an underground cell and was found after the rubble was taken away.

For those who are interested in taking a tour of St. Pierre, the **Cyparis Express** is a colorful passenger train that gives hour-long English speaking tours weekdays, and half-hour tours on the weekends. See St. Pierre from a different point of view for $8 for adults ($4 for children). Catch the train on the boardwalk at the base of the Vulcanological Museum.

When it is time for lunch, the author's favorite spot is the **supermarché** near the waterfront pier, with a superb deli offering sandwiches or baguettes. Street-side cafes also offer lunch to be enjoyed along the coastline, but the locals of St. Pierre do not speak much English. After lunch, plan to leave for Morne-Rouge by 1 PM.

3. After leaving St. Pierre, it only takes 15 minutes to reach **Morne-Rouge**, which has an excellent view of Mont Pelée. The quiet town is typical of rural communities throughout the island, and from here, you should begin your journey back to Fort-de-France. Signs leading **south** to Fort-de-France are posted along the road, and the highway becomes a winding pathway through the tropical rain forest common in the northern part of Martinique.

4. After 20-25 minutes of driving, a sign for the **Balata Botanical Gardens** will direct you to the right. The majestic gardens offer views of Carbet Peak, and the bay of Fort-de-France. Beautiful pathways lined with tropical plants, trees, and flowers show why Martinique is called the "Isle of Flowers." Passengers should arrive at the Botanical Garden between 2 and 2:30 PM, spending 30-45 minutes wandering through the tropical wonderland. The entrance fee is $6 for adults, and $2 for children.

5. A 15-20-minute drive back into Fort-de-France will bring visitors through the east end of town. Be sure to follow a town map to guide you safely when returning the rental car. After leaving the car, walk through the Market Square at **Place de la Savane**, and enjoy the beautiful park. At the completion of the tour, you should have spent between six and seven hours enjoying the outer regions of Martinique.

Diamond Waterfall, St. Lucia

St. Lucia

The "Helen Of The West Indies"

Island Description:

It is not known who bestowed the name of St. Lucia (pronounced *loo-sha*) on the island; historians doubt whether it was discovered by Columbus. The first known European to settle on St. Lucia was the pirate Francois De Clerc, known as "Wooden Leg." Legend says the peg-legged pirate buried his stolen Spanish gold on Pigeon Island, which later became the location of a British fortress.

When the English arrived in 1605, after being blown off course on their way to Guiana, they bought land from the Carib Indians to begin a settlement. Of the 67 English settlers who arrived on the island, only 19 survived subsequent Carib attacks, and were able to flee the island in a stolen Carib boat. The second wave of English settlers, led by Sir Thomas Warner, were also killed or driven out by the Caribs in 1639. A successful settlement was eventually established at Soufriere in 1746 when the French West India Company bought the island from the British in 1651.

The French choice of location for their settlement may have been fortunate. Soufriere is near the Sulphur Springs, which were deeply feared by the Indians who believed the boiling pools were occupied by the god of death. The nearby twin peaks, the Pitons, also represented the goddess of birth and the giver of food, both powerful and dangerous gods to the Indians. The British soon declared war on the French for assisting in the American Revolution, and St. Lucia was considered a prize—changing hands 14 times before the English prevailed.

A crucial naval battle for the English was waged from St. Lucia in 1782, when Admiral George Rodney learned of French plans for joining forces with the Spanish Armada to drive the English out of the Caribbean. Admiral Rodney kept watch daily from the Fort on Pigeon Island, for a signal of the French fleet sailing from Fort Royal in Martinique. Finally, 150 French ships containing 10,000 men departed from Martinique, and within two hours Rodney sailed with his own fleet of 100 ships in hot pursuit. The resulting defeat of the French fleet in the battle of Iles des Saints, secured

Twin Pitons, St. Lucia

ritish supremacy over the seas and its position of power in the Caribbean.

Castries, the capital of St. Lucia, was destroyed many times by hurricanes, military attacks, and catastrophic fires, so there are few historic structures remaining. Castries' large harbor, framed by stately mansions perched on hills facing the panoramic Caribbean, became a favorite port in colonial days. St. Lucia's natural vegetation, dramatic volcanic mountains, and fertile fields earned the island the name "The Helen of the West"–comparing the island to the beautiful "Helen of Troy."

In 1863 the coaling industry was introduced to St. Lucia to fuel the coal-driven steamships which called upon Port Castries. Indentured East Indians arrived on the island during the next 30 years to provide manpower for the coal industry, and many remained as island residents after their terms of indenture ended.

Agriculture is still St. Lucia's largest source of income, and a large portion of the countryside is cultivated with bananas. This single crop accounts for 80% of the island's economy and has earned the nickname "Green Gold." The islanders prefer to call their farms estates rather than plantations. Some privately owned estates are still in operation, offering tours to the public.

Having opened the new Pointe Seraphine Shopping Mall adjacent to the cruise ship port, St. Lucia hopes to attract more tourism. Pointe Seraphine is a beautiful, modern shopping mall luring some of the most stylish shops .

Island People:
St. Lucians are a mixture of British, French, African, and Indian blood which exemplifies West Indian culture. Eudovic, a master wood-sculptor and native, explains the meaning behind his "tree of life" wall carvings. These wooden plaques show the face of a man, a house, and a garden, all sheltered under the branches of a coconut tree.

According to Eudovic, when a baby boy was born, his father took the infant's naval cord and planted it along with a coconut. When the coconut palm grew, it would mark the area which would be the boy's land during his lifetime. When the boy became a man, he would build his house, raise his crops, and his family would live on the land under his tree. When the man died, the tree was cut down, symbolizing an end to the dual-life cycle.

Craftsmen like Eudovic care deeply for their island, their people, and their art. To find materials for his craft, he trudges through the rain forest in search of choice pieces of dead wood, and he plants new trees to help replenish the land. Eudovic also teaches the skills he has learned over a lifetime to apprentices so that his art is kept alive. He welcomes visitors to his work studio with a child-like pleasure, and his warm hospitality reveals an integral part of the West Indian character. (See shopping on the island.)

The government is improving St. Lucia by building new roads which link the major towns and tourist attractions with the cruise ship port. The government also realizes the value of its natural resources and a number of protected marine areas have been established, where it is illegal to go without written permission.

Sports in the form of soccer and cricket are important events on the island. It is not unusual for a traffic jam to occur near the local soccer field on a Saturday morning, and locals take pleasure in discussing the latest sporting events in the same way Americans talk about football or baseball. Island sports figures become national heroes, even though their nation may be smaller than most states in America.

Island Proverbs:
- "Fishermen don't say de fish stink." (People don't notice the bad in themselves.)
- "Who help you buy de big mule, don't help you feed it." (The one who helps get you in trouble doesn't help get you out.)
- "Head not made fer hat alone." (Use your brain.)

Holidays:
Pointe Seraphine's shops are open whenever a cruise ship is in port, and ship arrival dates and times are known by merchants and taxi drivers. St. Lucia loves a party, and most of their holidays give rise to a festival which makes visiting St. Lucia more enjoyable.

January: 1st–New Year's Day; Jan. 1st and 2nd–fiesta held in Vigie playground, Castries. Locals sell delicacies, and masquerade bands display dancing.

February: Early February–starting the Sunday before Ash Wednesday is Carnival, which lasts for over a week, ending on the Tuesday before Ash Wednesday; February 22–Independence Day.

April: 1st–Good Friday; 3rd–Easter; 4th–Easter Monday.

June: 29th– St. Peter's Day is a Fisherman's Feast where all the local fishermen celebrate by decorating their fishing boats.

August: 30th–Feast of St. Rose de Lima. Members of La Rose Flower Society parade the streets dressed in costume; Last Wednesday in August–Market Vendors' Festival.

October: 17th–Feast of St. Margaret Alacoque is celebrated by another local flower society parading in the streets in costume.

November: 22nd–St. Cecilia's Day is a musician's festival day.

December: 13th–National Day which celebrates the island's patron saint; 25th–Christmas; 26th–Boxing Day.

The Pier

The Elizabeth II Pier and three docking berths are located near the business district of Castries, used for receiving cruise ships when two or more enter the port. Facilities are not specifically designed for cruise ship passengers, but the pier is a short walk to the center of town where the general post office, banks, a Cable and Wireless office, and shopping can be found.

The newly built pier at Pointe Seraphine is located to the left when entering the harbor area from the ocean, and contains some of the best shopping found on the island. Castries, the largest town on the island, is a short taxi ride from Pointe Seraphine. The facilities were designed to appeal to cruisers, with a tourist information center, a money exchange, and an outlet of the Philatelic Bureau all on the premises.

Pier Phones:

The commercial piers are a short walk from a Cable and Wireless office that sells Phone Cards, and provides public telephones at its office. You should have no difficulty making long distance calls from St. Lucia. The excellent facilities at Pointe Seraphine include access to telephones at either end of the shopping mall. Certain phones are designated for AT&T direct dial access, for credit cards, or you can purchase a Phonecard in E.C. denominations to use with the specially marked Card Phones.

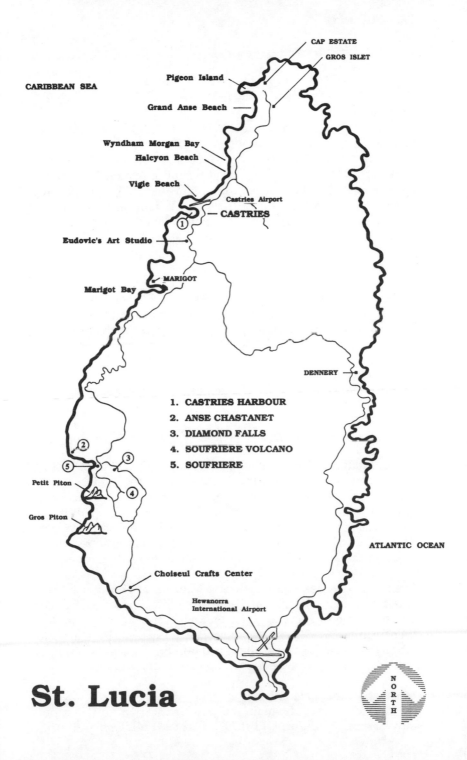

CAP ESTATE

GROS ISLET

Pigeon Island

CARIBBEAN SEA

Grand Anse Beach

Wyndham Morgan Bay

Halcyon Beach

Vigie Beach

Castries Airport

CASTRIES

①

Eudovic's Art Studio

MARIGOT

Marigot Bay

DENNERY

1. CASTRIES HARBOUR
2. ANSE CHASTANET
3. DIAMOND FALLS
4. SOUFRIERE VOLCANO
5. SOUFRIERE

②

③

⑤

Petit Piton

④

Gros Piton

ATLANTIC OCEAN

Choiseul Crafts Center

Hewanorra
International Airport

St. Lucia

NORTH

In Town

Currency:
The currency used on St. Lucia is the Eastern Caribbean dollar, E.C. tied to the U.S. dollar at about $2.70 E.C. to $1.00 U.S. Banking hours are 8 AM-3 PM weekdays, and until 5 PM on Fridays. Most banks are closed on weekends and holidays. A money exchange booth is available at Pointe Seraphine, however, major credit cards and traveler's checks are accepted by merchants and tour operators. It is wise to carry small denominations to avoid receiving large amounts of E.C. in change.

Postage:
The General Post Office is on Bridge Street in Castries, just two blocks away from the commercial piers, and is open 8:30 AM to 4 PM weekdays. A Philatelic Bureau is located in a room to the right inside the General Post Office, and an outlet of the Bureau is also at the Pointe Seraphine complex. Stamp collectors will find that the stamps offered by the Bureau make an excellent addition to their island collections. The cost to airmail a post card is 65 cents E.C.– approximately 25 cents U.S. (Do not use U.S. postage.)

Museums & Historical Sites

The **Cathedral of Immaculate Conception** is the most interesting building in downtown Castries. Built in 1894, the interior is covered in wood with intricate and beautiful paintings. The effect is quite unusual. Visitors are permitted to enter the cathedral, but shorts are not considered acceptable attire. Just outside the cathedral is **Columbus Square** where the oldest and largest tree on the island, a Saman tree, fills the square with its spreading branches.

The city of Castries, named after the Minister of The French Navy and the Colony, "Marechal De Castries," was ravaged by four enormous fires. Therefore, the buildings appear more modern than in other Caribbean capitals. The Cathedral, the Victorian Library, and the old French-designed buildings around Columbus Square are the best of the remaining historical buildings in town.

Morne Fortune, meaning "hill of good luck," is a large, hilly area which once housed the main military fortification for the important Castries Harbour. Old British barrack buildings and a few older French ruins are scattered over the Morne among modern luxury homes and hotels. Taxi drivers are happy to point out the historically important features of the Morne as you drive through the area.

Pigeon Island National Park is considered the most historically significant site on St. Lucia. Located to the north of Castries above Gros Islet, the park is now connected to the mainland by a man-made causeway. Due to its height and prominent location, Pigeon Island made an excellent lookout for pirates lying in wait for Spanish galleons heavily weighted with gold. Martinique was clearly visible to the north, so the site made a perfect location for an English military fort to defend against the French.

Today the Pigeon Island National Park is open to visitors daily. With the assistance of a map available at the entry gate, you can wander through a continual maze of stone and brick ruins, the remnants of Admiral Rodney's naval station. In addition, a museum and a splendid park filled with tropical trees and flowers are maintained for visitors to enjoy. (See Self-Guided Tours.)

Shopping

Pointe Seraphine Mall

The duty-free shopping at Pointe Seraphine is cool and comfortable. To insure duty-free prices, carry a passport and ship's boarding pass while shopping. When you complete a purchase the shop keeper supplies two copies of the sales invoice. The white copy is the your receipt, and the pink copy must be handed to the customs official when departing the island. Liquor and tobacco must be delivered directly to the ship, but other items may be taken at the time of purchase.

NOAH'S ARKADE offers a broad sampling of local crafts from St. Lucia within easy reach of tourists, including wood carvings, dolls, baskets, straw mats, hats, books, reproductions of old maps, and warri boards (a West Indian game).

ISLAND CONNECTION is a true West Indian boutique, bringing together gift items: the art of Jill Walker, internationally known names such as Naf Naf, Body Glove, and Jimmy Z, as well as a selection of children's clothes. This shop is also a good place to buy film. (Another branch is at the St. Lucian Hotel on Grand Anse Beach.)

BAGSHAW'S STUDIO carries silk-screened designs that are unique to St. Lucia (the designs are not exported). The brightly colored hand-printed cloth is made into wall hangings, shirts, dresses and tropical clothing. (The impressive Bagshaw Studio Factory, located on the Morne, is also open to the public. See Shopping on the Island.)

WINDJAMMER CLOTHING COMPANY specializes in quality casual clothing made from natural fabrics, linen, and cotton. The Windjammer line is designed and manufactured in St. Lucia, then exported internationally. (Other boutiques are at Windjammer Landing, Vigie Cove, and on Bourbon Street in Castries.)

COLOMBIAN EMERALD, part of the world-famous chain of jewelry stores in major cruise ship ports, guarantees the same price on its jewelry from island to island. Passengers who missed a "great buy" in St. Thomas or St. Maarten may be able to find the same item here. (See Introduction, Shopping.)

BENETTON (See Introduction, Shopping.)

IMAGES contains an excellent selection of international perfumes and cosmetics from Elizabeth Arden, Lancome, and Revlon as well as a wide selection of Rayban sunglasses.

Shopping Out On The Island

A visit to St. Lucia gives shoppers the opportunity to visit several working factories where quality merchandise is manufactured and sold on-site. By viewing the process used to create unique designs, shoppers can appreciate special purchases even more. It is easy to arrange for a taxi shopping adventure starting just outside Pointe Seraphine Mall by asking to see the following:

WINDJAMMER CLOTHING COMPANY is at Windjammer Landing Resort, a short drive from the cruise port. (To arrange a factory tour call 809-462-1041 before you go.) This factory manufactures fine quality sportswear using 100% cotton. T-shirts are a specialty and there is a large selection of shorts and shirts made of brightly printed fabrics in tropical motifs. The shop also carries Caribic ceramics and jewelry.

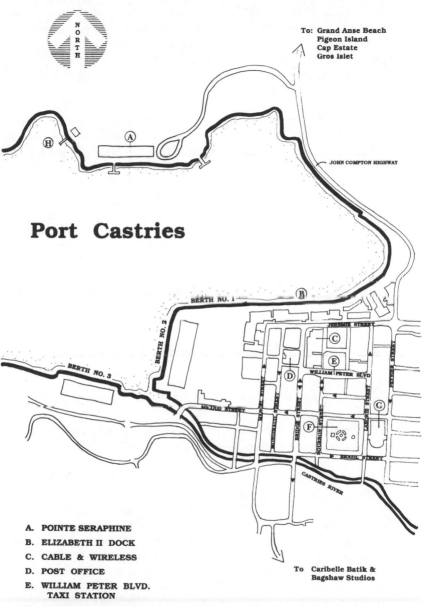

Port Castries

To: Grand Anse Beach
Pigeon Island
Cap Estate
Gros Islet

JOHN COMPTON HIGHWAY

BERTH NO. 1

BERTH NO. 2

BERTH NO. 3

BRIDGE STREET

BOURBON STREET

LABORIE STREET

PEYNIER STREET

MICOUD STREET

BRAZIL STREET

CASTRIES RIVER

WILLIAM PETER BLVD

To Caribelle Batik &
Bagshaw Studios

A. POINTE SERAPHINE

B. ELIZABETH II DOCK

C. CABLE & WIRELESS

D. POST OFFICE

E. WILLIAM PETER BLVD.
TAXI STATION

F. COLUMBUS SQUARE

G. CATHEDRAL OF IMMACULATE CONCEPTION

H. VIGIE BAY

BAGSHAW STUDIOS FACTORY is on the Morne just two miles outside of Castries, overlooking the ocean. This factory manufactures vibrantly colored silk-screened designs by local artists, Sydney Bagshaw and Virginia Henry. All the garments are made in St. Lucia from the finest materials.

***CARIBELLE BATIK FACTORY is on the Morne occupying the old Howelton House, which enjoys some of the best views on the island. This factory is one of two Caribelle Factories in the Caribbean (the other is on St. Kitts and offers different clothing designs). Marvel at the skill demonstrated by the Caribelle workers as they apply searing hot wax to ultra-fine cotton. Each color in a batik requires hot waxing, dying, and drying before the next color can be applied using the same process. A wall hanging containing many layers of color will therefore cost more than a fabric containing one or two colors.

After viewing the hot waxing process, shop for merchandise in the large showroom, containing T-shirts, shirts, dresses, wall hangings, skirts, shorts, and accessories in men's and women's sizes. On the veranda behind the building, you can buy a cool drink and see the dying rooms and colorful fabrics drying in the sun. From here there are also phenomenal views of Castries Harbor. Caribelle batiks are sold in outlets around Castries and in major hotels, but a visit to the factory may be the highlight of a trip to St. Lucia.

***EUDOVIC'S ART STUDIO is located on the Morne. This is the best wood-working studio found in the Caribbean. Meeting the owner, Vincent Joseph Eudovic, is part of the total experience. He will proudly show visitors his work and enchant them with his winning personality. Small, very affordable pieces are available in the main showroom, and the wall plaques depicting the "tree of life," are a genuine bargain. The artists use dead wood gathered in the rain forest from cobary, mahogany, red cedar, and lourier cannea trees. The most spectacular sculptures are Eudovic's large free-form pieces which can be seen in his second showroom. Be sure to ask to see these. They capture the strength and character of the wood itself, and the use of positive and negative space is reminiscent of the famous works by Henri Moore.

The pieces at Eudovic's are created by native artists with no formal art training, but no finer craftsmanship and imagination is displayed in any art museum. The prices reflect many hours of work, but a true art collector will recognize them as bargains.

CHOISEUL CRAFT CENTER is just outside the village of Choiseul between Soufriere and Vieux Fort. If you are on a tour to the southern part of the island, arrange to stop at the Choiseul Craft Center, where volunteers come from around the world to teach various skills to children and locals. The goal of the center is to encourage islanders to start businesses for themselves or sell their creations to local store owners and help to improve the local economy. The skills of basket weaving, pottery, and wood crafting are being preserved through the efforts of this center and the works are sold in a shop on the site.

Transportation, Excursions

Taxis:
Passengers arriving in St. Lucia will dock at either the Elizabeth II Pier and commercial berths on the edge of downtown Castries, or at Pointe Seraphine across the harbor. At both locations, taxis are waiting outside the pier area. Taxi rates are regulated by a taxi association and are priced for the whole taxi, including one to four persons. Rates may be given in E.C. dollars or U.S. dollars, so be sure to question the driver for the correct fare before getting into the taxi. Taxis are available for island tours or trips to the beach, and round-trip fares can be negotiated.

Taxi Chart:

Destination	Cost
Pigeon Island	$13.00
Marigot Bay	$19.00
St. Lucian Hotel	$10.00
Wyndham Morgan Bay	$6.00
Halcyon Beach Hotel	$4.00
Anse Chastanet	$50.00
New Vigie Beach Hotel	$3.00
Soufriere/Sulphur Springs (round trip)	$93.00
Rodney Bay Marina	$11.00
Cap Estate Golf Club	$15.00

All rates are for the whole taxi, one to four persons.

Rental Cars:
Driving is on the left in St. Lucia and the roads are constantly in repair, which makes driving difficult. The island is large and hilly, with many winding roads. Currently the main road from Castries

to Soufriere is under extensive repair to eliminate the large pot-holes and weather eroded pavement. The alternative road from Castries to the southern portion of the island has been re-paved half-way to the Hewanorra Airport. This road is quite long but easy to maneuver. You should think twice about renting a car for the day. You must be willing to drive slowly and cautiously, honk around the blind curves, and remember to stay to the left! Another factor to consider is that many of the local bus and taxi drivers drive extremely fast; they can add to the tension as you try to negotiate the winding roads.

Cars can be rented at the pier area or at Vigie Airport for $44-$60. You must acquire a temporary drivers license for $12, and the minimum age for rentals is 25. A collision damage waiver is avail-able for $12 a day, and a credit card will cover the $200 deposit for rental cars.

Rental Agencies: The area code for St. Lucia is (809), a long dis-tance phone call from the United States.

Avis 452-2700/2202
Courtesy Car Rental Ltd. 450-8140
National Car Rental 453-0085/452-8721

Self-Guided Tours

1. Pigeon Island National Park lies to the north of Castries and Rodney Bay. The 40 acres of protected land is dotted with ruins, forts, and hidden caves which may still contain pirate treasure. Before the island became a defensive military complex, the area was used as a hideout for the notorious French privateer, "Wooden Leg." The park contains some of the oldest historical ruins on the entire island, and visitors can spend hours wandering along the walkways. Although the name implies it is an island, Pigeon Island is actually part of a man-made peninsula connected to the main island of St. Lucia.

A 30-minute taxi ride will take you to the entrance of the park, and the walk to the top of the peak takes an hour for people in fair to excellent condition. An entrance fee of $1 U.S. helps to maintain the park, and a self-guided map is also available for $1 E.C. Pigeon Island is open to visitors from 9 AM to 5 PM daily and is located next to the excellent **Reduit Beach**. You can spend up to two hours exploring the ruins throughout the park, then take a swim along the reef of Reduit Beach.

2. A 30-minute drive south of Castries through the Cul-de-Sac Valley lined with mile after mile of green banana plants is the sheltered **Marigot Bay**. The winding road brings you into a private harbor area protected by steep mountains and lush foliage lining the three sides of the cove. You may recognize this as the harbor which was the location for the film, *Dr. Doolittle*. Today it is used by The Moorings, a major sailing center. The bay is the best hurricane shelter on the island and is always filled with small sailboats and dinghies. The **Hurricane Hole Hotel** is a great stop for lunch and a tropical rum punch while you enjoy the picturesque harbor.

A taxi ride down the coast to Marigot can also include a stop at Eudovics Art Studio (see Shopping). If you want to rent a car, remember to stay to the left and watch for the signs heading south out of Castries by way of Morne Fortune, down the hill through Cul-de-Sac to the entrance of Marigot Bay. Obtain a map at the car rental agency, and drive carefully.

Organized Tours & Activities

All prices are quoted in U.S. dollars

Sunlink International provides complete island tours at reasonable prices. Various tours allow you to see the very best St. Lucia has to offer within a half-day or full-day time schedule. Passengers on cruise ships should make prior reservations with Sunlink to ensure space availability. Contact Sunlink International by calling (809) 452-8232 or fax your requests to (809) 452-0459. Provide a credit card number to guarantee the reservation. Tours 1-3 below are offered by Sunlink International.

1. Visit **Soufriere** by land or by sea for a full day of exploring. The trip by land takes you on a wild ride over the hills and valleys to the town of Soufriere and surrounding sites. Scheduled stops at the Sulphur Springs (the "drive-in" volcano), the Diamond Waterfall, Diamond Baths natural spring, and Gardens are worth the winding bus ride. The return trip is by boat with a stop at Marigot Bay for a refreshing drink and a view of St. Lucia's Caribbean coastline.

The alternative trip to Soufriere is a cruise down the coastline on a powerful speedboat, followed by a tour of the sites by bus. The scheduled stops are basically the same–Sulphur Springs, Diamond Waterfall and Baths–but the tour also includes a visit to the Soufriere Estate, a former sugar estate open to the public. If time allows, the return boat trip to Castries will also include a trip around Marigot Bay and an opportunity to snorkel in the warm Caribbean sea.

Lunch at a local restaurant, all entrance fees, the boat trip with drinks, and an informative tour-guide are all included in both tours. The tours, costing $62 per person, leave by 8 AM and return at 4:30-5 PM.

2. A half-day excursion to the historical ruins of **Pigeon Island** is available at a cost of $25 per person. The tour begins at 1:30 PM and takes passengers past the large estates on Cap Estate out to the causeway leading to Pigeon Island. The two-hour guided tour transports visitors back to the exciting days of Admiral Rodney's naval station that once existed on the island. The tour returns to Castries at 5 PM, so you have half the day to explore the historical ruins on the 40 acres of the designated National Park or to swim and snorkel off the park's beach.

3. Take a day sail on a 140-foot replica of a 19th-century sailing ship. The Brig *Unicorn* leaves from Vigie Bay, next to Pointe Seraphine, and sails along the west coast to Soufriere. Once in Soufriere, you take a guided tour of the Sulphur Springs, Diamond Falls, and Botanical Gardens. The return voyage to Castries includes complimentary drinks, a buffet lunch, snorkeling, and a visit to Marigot Bay. The trip leaves at 9-9:30 AM, and returns at 4:30 PM, for a cost of $65 per person. You can make reservations through Sunlink International, or contact the *Unicorn* directly at (809) 452-6811.

4. One of the most exhilarating ways to see St. Lucia is by air, riding in one of **St. Lucia's Helicopters**. The tour operator offers a choice of two tours for cruise passengers leaving from Pointe Seraphine. The North Island Tour is approximately 10 minutes long, with views of St. Lucia's west coast, Rodney Bay Marina, Pigeon Island, then back over Castries to Pointe Seraphine. Fly over beach-side resorts, the ruins at Pigeon Point, and the jagged rocks along the Atlantic coastline. The flight is a quick but interesting view of the areas around Castries at a cost of $38 per person.

The South Island Tour is approximately 20 minutes long, with flights along the west coast of St. Lucia to Marigot Bay and Soufriere. The tour begins by flying over Castries Harbor, then to the bay at Marigot. You will then see Soufriere's Pitons emerging straight out of the water to 2,700 feet above sea level, which are most impressive from the air. Do not forget to bring your camera to capture these dramatic creations of nature on film. The return trip brings you inland over the island's volcano and bubbling sulphur springs. The flight back to Castries also allows you to view the jagged peaks and lush tropical rain forest which dominates St. Lucia's terrain. The entire trip is well worth the time and effort, for a cost of $75 per person. Both the North and South Island tours can be arranged at the tour desk located at Pointe Seraphine, or by calling St. Lucia's Helicopters (809) 453-6950.

St. Lucia Beach Chart:

	Facilities	Windsurfing	Snorkeling	Scuba Diving	Waverunners	Swimming	Parasailing	Sailing	Waterskiing	Nude/Topless
Grand Anse	●	●			●	●	●	●		
Wyndham Morgan Bay	●	●	●			●		●		
Vigie Beach	●		●			●				
Halcyon Beach	●	●			●	●		●		

Beaches

1. Beach-side resorts are located all along the St. Lucian coastline, so the beaches are often packed with hotel guests, tourists, locals and sports enthusiasts. The **Grand Anse** beach is home to the St. Lucian Hotel, and is one of the most popular beaches, with something for everyone. A volleyball net and water sports are available and the long stretch of beach for sunbathers and beachcombers may remind some of Miami Beach. A 15-minute taxi ride from Castries or Pointe Seraphine brings you to the entrance of the St. Lucian Hotel, and a walk through the property leads straight to the beach. The hotel has gift shops, restaurants and a beach-side barbecue hut serving hotel guests and daily visitors to the beach.

2. A new resort which has recently opened on St. Lucia is the **Wyndham Morgan Bay Resort** offering a stretch of private beach for its hotel guests. If want to spend the day at the resort, it is highly recommended that you inform the front desk at the hotel that you would like to use the facilities. Passengers willing to have lunch at the hotel and use the beach-side bar are welcome at the resort and beach as long as they conduct themselves like hotel guests. Water sports such as windsurfing, sailing, water-skiing, and snorkeling are also available for a charge to non-hotel guests. A 20-minute taxi ride brings you to the resort.

3. Vigie Beach, located near the airport and Pointe Seraphine, is a quick five-minute taxi ride for cruise passengers. The beach is a long stretch of grey sand with no water sports or congestion from beach-side resorts. The water is quite calm for swimming. The New Vigie Beach Hotel nearby offers a restaurant and facilities for beachcombers. Not the most popular beach on the island, Vigie Beach is close to the cruise ports and offers a quieter location for those who want peace and tranquility.

4. A smaller but equally beautiful beach is located at the **Halcyon Beach Hotel**. Only 10 minutes from Castries, Halcyon Beach is a stretch of white sandy beach offering water sports and beach-side facilities for visitors. Many of the resorts on the island which are not located along the beach send their own guests to the Halcyon Beach. The beach may tend to become crowded with sun-worshippers.

Island Sports & Ocean Sports

All rates are quoted in U.S. dollars

Golf:
To the north of Castries is a nine-hole golf course, the **Cap Estate Golf Club**, located among luxurious estates. Greens fees are $12 and club rentals are $6. The 20-minute taxi ride from Castries will bring you to the course at a cost of $15 for one to four persons.

Tennis:
The new resort which opened September, 1992 the **Wyndham Morgan Bay Resort** may offer the greatest tennis experience on the island. Make prior reservations for court times if you want to play on four of the newest courts on St. Lucia. Court fees range from $10 to $20 an hour and a tennis pro is on the property for lessons.

Contact the resort by calling (809) 450-2511 either prior to arrival or once you have entered Castries harbor or Pointe Seraphine, where phones are available.

Horseback Riding:
You can tour the North portion of St. Lucia on horseback. **Trim's National Riding** group offers daily beach rides along the Caribbean and Atlantic beaches, and scenic inland rides around the Cap Estate and Pigeon Island. The two-hour rides cost $25 per person and must be reserved prior to arrival on the island; for groups of eight or more, a beach barbecue can also be arranged at $45 per person. For reservations and further information contact director Rene Trim at (809) 450-8273.

Windsurfing:
In general, windsurfing rentals cost $15-$20 per hour and are available at the St. Lucian Hotel, Halcyon Beach Hotel, and the new Wyndham Morgan Bay. All the hotel locations along the Caribbean side of the island have excellent conditions for beginners and the waters near the rocky coastline are perfect for advanced windsurfers.

Scuba Diving:
One of the most dramatic coral reefs in St. Lucia begins at the beach off the Anse Chastanet Resort. With bright orange and yellow coral gardens, six-foot wide seafans, and a multitude of tropical fish, a dive at the Anse Chastanet Bay will be the highlight of a cruiser's time on St. Lucia.

Scuba St. Lucia has established a quality dive center at the resort and offers scuba trips for resort guests and daily visitors. Among the best dive locations is **Key Hole Pinnacles**, named for the keyhole shape cut into the rock marking its location. Four underwater pinnacles rise from the bottom of the sea to 10 feet below the surface. Here divers can spend all of their air time circling the rock formations that teem with underwater creatures, corals, and colorful fish.

The **Anse Chastanet Reef** is the next best location for diving, offering sites for every level of diver. The reef begins directly off the beach and descends to 140 feet. The shallow plateau makes an excellent area for snorkelers as well as for first time divers. The reef wall which has its best sights at 50-60 feet is alive with trunkfish, spotted drums, angel fish, and the occasional luminescent squid.

Divers should watch for, but should not touch, the bright orange fireworms crawling along the coral, and the shy but curious moray eels. Scuba St. Lucia takes you to various locations around Soufriere and the Anse Chastanet Resort that will amaze and impress even the most experienced divers. St. Lucia has so much to offer visitors below the surface that certified divers and snorkelers should make an effort to explore the island's coral wonderlands. Scuba St. Lucia offers a special two-tank dive package for cruise passengers arriving in Castries at $85 per person. The package includes: a boat ride to Anse Chastanet at 9 AM, tanks and equipment for a beach dive and a boat dive, lunch in the restaurant, and a return boat trip to Castries by 4 PM. Passengers interested in only snorkeling are offered the same boat trip to and from Anse Chastanet, lunch, and all-day snorkeling rental for $45 per person. For first-time divers, an Introduction to Scuba course is available at $85 per person, including the boat trip and diving. Scuba St. Lucia tries its best to accommodate cruise ship passengers and to make their time on the island the best experience possible. Reservations must be made in advance to coordinate boat pick-ups and space availability on the boat dives. Passengers who are interested in diving at Anse Chastanet should contact the resort at (809) 459-7000 and ask for the Scuba St. Lucia dive group. They plan to open a dive center at the Rodney Bay Marina in Castries, which will also offer dive trips and watersports.

An alternative dive group on St. Lucia which offers daily scuba diving trips is **Buddies**, at the Vigie Bay Marina near Pointe Seraphine. Buddies takes divers to Anse Chastanet and Anse Cochon for excellent coral-head diving and spectacular wall dives. A two-tank dive package for $65 per person includes all equipment and tanks. For visitors with their own equipment, a two-tank dive is available for $55 including tanks. Dive trips leave at 12:30 PM and return passengers at 4:30 PM Monday through Saturday, with no trips on Sunday. Buddies is near the cruise ship ports in Castries, and offers scuba courses for divers of all levels. For more information, contact the dive group at (809) 452-5288.

One-Day Itinerary

Passengers interested in seeing the best St. Lucia has to offer will need to travel from the Castries cruise ports down the coast to Soufriere to the only "drive-in" volcano in the Caribbean. The Sulphur Springs, Diamond Waterfall, Botanical Gardens, and the Anse Chastanet Resort are sites every traveler should visit on St.

Lucia. If you want to follow the one-day itinerary, you should plan your excursion ahead of time to ensure a successful day.

The dive operator at the Anse Chastanet Resort, Scuba St. Lucia, offers daily boat trips from Vigie Bay, near Pointe Seraphine, down the west coast to Anse Chastanet. You must first contact Scuba St. Lucia to arrange for space on the boat, which leaves daily at 9 AM, returning at 4:30 PM. Let them know you would like to spend one-two hours snorkeling on the reef off the resort's beach, and an hour for lunch in the hotel's restaurant. Boat reservations can be made by calling the resort at (809) 454-7000, and speaking with Scuba St. Lucia directly.

Before arriving at the Anse Chastanet Resort, you have two options for planning your day.

- You may book a half-day island tour with the resort for the Sulphur Springs, Diamond Waterfall, and Botanical Gardens.
- Once you arrive at Anse Chastanet, you can hire a taxi to take you to the specific sites.

If you give the resort prior notice, they may be able to arrange space on the half-day tour for their guests. When you phone Scuba St. Lucia to arrange for the boat ride, inquire about the availability of the land tour. The Anse Chastanet Resort will accommodate cruise passengers who use their establishment for lunch or who snorkel off the hotel's reef. One good turn always deserves another!

Costs for the tour, boat trip, and snorkeling are listed below:

- The boat trip is complimentary with a dive package, but otherwise will cost between $15 and $30 per person. Ask for the current rate when phoning for your reservation.
- A tour with the Anse Chastanet Resort or with a hired taxi costs approximately $20 per person, and takes 1 1/2-2 hours.
- The entrance fee to the Sulphur Springs is $3 E.C. or $1.15 U.S.
- The entrance fee for the Diamond Waterfall and Botanical Gardens is $5 E.C. or $2 U.S., and $6.50 E.C. or $2.50 U. S. for a mineral bath.
- Snorkeling equipment costs $15 per set.

Cost for the entire day will range from $65 to $80 per person.

What to Bring:
For the trip to Soufriere, passengers should bring along sunscreen, a hat, a light-weight jacket for a possible rain shower, and a camera for the spectacular sites. If you have your own snorkel equipment, bring along the gear and a towel for drying off. Lunch is served at the Anse Chastanet resort, with moderate prices and excellent food.

Directions:
Refer to the island map for numbers corresponding with the suggested sites described.

1. Scuba St. Lucia will either pick you up at Pointe Seraphine, at the Castries commercial pier, or send a taxi to bring you to the pier at Vigie Bay. The shuttle boat leaves at 9 AM, arriving at Anse Chastanet at 9:45 AM. The trips down the west coast of St. Lucia will pass dramatic cliffs, the hurricane-safe port of Marigot Bay, and allow you to see a great view of the twin pitons emerging from the water in front of the town of Soufriere.

2. When the dive group drops you off at the Anse Chastanet Resort, you can either take the tour with the hotel, or call for a taxi driver to take you to the specific sites.

3. The first stop on the tour is a 10-minute drive to the Diamond Botanical Gardens, Waterfall, and Mineral Baths. You can request a guide at the entrance of the private estate to take you through the gardens, point out the various island plants, and escort you to the waterfall. Originally built in 1785, the estate features special mineral baths which are believed to help skin inflammations and other ailments. The baths have been carefully restored and you can take a dip for a nominal charge. The beautifully manicured gardens contain a wide assortment of colorful flowers and trees unique to the Caribbean.

The Diamond Waterfall is a popular photo attraction with its water streaming over the orange volcanic rocks. The orange coloring is not a moss, but a chemical reaction from the hot water reacting with the iron composites in the volcanic rock. The waterfall is unsafe for bathing because of harmful bacteria caused by small snails living in the water.

4. The next location is a 10-minute drive to the Sulphur Springs, St. Lucia's original "drive-in" volcano. The bubbling sulphur springs are alive with steam and black molten lava. A guide will take you on an half-hour tour explaining the creation of the springs, and allow you to see the remains of the once-active volcano at close range.

5. The tour may include a stop at the Soufriere Estate, which was originally part of a 2,000-acre estate granted to the Devaux family by King Louis XIV in 1713, and is open to the public for tours of the minizoo, and the machinery which once harvested copra and cocoa fields.

6. Between 12:40 and 1:00 PM, you can return to the Anse Chastanet Resort for lunch in the exquisite beach-side restaurant. After lunch, take an hour or two to snorkel over the colorful reef that lies just 20 feet off the beach. Snorkel equipment can be rented from Scuba St. Lucia, and there are lockers, showers, and rest rooms for changing.

7. At approximately 3:40 PM the boat departs from the resort to return passengers to Castries, arriving by 4:00-4:20 PM. Passengers are returned to Pointe Seraphine, Vigie Bay, or the Castries commercial pier, and the total trip should just over seven hours.

Barbados

1. HARRISON'S CAVE
2. FLOWER FOREST
3. BARCLAYS PARK BEACH BAR
4. MORGAN LEWIS MILL
5. BARBADOS WILDLIFE RESERVE

Speightstown

ATLANTIC OCEAN

Folkstone
Underwater Park

Sandy Lane Golf
Course & Resort

Oughterson
Wildlife Park

Gun Hill
Signal Station

Sam Lord's
Castle

Crane Beach

BRIDGETOWN

Barbados Museum

Hilton Hotel

Rockley Golf and
Country Club

Grantley Adams
International Airport

CARIBBEAN SEA

NORTH

0   MILES   2

Barbados

Little England

Island Description:
The first Europeans to land on Barbados (pronounced bar-bay-dohs) were Portuguese sailors, who stopped at the island in 1536 to secure provisions on their route to Brazil. The sailors dubbed the island Los Barbados (meaning the bearded ones) because the local fig trees have aerial roots hanging from the tree's branches which resembled an old man's beard.

Arawak Indians were still living on the island when the Portuguese landed, but the island was uninhabited by the time Captain Henry Powell landed in 1625. He stumbled on the island due to navigational errors and he promptly claimed it for the British. In 1627 Powell returned with 80 settlers and a number of slaves, landing at Holetown, named after an area in England. Bridgetown, the capital of Barbados, was founded in 1628 and named after an old Indian bridge.

Early settlers planted cotton, tobacco, yams and cassava, but after ten years of difficulties, Sir James Drax introduced the alternate crop of sugar cane. There was high demand for sugar in Europe, and the crop thrived in Barbados. The original system of using indentured servants to man the vast plantations proved inadequate, and plantation owners soon imported slaves from Africa to fill the shortage. The great wealth amassed by the harsh system largely remained on the island and funded the its infrastructure.

A unique factor in the history of Barbados is that the British remained in continuous control for over 300 years. The islanders established their own Parliament in 1652 and earned the nickname "Little England" since the laws, traditions, and even the appearance of the cities in Barbados mirrored the mother country. Today, the Barbados Parliament has the distinction of being the third oldest continuous government in the British Commonwealth.

Barbados is located slightly outside the arc of islands which make up the Windward Island chain, and is shaped like a pork chop with its majority population in the capital of Bridgetown. The island consists of a very old coral and limestone geological base which sometimes exceeds 300 feet in depth. The coral helps to filter natural rainfall into a system of underground streams and caves, making the water pure and clean.

Barbados is still agricultural, producing sugar cane, and other cash crops. Surprisingly enough, the most serious threat to the agriculture industry, has come from the green monkeys which were imported from Africa as pets during colonial times. Monkeys enjoy eating mangoes, papayas, guavas, and bananas, but to test for ripeness, a monkey takes small bites out of many fruits, spoiling them all in the process. Government studies indicate the monkey population, which has increased tremendously over the last three decades, may be responsible for crop losses as high as 40%. Although the government pays a bounty for dead monkeys, the Barbados Primate Research Center pays more per monkey, $50 if captured alive and unharmed in cage traps supplied by the center. The research center operates the Barbados Wildlife Reserve where wild monkeys and people may roam freely together and stare at one another with equal curiosity. The monkeys mingle with the other fauna in the sanctuary, hares, tortoises, deer, and river otters. The animals live in a well-provisioned natural environment, and crop damage has already decreased due to the Research Center's efforts.

Although agriculture is important, tourism has become the largest industry on Barbados. In 1986, the government began a program to educate its population about the importance of tourism, beginning in the schools, and ultimately involving every walk of life. With its slogan that "tourism is everybody's business," the program's success is evident in the improved tourist attractions and the friendly islanders who are eager to help make the tourist's stay on Barbados memorable.

The Island People:
With cultural roots grounded in 300 years of British heritage, the Bajan (pronounced bay-shun) people are more British in tradition than other Caribbean islands. British names appear on landmarks, local parish sectors and churches, while their Houses of Parliament and Trafalgar Square are modeled on London. Echoes of the era when slaves worked the plantations are still evident throughout the island. The slave trade was abolished by Britain in 1807, due to increasing world condemnation of the cruel system. But full emancipation of the slaves on Barbados did not take place until 1838.

Many slaves remained on plantations and experienced little change in their lives, while other slaves left the plantations and created a new middle class on the island. Samuel Jackman Prescod became the first non-white member of the House of Assembly in 1843, although universal suffrage was not granted until 1950, after 117 years of struggle and social turmoil.

Visitors to Barbados may notice small wooden houses sitting above the flood plain on concrete blocks. These structures are called "chattel houses," derived from an old term meaning "movable personal property." In the early days, changing a job meant moving the entire house, which needed to be small enough to transport by mule cart. The wooden chattel house could be expanded by adding on sections (each movable separately) or by adding a veranda. As the owner prospered, the house could be made to look very grand by adding new sections, elegant carved detailing, and bright cheerful paint. Few examples of chattel houses have survived, but tourism has revived an interest in the architecture of "the working man's house." As a result, some chattel houses have been preserved and converted into boutiques or shops. (See Shopping, Chattel House Village.)

Island Proverbs:
Bajans speak English with a very understandable accent, but over the years they have developed their own slang. Here are a few examples:

- "Cheese on!" (Right on!)
- "Fingersmith" (Pickpocket)
- "Being in goat heaven" (Being in hog heaven)
- "Rest off" (Take a coffee break)
- "A lick-mout" (A gossip)
- "Jam" (Eat like a pig)
- "A yard fowl" (A yes man)

Holidays:
Museums, post offices, and banks close on national holidays, but are open during festivals. You will find shops and tourist attractions open unless otherwise noted in the description of the attraction. Festival periods are often the most fun time to visit the island.

January: 1st–New Year's Day; 21st–Errol Barrow Day
February: 20th-27th–Holetown Festival (Holetown celebrates the arrival of the first settlers with a week of medieval revelry)

April: 1st–Good Friday; 4th–Easter Monday; (Oistins Fish Festival on Easter weekend pays tribute to the skills of the island's fishing industry with two days of boating events and excitement.)

May: 2nd–May Day; 23rd–Whit Monday

July: 9th to August 1–Crop Over Festival (celebrates the completion of the sugar cane harvest with calypso music, dancing, drama, and contests)

August: 1st Monday–Kadooment Day. The climax of the Crop Over Festival is a national holiday with costumed bands in the streets and fireworks.

October: 4th–United Nations Day

November: 30th–Independence Day; The National Independence Festival of the Creative Arts. The entire month is filled with events featuring the creative arts, with the final exhibitions on the national holiday, Independence Day.

December: 25th–Christmas; 26th–Boxing Day

The Pier

Barbados has built one of the finest docking facilities in the islands, located in the Deep Water Harbour a short distance from its capital city, Bridgetown. The concrete pier has room to dock many ships at once, allowing you to walk straight from the ship to the excellent facilities inside the port building. A fully staffed tourist bureau is conveniently located inside the building with brochures and information about the island as well as local postage to mail letters and cards.

Pier Phones:

Plenty of clearly marked phones are found inside the port building with U.S.A. Direct and Credit Card Phones available for calls to the United States. The island Phone Card machines are clearly marked with instructions. Phone cards are available for purchase at the port authority in Bajan dollars. Keep in mind that a call to the U.S. will cost a minimum of $5 U.S. just to make the connection, so be sure to purchase a card with sufficient credit in the local currency to cover the cost of the call.

Shopping At The Pier:

A few shops are at the pier terminal, including a duty free shop, a craft shop, and a flower shop, Exotic Blooms (a florist who can deliver fresh flowers right to the ship for special occasions). Barbados is one of the first islands to recognize the importance of encouraging crafts as a means of providing full employment for its citizens. Pelican Village, a complex designed to house 37 local craft shops, is a five-minute walk from the pier. (See Shopping.) In order to reach the village, leave the harbor area through the main gates, continue along Princess Alice Highway towards Bridgetown, and look for Pelican Village on the left-hand side of the road. Remember, duty free means there is no tax added to imported items, but locally made items are more interesting and less expensive.

In Town

Currency:
The Bajan dollar (BDS) is the official currency of Barbados and the Bajans use the same denomination system as used in the U.S. However, most stores on Barbados price their items in both Bajan and U.S. dollars to assist visiting tourists. The exchange rate is approximately $2 BDS for $1 U.S., but the value of the Bajan dollar fluctuates, so check with the Tourist Information desk at the pier for the current exchange rate. Both E.C. and U.S. currency are accepted in Barbados, but try to avoid receiving Bajan currency in change. Credit cards should be used whenever possible, but be sure the credit card slip is clearly marked to indicate BDS or U.S. dollars.

Banks are open from 8 AM to 3 PM weekdays and until 5 PM on Fridays. The Caribbean Commercial Bank is open until noon on Saturdays, and the Royal Bank of Canada has machines to access Visa and Plus System ATM cards for cash advances in Bajan dollars.

Postage:
A window selling postage stamps is open at the cruise pier facility from 8 AM to 3PM. The air mail rate to send a post card is 65 cents BDS, about 33 cents U.S. Remember that Caribbean islands will not accept mail using U.S. stamps.

Museums & Historical Sites

The island is filled with historical, cultural and ecological sites. The Barbados National Trust offers a voucher system called the Heritage Passport which allows visitors to explore the rich culture and heritage of the island at almost half the cost normally charged for the same attractions. The passport costs $25 U.S. and may be ordered in advance by calling the Board of Tourism at (800) 221-9831. A booth for the Barbados National Trust is also located at the cruise ship terminal building to the far left and is clearly marked.

The **Parliament Buildings** are on Bridge Street in the center of Bridgetown. The buildings were constructed in 1871, nearly 240 years after the Parliament was established. Entry to the buildings may be restricted on weekdays, as government business is taking place.

British Admiral Lord Horatio Nelson was especially important in protecting the island of Barbados from foreign invasion. When Nelson was in the process of assembling his fleet in the Barbados harbour for the battle of Trafalgar, the French and Spanish combined their fleets to execute a secret attack on Barbados. When they caught sight of Lord Nelson's formidable fleet, they knew they were outgunned and fled. Nelson's imposing presence saved Barbados from attack, and a statue commemorating the courageous British Admiral was erected in Bridgetown's **Trafalgar Square**.

The **Jewish Synagogue and Cemetery**, located at Coleridge Street and Magazine Lane, represents the oldest synagogue in the western hemisphere, built in 1654. The Jewish community had a great influence on the island economy, having introduced the crop of sugar cane. The adjoining cemetery has tombstones dating back to 1630, and is open to the public Monday-Friday from 9 AM to 4 PM.

The **Garrison Historic Area** contains many colonial buildings of architectural and historic value, including the Bush House where George Washington visited his ailing half-brother in 1751. Barbados was the only island Washington ever visited outside the continental United States. The **Barbados Museum**, located in the Garrison Historic Area, is housed in the 19th-century Military Garrison, a former prison. The museum is arranged in a circular walking pattern starting with a natural history section, ending with several island art galleries. A superb collection of plantation house furniture is particularly interesting and represents the lifestyle common to the wealthier families on the islands throughout the Caribbean. The exhibits are arranged to represent complete rooms which might have existed in a colonial mansion. Settlers were eager to establish a European environment to make their secluded life in the islands more bearable. Victorian-style furniture was shipped from England at great expense, or meticulously copied by craftsmen on the islands, using highly polished mahogany and lavish imported fabrics.

The Domestic and Decorative Arts display includes intricate examples of shell-craft called a "Sailor's Valentine." Sailors would buy or commission shell-paintings, flowers fabricated from shells, and decorated boxes or mirrors from local artisans as gifts to take home to their wives and sweethearts.

The most intriguing section is the Children's Gallery, designed to familiarize children with the Barbados heritage, especially the influence of slavery. Included is a full-scale model of the slaves' living quarters, showing the meager conditions in which they lived.

Other exhibits in the museum include contemporary art, military history, old maps and prints, period paintings, and an example of a prisoner's cell. Do not miss the museum shop and library where unique island merchandise and collector's stamps are offered for sale. The museum is open Monday through Saturday 10 AM to 6 PM except holidays. Admission is $3.50 U.S. Visitors should make the effort to visit the most interesting museum in the Caribbean.

Shopping

It is not necessary to shop downtown to obtain duty-free prices, but be sure to carry a passport and ship's boarding pass to qualify for the duty-free discounts. Up to 40% can be saved with proper I.D. and using credit cards or traveler's checks to pay for purchases. Be sure to place the duplicate copy of the sales receipt in the custom's box at the cruise terminal before boarding the ship.

The shopkeepers in Barbados have also established outlets in many of the major hotels near or on the route to tourist attractions.

Shopping In Bridgetown

***PELICAN VILLAGE is on Princess Alice Highway, a five-minute walk from the pier. The complex is the best of its kind, and other islands would do well to encourage local artisans to form a similar enterprise. The 37 shops include expert woodcarvers, coral jewelry, handmade baskets, pottery, original fine art, dolls, hand

Bridgetown

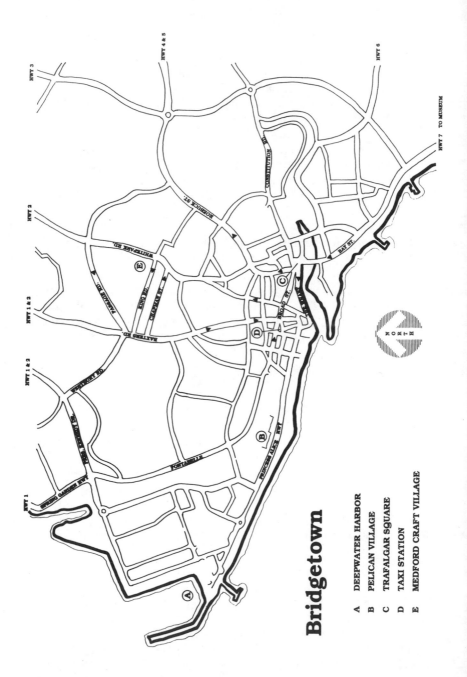

A DEEPWATER HARBOR
B PELICAN VILLAGE
C TRAFALGAR SQUARE
D TAXI STATION
E MEDFORD CRAFT VILLAGE

made clothing, and unique souvenirs–all made on Barbados. Shopping at Pelican Village supports the local economy and provides exceptional gifts for family and friends at reasonable prices. It is easy to hale a cab outside Pelican Village, or continue walking into Bridgetown after shopping.

LOUIS L. BALEY in De Costas Mall carries the same type of merchandise that Little Switzerland shops offer on other islands, including Rolex watches at special Caribbean prices. The camera department is renowned for excellent service and expertise.

GREAT GIFTS in De Costas Mall is one of the shops on the island featuring the artwork and crafts of Jill Walker. This savvy lady may be responsible for the craft revival on Barbados, which is spreading through the Caribbean. Original fine art, prints, posters, trays, coasters, and other merchandise is decorated with Jill Walker's Caribbean scenes. Other shops that carry Jill Walker merchandise are located in prime tourist attractions like the Flower Forest, Sam Lord's Castle, and Andromeda Gardens.

RAIN FOREST is a new store designed to resemble a rain forest, with painted wooden parrots, animals, and tropical fish for sale. The merchandise originates in the Caribbean and South America and shows superb workmanship.

HARRISON'S resembles a fine department store in the U.S., offering all the major names in crystal, perfume, and ceramics. Fine leather products are also available, including Gucci, Land, and Gold Pfeil, which are exclusive to Harrison's on Barbados. There are two locations downtown and outlets in hotels around the island with the same prices.

CAVE SHEPHERD is another major department store in Barbados, competing with Harrison's for the duty-free business. Cave Shepherd has virtually every kind of product from housewares to crystal, shoes to sporting goods, books to dress fabrics–all at duty-free prices. The store is large, roomy, and bargains are easy to find in every department.

Shopping Out On The Island

CHATTEL HOUSE VILLAGE is a collection of restored chattel houses which have been converted into charming shops. The village is located in St. Lawrence Gap, on the route to Sam Lord's

Castle. The village is worth a stop for the handicrafts and to see the picturesque cottages.

DAPHNE'S SHELL SHOP is at the graceful old plantation great house of "Congo Road" in St. Philip, which is on the route to Sam Lord's Castle. The shop features shell artwork, baskets, mirrors, picture frames, and flower-like creations. This shop was started in 1980 by Daphne Hunte, who has since been joined by her daughters in creating shell-craft.

SHELL GALLERY is at the Carlton House in the parish of St. James, the home of the owner/designer Maureen Edghill. The gallery is famous for elegant shell mirrors and a spectacular display of shells from countries all over the world. In 1984 the Barbados Museum commissioned Maureen to make a "Sailors Valentine" for Queen Elizabeth II. The gallery is open 9 AM to 4 PM Monday through Friday. Call (809) 422-2635 for weekend schedules.

MEDFORD MAHOGANY CRAFT VILLAGE, just outside Bridgetown at Barbarees Hill, is the residence of Dr. R. Medford. Mahogany woodcrafters create wood items of all sizes from massive tree roots, along with other handmade crafts which are displayed for sale.

FAIRFIELD POTTERY & GALLERY in the parish of St. Michael is a pottery complex operated by the Bell family. Local red clay is used in making the large pottery and the special works of Chalky Mount and Castle Potteries are also available at the gallery. Located at Fairfield Cross Roads, (809) 424-3800.

Transportation, Excursions

Taxis:
Taxis in Barbados are abundant and easily identified by the taxi sign on their roof and the "Z" on their license plates. They are not metered, but follow an established rate system set by the taxi association. Fares are based on one to five persons, but it is very important to establish the rate before entering the taxi! A taxi rate board is posted outside the cruise terminal listing the current rates for the whole taxi. This can be used when bargaining for fares. Trips to town are not negotiable, but the price for excursions out on the island can be negotiated. Again, the more people in the taxi,

Monkeys at the Barbados Wildlife Reserve

Harrison's Cave, Barbados

St. George Harbour, Grenada

Northern coastline, Grenada

the lower the price per person. Due to the fact that there are so many taxi drivers available, if one does not bargain or follow the regulated fares, try another driver. Drivers as a rule are friendly and courteous to tourists, but there are some who need lessons on polite behavior. Taxis offer a regulated island tour at $17.50 U.S. per hour for one to four people.

Taxi Chart:

Destination	Cost
Sandy Lane	$11.00
Harrison's Cave	$15.00
Crane Beach	$17.00
Sam Lord's Castle	$19.00
St. Lawrence	$9.00
Hilton Hotel	$6.00
Paradise Beach	$6.00
Carlisle Bay	$12.00
Flower Forest	$15.00
Barbados Wildlife Reserve	$20.00

All rates are for the whole taxi, one to four persons.

Taxi Facts:
- Tipping is not required when driving from one location to the next within Bridgetown.
- When a driver arranges a round-trip rate for a trip to a beach or outer island site, a 10% tip is appreciated.
- Drivers, when bargaining, may quote their rate in Bajan dollars, so be sure to establish which currency is being used
- Never have a taxi driver wait when traveling to a beach. The driver will charge a separate rate while he waits. Instead, arrange to have him come back for the return trip, or take another taxi.
- For round-trip fares, pay the driver at the end of the trip to ensure the same driver returns.

Local Buses:
Barbados has two types of local transportation. One is the government regulated Transport Board system. The other consists of minibuses driven by private operators. The Transport Board uses vehicles painted yellow with a dominant blue trim, the colors of the national flag. The privately operated minibuses are clearly marked with a "ZR" on their license plates, and have signs in their front window and on the side of their vans designating their

destination. The Transport Board buses also display their destination on a sign above their front windshields.

The cost is $1.50 BDS or 75 cents U.S. for either bus to any part of the island. The minibuses can be flagged down on the main roads or at the main terminal on River Road in Bridgetown. The large Transport Board buses can be waved down at any Bus Stop sign marked To City or Out of City. Passengers must wave to have the bus stop or it will drive on by. The buses may be inexpensive and easy to track down, but they make numerous stops along the roads and travel slowly. If time is not a consideration, try them out.

Rental Cars:
Driving on Barbados is on the left, with English-style turnabouts and many unmarked roads. Acquire a map from the tourist bureau or from the rental agency to assist in navigating the roads.

Rental cars are easily accessible on the island if you reserve ahead. Agencies can have a car waiting at the pier terminal when you arrive if contacted before entering the port. You must acquire a temporary driver's license for $5, available at the police station in downtown Bridgetown or from selected stations arranged through the rental agency.

Prices for four-door cars range from $50 to $60 per day, and the popular mini moke (an open air jeep-type car) is $60-$85 per day. Collision insurance is also available for $5, and gasoline, not included in rental, is currently .63/litre. A credit card is usually required to cover the damage deposit, and the minimum age to rent a car is 23.

Driving in Bridgetown is congested with traffic and taxi drivers, but once you get out on the island, the open roads become easier to maneuver. Unfortunately, many of the outer island roads do not have proper signs or direction markers, but adventurers can usually find the way to their destination. Ask for a current map from the Tourist Information desk at the pier terminal or from the rental agency. Remember to stay on the left at all times!

Rental Agencies: The area code for Barbados is (809), an overseas phone call from the United States.

L.E. Williams Tours 427-1043/6006
National Car Rentals Ltd. 426-0603

Sunny Isle Motors 435-7979
P&S Car Rentals 424-2052

Self-Guided Tours

1. Animal lovers arriving on Barbados must plan a visit to the **Barbados Wildlife Reserve**. Open daily 10 AM to 5 PM, the reserve is the only location in the Caribbean where you walk freely among the animals. The shady pathways are full of animals, some close to extinction, and others living a protected life in their own environment. Walk quietly so as not to scare away creatures at home in their "own world," or sit on a bench to see what may wander your way.

Everything from brocket deer, regal peacocks, armadillos, wallabies, porcupines, hares, red foot tortoises, and iguanas will cross the pathways, and scatter to safety under the large mahogany trees. Caymans (South American alligators) and pelicans coexist peacefully in the same exhibit and nearby is a family of playful river otters. The salt water aquarium exhibits a wide variety of tropical fish, and the walk-in aviary houses exotic birds like macaws, cockatoos, cockatiels, pheasants, toucans, parakeets, and the near-extinct St. Vincent parrot. The only animals securely contained away from visitors are a pair of reticulated pythons.

A special laboratory and quarantine area, which may be viewed by appointment only, breeds and researches the population of green monkeys brought into the reserve. The mischievous monkeys derive their name from the color of their coat, which is brownish grey with flecks of yellow and olive green. When sunlight hits the coat, it appears entirely green. These curious and humorous monkeys are the highlight of the park and are most active in the afternoon from 2 to 3 PM, when the park rangers bring out bunches of bananas at feeding time. The monkeys may come right up to visitors, but they are still considered wild animals and may bite. Be cautious, but not afraid. The monkeys make great subjects for pictures, but watch out–they have been known to steal people's glasses right off their heads.

The park has paths designed for the handicapped and small children, and has a friendly staff available to answer questions concerning the wildlife. An entrance fee of $5 for adults and $2.50 for children under 12 helps to maintain the grounds and the natural atmosphere for the animals. A trip to the reserve takes between 45 minutes and an hour. Combined with an island tour, a stop at the reserve makes for a terrific day.

2. A trip to Barbados would not be complete without a visit to **Harrison's Cave**. A motorized tram transports visitors underground for a guided view of caverns, bubbling streams, and waterfalls cascading into natural pools. The mile-long cave tour allows you to see stalagmites rising from the floor to touch stalactites hanging from the crystallized ceiling of the caves. The experience cannot be matched anywhere in the Caribbean. Artificial lighting inside the cave system allows photographs to be taken with a flash or with a video camera. Cave tours are available through organized tour operators or by reserving in person at the Harrison's Cave's front desk. The park is open seven days a week, rain or shine, and offers 8-16 tours a day starting at 9:30 AM. The 30-minute tour costs $7.50 per adult and $3.75 for children. A 35-minute taxi ride can take you to the cave. The cave park also contains a food stand, rest rooms, and a gift shop where you can browse before and after the tour. Harrison's Cave is an attraction not to be missed!

3. Colonial plantations on Barbados have some of the most lush gardens and flowering vegetation on any island in the Caribbean. One of the most beautifully manicured garden estates is called the **Flower Forest**. Located at the Richmond Planation in St. Joseph's Parish, the 50-acre estate displays every variety of plants and trees found in the hot houses of the Caribbean. You can spend up to 45 minutes wandering the trails and pathways. All plants and trees have been clearly identified with labels giving the botanical, Latin, and common names in English. A map and explanation of plants are available at the entrance in English.

Entrance to the park is $5 for adults. They are open daily from 9 AM to 5 PM. A snack bar, rest rooms, and a gift shop featuring Jill Walker prints, watercolors, gifts and crafts are at the main entrance building. Look for Walker's special prints of the Flower Forest! A 35-minute taxi ride brings you here to the most beautiful spot on the island.

4. Gun Hill Signal Station is a beautifully restored historical site only 15 minutes above Bridgetown. The station was originally built in 1818, and its excellent location provides sweeping views of Barbados' rolling sugar cane fields. Restored in 1982, the station is currently open to visitors Monday through Saturday, 9 AM to 5

PM except public holidays. A $2.50 entrance fee is charged to maintain the gardens surrounding the station. Remember to visit the famous British Military Lion, carved from coral limestone by British soldiers in the 19th century. It sits below the station on the hillside. The lion makes a great picture-taking location, and is a grand reminder of Barbados.

Organized Tours & Activities

1. Barbados, being a coral island, is surrounded by miles of coral reefs alive with colorful fish, exotic plant-life and sunken wrecks. Unless you are an experienced diver, however, you will see little more than a variety of tropical fish by snorkeling. If you take an **Atlantis Submarine** excursion, you will be able to view the mysterious undersea world to a depth of 150 feet. Spend an hour viewing vibrant orange fire corals or watching the multicolored parrot fish and angelfish, all in an air-conditioned submarine.

Most cruise ships offer one or two tour times for the submarine trip through their own Shore Excursion Office. Passengers can either book a tour through their ship or take one of the other seven scheduled dives by booking through Atlantis Submarine's main office. The main office is on Lower Broad Street, leading away from the cruise pier terminal towards downtown Trafalgar Square. A 15-minute walk, or a five-minute taxi trip will take you there. However you book the trip, you should not miss it.

Reservations can be made prior to arrival by calling toll-free 1-800-253-0493. The cost for the dive is $68 for adults, $34 for children ages 13-18, and $25 for children ages 4-12. You should arrive 15 minutes before the scheduled two-hour tour to receive a brief orientation. A submarine dive with Atlantis is definitely worth the time and effort.

2. Barbados can also be explored from above via **Bajan Helicopters**. Fasten your seat belts for a ride over the rolling hills and beach-lined coastlines of Barbados. A sightseeing guide who is also the pilot, points out island attractions as he flies you over beaches and tropical gardens. The 10 flights scheduled daily are either 20 minutes for $60, or 30 minutes for $90 per person. Reservations can be made by calling (809) 431-0069 Monday through Saturday, 10 AM to 5 PM. Only four passengers are allowed per flight, so make the reservation early.

3. An 80-mile coastal island tour around the entire circumference of Barbados is available though **L.E. Williams Tour Co. Ltd**. This bus tour gives you the opportunity to see the outer island attractions and to visit the communities which make up the sugar cane isle. Travelers arriving at the Deep Water Harbour are picked up 9 AM to begin the 6 1/2-hour island tour. The first stop is at the "Holetown Monument," the point where the first settlers landed in 1627. The second stop, past the town of Speightstown, is the Animal Flower Cave where you are allowed 20 minutes to tour the natural sea cave. The bus continues to Cherry Tree Hill for a complimentary drink and views of the dramatic East coastline. The following stop is at Morgan Lewis Sugar Mill, where you can examine the only remaining fully intact mill of its kind in the West Indies. Lunch is served at the Atlantis Hotel, offering authentic Bajan dishes.

After lunch, a 15-minute stop at St. Johns Parish Church allows you to explore the grounds and take pictures of a beautifully constructed church built over 150 years ago. The next location on the tour is Oughterson Zoo Park in St. Philip offering visitors a complimentary drink while they wander around the Plantation House and Zoo. A 30-minute stop is scheduled for the Zoo and Plantation, then the final stop is Sam Lord's Castle, one of the delightful resorts on the island. The grounds contain a gift shop, a monkey exhibit, shark exhibit, and beautifully manicured gardens. Passengers are allowed 30 minutes to explore the facilities or wander along the hotel's beach.

The tours are conducted by experienced and friendly guides. The tour buses are air-conditioned and can accommodate 27 people in comfort for a cost of $50 per person including lunch, drinks, and entrance fees. Advance reservations are required. Contact (809) 427-1043/6006. Office hours are Monday-Friday 8 AM-7 PM, Sat. 8 AM-4 PM, and Sun. & holidays 9 AM-4 PM.

4. There are three different types of cruises on Barbados which allow you to spend the whole day at sea. The first is the famous *Jolly Roger* **cruise** including the pirate's walking the plank, a rope swing, and lethal rum punches. The four-hour Jolly Roger cruise takes its passengers up the west coast for watersports, snorkeling, beachcombing, or simply jumping off the decks of the ship into the warm Caribbean sea. During the break, a barbecued chicken, steak, or pan-fried flying fish lunch is served with drinks. After everyone has eaten, the party really begins. Calypso music and international hits start everyone dancing and celebrating. The cruise is quite popular, so advance reservations are needed. Call (809) 436-6424. The price for the daily cruise is $51.50 per adult and $22.50 for children under 12.

The second possibility is the infamous **Bajan Queen** party boat. Ask any local on the island, and they will agree the *Bajan Queen* is the "Queen of Party Cruises." The four-hour cruise takes passengers along the west coast to a stop at Carlisle Bay for watersports and snorkeling over the 70-year-old *Berwyn* wreck. The stop is only an hour; then the party and music begins. The next two hours is devoted strictly to dancing, drinking, and having more fun than some people can handle. By the time the boat has come back to port, every passenger will be proficient at performing the Caribbean "Dollar Dance!" If you have never been on a "booze cruise," you must make the time to party on the Bajan Queen. Cruises run from 10 AM to 2 PM weekdays and they may be available through the ship's Shore Excursion Office. Reservations can be made by contacting (809) 436-6424. Price for the day cruise are $25 per person including an open bar and snorkeling. A $10 deposit is required for snorkelers and the money is returned when the equipment is returned. The boat can hold up to 250 passengers, so be sure to make a reservation to ensure space on the best party cruise in the Caribbean!

The third option for cruising is on a 36-foot catamaran, the *Why Not*. Daily cruises leave at 10 AM and return at 2:30 PM. Transportation, a Bajan buffet lunch, open bar, and snorkeling is included for $42.50 per person. Snorkeling is available over the sunken wreck at Carlisle Bay, the *Berwyn*, which lies in only 25 feet of water. Cruisers are also allowed to snorkel at various stops along the reef on the west coast. There is space for only 16 passengers , so all have their own deck space for tanning or resting in the shade. Reservations can be made by calling L.E. Williams Tour Co., Ltd, (809) 427-1043/6006.

Beaches

1. It may be a 30-minute drive from the Deep Water Harbour, but **Crane Beach** is the most beautiful cove on the entire island. Situated on the eastern coastline, the Crane Beach Hotel sits high above the cove of white beach and pounding Atlantic waves. An entrance fee of $2 is charged to non-hotel guests, but you can redeem the fee at the hotel bar with a free drink. A set of stairs leads from the hotel down to the beach for fun in the sand and surf. Watersports are not available, but you will spend most of your time relaxing on the beach or frolicking in the blue-green waters. The Crane Beach Hotel also has a restaurant for lunch, and is a perfect getaway for lovers or cruisers escaping to a piece of paradise!

2. The **Hilton Hotel beach** is close to the pier area. You can take a 15-minute taxi ride through Bridgetown to the Hilton, then walk down to the beach area. There are watersports available on the beach, as well as food stands and rest room facilities. Check with the watersports group about their "Watersports Bonanza" package that includes four-five hours use of water-skiing, knee boards, boogie boarding, Hobie cat sailing, windsurfing, wave runners, and a snorkeling trip–all for $42. Visitors must bring their own towel, and the pool area is reserved for hotel guests. The beach at the Hilton Hotel is not as crowded as some other hotel beaches and is wide enough to provide a little bit of privacy for every beach-comber.

3. A snorkeler's paradise can be found at the **Folkstone Underwater Park**, and the nearby **Sandy Lane Hotel** has a popular beach. Folkstone is 20 minutes from the Deep Water Harbour and has a protected inshore reef with an underwater trail designed for snorkelers of all levels. An aquarium and museum on the premises displays corals, sponges, and photographs of marine life native to Barbados. Admission to the museum is 50 cents, and it is open from 10 AM to 5 PM Sunday through Friday. The Folkstone Park rents snorkeling gear for approximately $15 per set. You will find food vendors and rest room facilities here as well.

A few yards down the coast from the underwater park is the famous Sandy Lane Hotel, with a championship golf course. The beach is public and offers a wide variety of watersports including wave runners, snorkeling, sailboats, and windsurfing. Glassbottom boat rides are also available for $6-$10 per hour around the bay. There are no food vendors on the beach and the hotel restaurant can be quite expensive. The beach may be crowded due to its popularity and close proximity to other hotels.

4. Sam Lord's Castle, located on the Atlantic side of the island, is a perfect place to spend the whole day. A 45-minute drive through sugar cane fields and open countryside will bring you to the entrance of Marriott's Sam Lord's Castle. The grounds contain much more than an old plantation turned resort. There is a monkey, parrot, and shark exhibit to intrigue daily visitors. A gift shop, frozen yogurt stand, restored "Castle" building, colorful gardens, and a beautiful stretch of beach are among the many features available for a $2.50 entrance fee. The beach-side food stand has excellent Bajan dishes as well as tasty sandwiches. Bring a camera for photos of one of the most picturesque resorts on the island and spend the entire day enjoying a piece of Bajan paradise.

If you are taking a taxi to the hotel, do not have the driver wait for the return trip. Instead, have him return for you at a pre-arranged time. Drivers always charge a "waiting fee," if not instructed to return later.

Barbados Beach Chart:

	Facilities	Windsurfing	Snorkeling	Scuba Diving	Waverunners	Swimming	Parasailing	Sailing	Waterskiing	Nude/Topless
Crane Beach	●					●				
Hilton Hotel	●	●	●	●	●	●		●	●	
Sandy Lane	●	●	●		●	●	●	●	●	
Sam Lord's Castle	●					●				

Island & Ocean Sports

All rates are quoted in U.S. dollars

Golf:
The most prestigious golf course on the island is at Sandy Lane, set along the west coast. The **Sandy Lane Golf Club** offers an 18-hole course for its hotel guests, but cruise passengers can reserve tee times by calling prior to arrival on Barbados. Green fees are $25 (9 holes), plus $15 for club rental. The Sandy Lane Golf Club can be contacted by calling (809) 432-1145/1493.

Another challenging course is the **Rockley Golf and Country Club**. The 9-hole course is located to the southeast of Bridgetown, and is open between 7 AM and 3 PM weekdays. (Weekends must be pre-arranged) The greens fees are $20 (9 holes) or $30 (18 holes). Clubs and cart rentals are $15 (9 holes) or $20 (18 holes). Contact Rockley Golf Club at (809) 435-7873 for tee times. A 15-minute taxi ride will bring you to the Club for $12 (one-four persons).

Tennis:

Tennis courts are found at almost every resort on the island, but one of the most exotic locations is at the **Crane Beach Hotel**. Visitors can play a set of tennis, then spend the rest of the day relaxing on the enchanting beach. You can also play tennis for a small court fee at the Rockley Golf and Country Club, Sandy Lane, Sam Lord's Castle, and the Barbados Hilton. Fees run $15-$20 including racquet rental.

Horseback Riding:

Barbados has long stretches of beache perfect for horseback rides. **Wilcox Riding Stables** offers daily rides between 6 AM and 6 PM. Reservations must be made ahead of time by calling David or Arleen at (809) 428-3610. The one-hour beach ride includes round-trip transportation from the pier area for a cost of $27.50 per person. Call for more information.

The **Beau Geste Farm** offers a horseback ride for daily visitors interested in seeing the Bajan countryside. Rides are scheduled at 9:30 AM and 3 PM, taking passengers on a tranquil ride through sugar cane fields and past historic sites. The one-hour ride through the parish of St. George costs $27.50 per person.

Another two-hour ride takes you through the grounds of the **Francia Plantation House** for $50 per person. You are allowed 30 minutes for exploring the restored Plantation House and gardens, then you resume the horseback ride through the countryside. Long pants are recommended for riding tours, and transportation to and from the pier is provided. Advance reservations are required. Call Allison Cox at the Beau Geste Farm, (809) 429-0139.

Bicycles:

M.A. Williams Rentals offers one of the best ways to see Barbados—on a bicycle. The 12-speed cross trainers are perfect for cruising the flat countryside through sugar cane fields and old ruins. They will provide a map outlining a bicycle route to follow for a full day of fun. Rentals are $12.50 per day, with a $50 deposit which is refunded at the end of the day. With prior notice, the company can pick up passengers from the pier. For reservations contact (809) 427-3955; office hours are Monday-Friday 8:30 AM-4 PM and 9 AM-3 PM on Saturdays and Sundays.

Ocean Sports

The following hotels and beaches offer a full variety of watersports as detailed below: The Hilton, Sandy Lane, Paradise Beach and Carlisle Bay–all 10-15 minutes from the Deep Water Harbour. All rates are quoted in U.S. dollars but, when bargaining with water-sports vendors, confirm whether the price is quoted in U.S. or Bajan dollars.

Windsurfing:
Windsurfer rentals are available for $12-$20 per hour. Each hotel is located on the west coast, offering calm to choppy water conditions for beginners and intermediates.

Wave Runners:
Wave runners are available through the watersports operators or from locals on the beach. The rates are $12-$15 for 15 minutes. Better rates can be negotiated for wave runners when there are two or more persons in a group wishing to rent the equipment.

Water-skiing:
Speed boats offer water-skiing at $12-$20 for 15 minutes of skiing. They are only available when there are several people to fill the boat.

Parasailing:
Flights are available from free-floating platforms situated off the beach at $30 for 10-15 minutes, and $45 for 25-30 minutes. The boats are safe and instruction is provided before "lift-off."

Sailing:
Hobie Cats are offered at $15-$18 for 30 minutes of sailing, and Sunfish boats are available for one or two people at $12-$20 per hour. Lessons are also offered, but after a few minutes it is easy sailing.

Scuba Diving:
Barbados boasts an abundance of shipwrecks in 20 to 100 feet of water. There are 15 wrecks right off the coast of Bridgetown–all easily reached by a dive boat. The dive operators work directly

with the beach-side resorts, but they can also make advance arrangements directly with cruise ship passengers.

ExploreSub Barbados, in St. Lawrence Gap, is the only PADI training center on the island and employs the most experienced and qualified dive masters. Customized dive boats, underwater camera equipment, and quality dive gear are available with advance reservations. All levels of divers are welcome to experience the colorful reefs, numerous wrecks, and popular sites around Barbados. Two-tank dives are available for $60 per person, and with advance notice the dive operator can arrange transportation for cruise passengers. Contact ExploreSub Barbados for the best diving experience on the island.

The Dive Shop has an office near Bridgetown, offering a two-tank dive for $50 per person, including rental gear. Morning dives leave by 9:30 AM and afternoon dives are scheduled at 2:30 PM. They will pick up passengers at the pier for dives off the western coast. Contact The Dive Shop at (809) 426-9947 for further information and to arrange a quality dive excursion.

Dive Boat Safari is close to the cruise pier, with a dive shop at the Hilton Hotel beach. Dives are scheduled at 10 AM, 12:30 and 2:30 PM. A one-tank dive is $35 including dive gear rental, or $30 without gear. A two-tank dive package is $60 including gear, or $50 without rental gear. It is recommended that only experienced divers use this dive operation. Some of the instructors may be experienced divers, but they are not necessarily people oriented and give little help to beginning divers. The boats are no larger than dinghies, and may not be acceptable for begining divers.

One-Day Itinerary

To spend a whole day on Barbados and see all the natural wonders it has to offer, hiring a taxi for the day is the best option. The roads on Barbados are not hard to maneuver, but they are not clearly marked and you may run into delays as you try to orient yourself. Start the adventure by hiring one of the many drivers waiting for fares outside the pier terminal at the Deep Water Harbour. Because you will be spending the whole day with the driver, you should interview several before making your final choice. Be sure to tell the drivers about the itinerary you prefer to follow, and that the total trip will be seven hours.

The cost for the taxi can be negotiated, but you should be prepared to pay $75-$95 covering four to six persons for the seven-hour trip. (Government regulated fares are $60-$85 for five hours, four to six people, plus $7.50 for each additional hour.) The more people in the group, the cheaper the total fare per person, but remember to bargain for the whole taxi in U.S. dollars. Once you have set the price, get ready for the best island adventure on Barbados.

The sites, driving time from one location to the next, and the entrance fees in U.S. dollars per person are listed below. The total fees come to $18.50 per person.

Harrison's Caves	35 minutes	$7.50
Flower Forest	15 minutes	$5.00
Barclay Park	20 minutes	lunch moderate
Morgan Lewis Mill	15 minutes	$1.00
Barbados Wildlife Reserve	15 minutes	$5.00

What to Bring:
A camera is a necessity to capture the beauty of the island. If there are clouds, bring along a lightweight jacket and hat to protect against the rain. The showers on Barbados are brief and should not prevent you from enjoying the attractions.

Directions:
Refer to the island map for numbers corresponding with the suggested sites described.

1. Begin the excursion at 9 AM. You will spend 35 minutes driving across the countryside to **Harrison's Caves**. The cave park begins the first tour at 9:30 AM and you have a better chance to get on the first tour if you arrive early. The tour of the caves lasts 30 minutes. If you are unable to go on the first tour at 9:30 AM, but can reserve a later tour, skip to number 2 on the itinerary (the Flower Forest) and return later for the cave tour.

2. The **Flower Forest of Barbados** is the most immaculately manicured garden plantation in the Caribbean and only a 15-minute drive from Harrison's Cave. The pathways are clearly marked with the names of each plant, tree, and colorful flower grown on the grounds. Spend up to an hour wandering through the estate and be sure to visit the gift shop for island-made crafts and watercolors by Jill Walker.

3. A 20-minute drive from the Flower Forest along the east coast allows you to arrive in time for lunch at **Barclays Park Beach Bar**. The bar serves truly authentic Bajan and Caribbean dishes like Flying Fish, Curried Lamb or Chicken, and Garlic Shrimp. A special buffet lunch is served on Saturdays and Sundays. If the driver is not familiar with Barclays, tell him it is on the East Coast Road in the St. Andrew Parish. Phone number is 422-9976. Spend an hour enjoying lunch, then drive 15 minutes down the road to the Morgan Lewis Mill.

4. The **Morgan Lewis Mill** is the only complete sugar windmill with its original parts intact in the Caribbean. You can examine the structure and machinery typical of mills that once dotted the landscape were essential to the processing of sugar cane. The canvas sails which once caught the wind and turned the grinding mechanism are no longer stretched across the arms, but with imagination you can picture how the structure once appeared. From the top of the mill, you can enjoy magnificent views of the countryside and coastline. Spend 15-20 minutes viewing the old mill and then a 15-minute ride will bring you to the last and best stop of the day.

5. For animal lovers or those tired of visiting ordinary zoos, the **Barbados Wildlife Reserve** is certainly the best attraction on Barbados! The optimum time to visit is between 2 and 3 PM, when the green monkeys are fed by the park rangers. The monkeys seem to come down from every tree. When wandering through the park, look up, down, and carefully inside the bushes for all sorts of animals. The reserve creates a natural environment where the animals are free to roam uncaged, so it is the tourists who become the visitors in the "animals' world."

Spend up to two hours wandering through the park and taking pictures of the animals, but do not get too close or make sudden movements. The return trip to the Deep Water Harbour takes 45 minutes to an hour, so plan your time accordingly. The Barbados Wildlife Reserve is the best example of a natural animal habitat in the entire Caribbean.

6. At the end of the excursion, you should have spent seven hours exploring and experiencing nature in its most natural environments. Barbados has developed and maintained excellent tourist attractions, which cruise passengers and travelers must experience for themselves.

Grenada

The Spice Isle

Island Description:
Green rolling hills and snug harbors prompted homesick Spanish
sailors to name the island Granada when they first landed on the
island near the bottom of the Caribbean. When the British arrived
and settled on the island, they converted the name to Grenada as
we know it today. The British attempted to settle Grenada in 1609,
but were chased off by savage Carib Indians. In 1650 a French
expedition bought extensive land from the local Caribs for a few
beads and knives, and built a settlement near the current town of
St. George's. The site proved to be a poor choice because the
buildings became mired in a swamp during the rainy season, and
the Caribs became hostile within the year. The ensuing military
campaign against the Caribs ended in 1651 when the last 40 Indians chose to jump from a cliff at the northern end of the island,
rather than live under French rule.

The French and the British fought for control of the island until
1783, when Grenada was finally ceded to the British. Under English rule, Grenada established a parliamentary government and
became an independent British commonwealth in 1974 under the
leadership of Sir Eric Gairy. Gairy's main political opponent,
Maurice Bishop, seized control of the government while Gairy was
away from the island in 1979. Maurice Bishop became dictator and
invited the Cubans and Soviets onto the island to build military
facilities and a new airport. Private property was seized, including
a luxury hotel which Bishop commandeered for his residence and
governmental headquarters. In 1983 a radical faction within
Bishop's government placed him under house arrest and took
control, executing several of Bishop's aides. Due to the perceived
threat to U.S. medical students and the urgent pleas of governments in the Eastern Caribbean States, the U.S. military became
involved. Combined forces from America, Barbados, and the Eastern Caribbean States launched a "rescue mission" in 1983 to restore
peace and democracy to Grenada. The successful mission met with
overwhelming support from the local Grenadian population, and
in 1984 the first free elections were held since 1979.

Americans find it fascinating to drive past the now famous medical school located on Grand Anse Beach near the Ramada. The school is thriving, with 550 American students currently attending classes and has plans to expand enrollment to 750 students. Pictures and documents in the local museum record the events leading up to the intervention, when barbed wire was strung across Grand Anse Beach. The empty shell of the bombed-out residence occupied by Maurice Bishop stands in ruins on the hill overlooking the harbor as an eerie testimonial to Grenada's troubled past.

Grenada is oval in shape with tall mountains and dense rain forest in the northern portion of the island, and a little tail at the southern end where the Pt. Salines International Airport is located. Grenada's extinct volcano, the Grand Etang, formed an interesting round bottomless lake where the National Park Visitor's Center has been established. The island's rich volcanic soil is perfect for agriculture, yielding more spices per acre of land than anywhere else in the world. Grenada's number 1 industry is nutmeg production, and throughout the island you can sample and purchase delectable smelling spices. The capital of St. George's conveys an atmosphere akin to the French Riviera, with red tile roof buildings climbing the hills and cathedral spires that reach to the blue skies. Massive greystone fort walls emerge above narrow, winding streets to provide a sense of romance and drama. The streets are so narrow that the police officers must direct traffic using white gloves. Watch for the elevated traffic station where officers stand above the street, blowing their whistles and waving directions at drivers.

Island People:
French and English cultures meld together on Grenada with towns and landmarks bearing titles from both languages. Grenadians are proud of the spices grown in abundance throughout the countryside and a visit to the Nutmeg Processing Plant or a spice plantation is an extraordinary experience. Machinery is not widely used, so traditional methods of cultivation and processing the valuable spices can still be seen and appreciated for their ingenuity. Honest labor produces a surprising variety of spices, cinnamon, bay leaves, cloves, allspice, cocoa, and tarragon–but nutmeg is the principal spice, grown, processed, and exported from Grenada. Locals have learned over the years to use every part of the nutmeg. The outer fruit which resembles a peach, is made into jam and liqueur, and the orange membrane surrounding the nut is used as a separate spice called mace. The interior nutmeat of the fruit is

ground to produce nutmeg, while the shells are used like gravel to line walkways and driveways. In addition, alcohol derived from sugar cane production is mixed with nutmeg and other spices to create exotic perfumes, lotions, and body oils in a local factory.

Grenada has become a popular retirement destination for Europeans, Canadians, and Americans. The rugged Caribbean coastline is lined with exclusive retirement homes, and some residents can be seen hiking, running, or just walking in groups every other Saturday. The "Hash House Harriers" began as a group wanting to get back in shape, and have now formed a club with a newsletter and growing membership. The Harrier's fun-loving attitude exemplifies the attraction of the island, a place where hiking, swimming, boating, and diving can be enjoyed all year.

Island Proverbs:
If these few samples of island proverbs have piqued your interest, be sure to look for books in the islands that specialize in island folklore, proverbs, and language.

- "If de goat wanna roll, it can roll up de hill." (If someone is bent on doing something, no obstacle will hold him back.)
- "Yuh don't got to eat the whole pig to know yah eatin' pork." (A sample is all you need to know the value of the product.)

Holidays:
Ships docking on a Sunday or holiday may find just a few shops open for shopping and souvenirs, although vendors and taxi drivers are always on hand when a ship is due in port.

January: 1st–New Years Day
February: 7th–Independence Day; 5th to 15th–Carriaco Carnival Celebrations (disguise shows, parades, dancing)
April: 1st–Good Friday; 3rd–Easter
May: 2nd–Labor Day; 23rd–Whit Monday
June: 13th–Corpus Christi (religious procession; 29th–Fisherman's Birthday Celebration to bless boats
October: 25th–Thanksgiving Day
December: 25th–Christmas; 26th–Boxing Day

The Pier

Ships dock or tender boats into St. George's cozy harbor, the picturesque town with red tile roofs climbing the hills surrounding the horseshoe-shaped harbor. A gift shop with local crafts, T-shirts, and jewelry is at the pier, along with a Tourist Information Center. The main Grenada Tourism Office is located across from the Pedestrian Plaza on the Carenage (pronounced car-nah-jsh), but plans are underway to expand the current docking facility and move the Tourism headquarters. The Carenage is a short walk from the cruise ship terminal and offers a variety of shops, restaurants, and historical sites for visiting tourists.

Pier Phones:
Island Phone Card machines and telephones accepting major credit cards are at the cruise ship dock. Phone Cards may be purchased in E.C. currency denominations at the Tourist Information Center at the pier, or from the Grentel office located on the Carenage near the Pedestrian Plaza. The Grentel office also has a calling station for tourists, and the number to dial to access the AT&T U.S.A. direct calling service from Grenada is 872.

Arts & Crafts On The Pier:
The walk from the ship to the Carenage is lined with booths where local vendors sell spice baskets and a variety of handicrafts. The spice baskets are the most reasonably priced gifts to take home to friends, often decorated with shells or hand-stitched designs. Buy baskets from locals to save money (six baskets were offered for $10 U.S.) to encourage a local cottage industry. The Carenage is home to cheery island shops offering a variety of local crafts, perfumes, batiks, and art perfect for island souvenirs.

In Town

Currency:
The local currency is the East Caribbean dollar (E.C.) which is tied to the U.S. dollar at approximately $2.70 E.C. to $1.00 U.S. Shops and restaurants accept U.S. currency but do not give the best rate of exchange. Several banks are a short walk from the Carenage for those who wish to cash traveler's checks or exchange currency. To find the nearest bank turn right on Young Street and walk to Church Street or Cross Street. Banking hours are Monday through

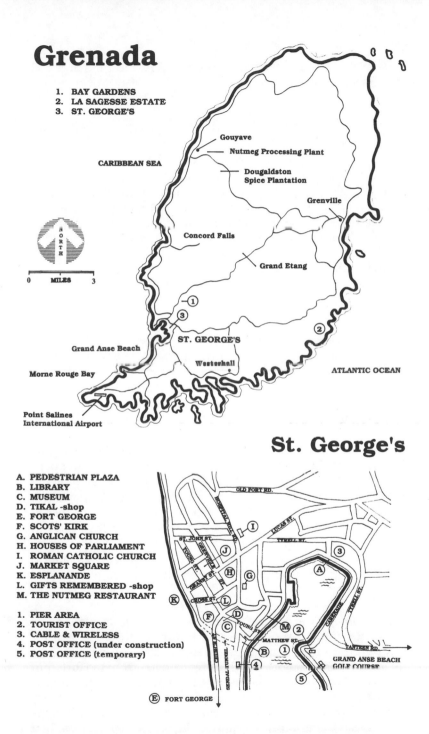

Grenada

1. BAY GARDENS
2. LA SAGESSE ESTATE
3. ST. GEORGE'S

Gouyave

Nutmeg Processing Plant

Dougaldston
Spice Plantation

CARIBBEAN SEA

Grenville

Concord Falls

Grand Etang

NORTH

0   MILES   3

① ③

②

ST. GEORGE'S

Grand Anse Beach

Westerhall

Morne Rouge Bay

ATLANTIC OCEAN

Point Salines
International Airport

St. George's

A. PEDESTRIAN PLAZA
B. LIBRARY
C. MUSEUM
D. TIKAL -shop
E. FORT GEORGE
F. SCOTS' KIRK
G. ANGLICAN CHURCH
H. HOUSES OF PARLIAMENT
I. ROMAN CATHOLIC CHURCH
J. MARKET SQUARE
K. ESPLANANDE
L. GIFTS REMEMBERED -shop
M. THE NUTMEG RESTAURANT

1. PIER AREA
2. TOURIST OFFICE
3. CABLE & WIRELESS
4. POST OFFICE (under construction)
5. POST OFFICE (temporary)

OLD FORT RD.

HOSPITAL HILL RD.

LUCAS ST.

ST. JOHN ST.

TYRELL RD.

③

Ⓘ

Ⓙ

Ⓗ

Ⓖ

Ⓐ

GRENVILLE ST.

YOUNG ST.

Ⓚ

GRANBY ST.

Ⓛ

CROSS ST.

Ⓜ ②

Ⓕ

Ⓓ

CARENAGE

TYRELL ST.

Ⓒ   YOUNG ST.

MATTHEW ST.

Ⓑ ①

TANTEEN RD.

④

SENDAL TUNNEL

GRENVILLE ST.

⑤

GRAND ANSE BEACH
GOLF COURSE

Ⓔ FORT GEORGE

Thursday 8 AM to 2 PM, and Fridays from 8 AM to 1 PM and 2:30 PM to 5 PM.

Postage:
The General Post Office in St. George's is open Monday through Thursday 8 AM to 3:30 PM, and until 4:30 PM on Fridays. The cost to airmail a post card is 75 cents E.C., about 29 cents U.S. The temporary quarters for the post office is in a warehouse near the cruise ship pier to the right of the Carenage, although the permanent location is on the opposite end of the Carenage near the National Library. A section of the Post Office is set aside for the Philatelic Bureau, which offers an incredible variety of stamps for the collector. Ask at one of the main windows if the sign for the bureau is not clearly visible.

Historical Walking Tour

The horseshoe-shaped inner harbor of the Carenage is a short walk from the historical sites in the town of St. George's. The distance of the walking tour is about one mile, with a moderately steep slope and some stairs to be climbed. At an average walking speed the entire walk should take about 1 1/2 hours, not including stops at special shops enroute.

A. From the cruise ship pier walk to the middle of the horseshoe that forms the **Carenage**. The harbor is always filled with boats, and rows of sailing sloops for hire. The walking tour begins at the center of the Pedestrian Plaza near the statue of "**The Christ of the Deep.**" The statue was given to Grenada by Costa Cruise Lines in appreciation for the heroic rescue of passengers and crew in 1961, when the *Bianca C* burned and sank in the outer harbor of St. George's. When the harbor alarm sounded, every boat available in St. George's from fishing vessels to small dinghies went to the rescue.

Continue to walk along the Carenage, passing local businesses, restaurants, and gift shops. The tour returns to this area later for an opportunity to eat and shop. When passing Young Street, be sure to notice the cannons which were removed from the forts, but are currently used as bollards to tie up ships. The tile-roofed warehouses at the end of the Carenage are 18th- and 19th-century brick structures. The red fish-scale tiles were brought to Grenada on European trade ships, which used the tiles as ballast to weight down the ships.

B. At the corner of Matthew Street is the **National Library**, housed in a former brick warehouse. The library was established in 1846 and has occupied this location since 1892.

C. Turn right on Matthew Street and walk uphill to the top of the short street. At the corner of Matthew Street and Young Street is the **National Museum**, in a building originally erected in 1704 by the French as an army barracks. Later the building was used by the British as a women's prison, then transformed into the Antilles Hotel. Notice the rare metal balcony on the exterior, one of four still remaining in St. George's from the French occupation period. The museum charges admission of $1.00 U.S., and contains a fine collection of Indian artifacts, military pieces, Josephine Bonaparte's marble bathtub, island documents, African and slave relics, the actual cells which were used to house women prisoners, and an exhibit showing pictures of the revolution and rescue mission of 1983. The museum's collection may tempt visitors to linger and talk with the friendly staff who are eager to help with a variety of books and pamphlets on Grenada's history and culture. Upon leaving the museum turn left onto Young Street.

D. Next door to the museum is the Tikal, a boutique which is worth stopping at to browse and shop. (See Shopping.) There are several other shops on the way to Church Street where you turn left again, and climb to **Fort George**. At the top of the street, take the steps to the left leading to a viewing platform which is a wonderful place to photograph the red tile roofs of the town and picturesque harbor.

E. Fort George was originally built by the French in 1705 and called Fort Royal. Later additions were constructed by the British to expand the fort, and the area is used today as barracks for the local Grenadian police. Visitors may walk through a tunnel and climb to another viewing location to the right, but a full tour of the fort is not currently available.

F. Leaving the fort, walk back down Church Street. Notice the St. Andrew's Presbyterian Kirk on the left, popularly known as the **Scots' Kirk**. The church was built in 1831 with the assistance of the Freemasons.

G. Continuing on Church Street another block, you will reach **St. George's Anglican Church**, a beautiful stone and pink stucco building. (This is another good place for a scenic view.) The church was built by the British in 1825 and contains an array of historical plaques and statues.

H. Continue walking up the hill on Hospital Hill Road, and notice the residences with exterior porches. At one time the specially designed porches were used to keep visitors dry when exiting their carriages during the rainy season. When passing Market Hill, you can see the brick **Houses of Parliament**, the center of Grenada's government, on the left.

I. Straight ahead on the right is the Roman Catholic **Cathedral of the Immaculate Conception**. The tower was built in 1818, and the cathedral was built in 1884 on the site of an older church built in 1804. Due to the fact that Grenada was tossed back and forth between French and English rule, the French Catholics were forced to move their church to the remote site on top of the hill by the Anglicans. The two religious factions had endured years of animosity and physical violence, though religious tolerance and cooperation have flourished over the past hundred years.

J. Turn left on St. John Street, and walk to Grenville Street leading to **Market Square**, the gathering place for locals selling produce and spices. The square is also the popular location for parades, political speeches and religious activities.

K. After leaving Market Square, walk down either Hillsborough Street or Granby Street to Melville, and turn left. Across the street is the **Esplanade**, the commercial waterfront for the outer harbor in St. George's.

L. Turn left on Cross Street and stop at the **Gifts Remembered** shop, and the **Yellow Poui Art Gallery** upstairs. (See Shopping.) Turn right on Young Street and walk downhill back to the Carenage. Turn left and walk back along the Carenage.

M. A wonderful place to stop for refreshments is **The Nutmeg**, located about half a block from Young Street on the left-hand side of the harbor. Locals, yachtsmen, and tourists all enjoy the congenial atmosphere of The Nutmeg with its excellent food, service, and harbor views. The walking tour ends at the Carenage, where shops are available for those who wish to buy island souvenirs.

Shopping

Shops On The Carenage

Shops are generally open weekdays 8 AM-12 PM and 1-4 PM, 8 AM to noon on Saturdays, and closed on Sundays unless indicated.

BON VOYAGE is a duty-free, air-conditioned shop featuring china, crystal, porcelain figures, and jewelry.

CREATIONS AND CRAFTS has straw work, ceramics, bamboo, carvings, jewelry, and paintings by locals. Imported artwork from other islands, Latin America, and Africa are also available.

TOURIST SHOPPING CENTRE features souvenirs, T-shirts, jewelry and hand crafts. The shop is open Sundays and holidays when cruise ships are in port.

FRANGIPANI displays local watercolors, hand-painted clothing, batiks, T-shirts, and handicrafts.

SEA CHANGE BOOK & GIFT SHOP is located below the Nutmeg Restaurant, and carries a wide selection of American and British books, island books, children's books, and international newspapers.

SPICE ISLAND PERFUMES features locally made perfumes, herbal teas, body oils, spices, craft items, T-shirts, and clothing.

WHITE CANE INDUSTRIES is located next to the Delicious Landing Restaurant, and features the work of blind native artisans, including bags, hats, straw mats, and postcards framed into serving trays. (Credit cards are not accepted.)

St. George's Shopping

***TIKAL is located next to the National Museum, and is the author's pick for the most interesting shop in St. George's. The owners have gathered a wide selection of quality products from Grenada and Latin America, including dolls, batiks, paintings, sculpture, jewelry, woven baskets, and clothing.

YELLOW POUI ART GALLERIES has two locations, one next to Barclays Bank at Church St. and Halifax St., and the other above the Gifts Remembered shop on Cross Street. These galleries contain a wide variety of Caribbean prints, maps, engravings, watercolors, drawings, and sculptures by local artists.

GIFTS REMEMBERED is on Cross Street, containing local arts, straw goods, postcards, spice baskets, film, T-shirts, and local batik prints.

GRAND ANSE SHOPPING CENTER is across from the Ramada and Grand Anse Beach outside St. George's.

THE GIFT SHOP sells the widest variety of imported watches, Land leather bags, crystal, china, and name-brand figurines at duty-free prices. Passengers should carry a passport and ship's I.D. to guarantee duty-free prices.

POCOLOCO BOUTIQUE carries casual wear, shoes, sandals, accessories, beachwear, and crafts. All items in the shop are made in the Caribbean.

IMAGINE contains a variety of Caribbean handicrafts, dolls, straw ware, clothing, stamps for the collector, and local batiks.

Transportation, Excursions

Taxis:
Cruise ships docking at the St. George's pier area or tendering their passengers to the pier have taxis available along the Carenage for trips around the island. The majority of cars used as taxis are minivans with clearly marked taxi signs or with the symbol "H" on the windshield or the roof. Taxis are not metered, but use regulated taxi fares dictated by the government, with a rate schedule posted at the pier. Fares are often quoted in E.C., and priced for the whole taxi, carrying one-five persons. Passengers should negotiate a price in U.S. dollars before entering the van or taxi. Feel free to negotiate fares for excursions out on the island, but understand that Grenada's taxi drivers are friendly, honest, hardworking, and follow the government regulated guidelines. Tipping is not required for short trips around St. George's, but outer-island excursions deserve a 10% tip.

Taxi Chart:

Destination	Cost
Bay Gardens	$16.00
Grand Anse Beach	$7.00
Morne Rouge Beach	$7.00
La Sagesse	$25.00
Gouyave Spice Factory	$40.00
Grand Etang	$30.00
Golf Course	$6.00
All rates are for the whole taxi, one to four persons.	

Rental Cars:
Driving in Grenada is on the left, and only for the very adventurous at heart. Roads are steep with sharp turns, and are not in very good condition. If you are brave enough to try driving, remember to stay left after dodging a pothole! Cars are available for $35-$50 per day, and collision insurance is optional. A temporary driver's license is required at a cost of $11 and can be obtained from the traffic department next to the Fire Station on the Carenage, or from the larger rental firms. Minimum age to rent a car is 23, and a credit card is recommended for covering the damage deposit required through most agencies.

Rental Agencies: The area code for Grenada is (809) and it is considered an overseas call from the United States.

Avis (Spice Island Rentals) 440-3936/2624
Budget Rent-a-Car 444-1620/440-2778
David's Car Rentals 440-2399/3038

Self-Guided Tours

1. La Sagesse Nature Center, located 20 minutes from St. George's, is nestled between two protective peninsulas in St. David's parish. La Sagesse, which means "the wise woman" in French, is a quiet seaside plantation estate containing a mangrove estuary, three beautiful beaches, coral reefs, and acres of thorn scrub cactus woodlands for visitors to explore. A restaurant on the property serves delicious seafood and continental cuisine ideal for an afternoon lunch. You can either take a taxi straight to La Sagesse, or join an island tour with Arnold's Tours, which includes a stop at La Sagesse Nature Center. (Also see Organized Tours) Between 10

AM and 2 PM, La Sagesse offers a guided nature walk which includes lunch and transportation to the property for $25 per person. Reservations for the walking tour can be made by contacting the owners prior to arrival on Grenada. Phone Mike Meranski at (809) 444-6458 to arrange a day at one of Grenada's best hidden secrets.

2. Located just outside St. George's is **Bay Gardens**, a botanist's paradise. Keith St. Bernard is the proprietor of the gardens, and has personally planted and overseen the placement of all the exotic plantlife and colorful flowers on the estate. Keith will take you on an informational walk through the winding pathways, pointing out plants and trees unique to the Caribbean. He has also personally created new varieties of plants by crossing flower types together to form hybrids. The estate is currently building a pathway access for wheelchairs and labeling for the trees and plants along the walkways. The garden is always changing and developing, and you will be amazed at the exceptional plant specimens Keith and his workers have established! A taxi to the gardens takes 15 minutes and the round-trip costs $16 for one to four persons. A $2 admission fee helps maintain the pathways and promotes the ongoing presentation of new plants and trees. Be sure to ask Keith to guide you through his property, one of the best botanical gardens in the Caribbean!

Organized Tours & Activities

All prices are quoted in U.S. dollars

1. One of Grenada's premiere tour operators, **Arnold's Tours** offers a wide selection of island tours.

• **Tour D.** "Scenic Fun" guides passengers to the historic Fort Frederick for the best overlook of St. George's and the Carenage. The next stop at De La Grenade Industries allows visitors to sample world famous liqueurs, rum punch, nutmeg jams and jellies. Next stop is at Bay Gardens. The tour continues along the Atlantic coastline to La Sagesse Nature Center. A guided walk through the banana plantations, mangrove estuary, and private beach will make you want to stay on the island forever. Lunch is served at the La Sagesse restaurant, and you are invited to swim and relax in the Atlantic sea cove before venturing to the next location on the tour. On the way back to St. George's, a scheduled stop at Fort Jeudy is at the southernmost tip of the peninsula. If the season is right, a guided tour is also available of the Westerhall Rum Distillery, which dates from the 1800's. The "Scenic Fun" tour lasts five hours, departing at 10 AM and returning at 3 PM. The cost is $22 per person including lunch at La Sagesse. Call ahead to reserve the tour (809) 440-0531/2213.

• **Tour #1**, also from Arnold's, consists of a day tour and cruise. They leave St. George's at 9 AM for a bus ride to Annandale Falls. Then they climb almost 2,000 feet above sea level to the Grand Etang Lake, the crater of an extinct volcano. Be sure to visit the Mona monkey exhibit, and watch for wild monkeys that come out of the trees to steal the food from the caged monkeys. These are the most striking monkeys found in the Caribbean, with a dark brown coat and white and black stripes down the front. Don't get too close to the monkeys or they may steal your glasses right off your head. The next point of interest is the Nutmeg Processing Plant in the coastal town of Gouyave. Grenada is known as the "Isle of Spice" and you will see what it takes to produce the number 1 export, nutmeg. A worker from the plant will guide you through the various rooms and explain the nutmeg processing. Islanders are busily sorting, cleaning, and roasting the nutmegs. A tour through the plant is like stepping back in time before the Industrial Revolution, as the spice is processed almost entirely by hand. The Dougaldston Spice Estate comes next–a surviving piece of Grenada's past where spices are grown and processed. A guide will display the different spices grown on the island, and allow you to sample them. The return trip to St. George's is aboard the *M.V. Welshman* departing from Gouyave. Complimentary fruit and rum punch drinks are served while passengers sit back and enjoy the coastal views from the boat.

The total trip takes five hours and can also be done in reverse order. It is available on Mondays, Wednesdays, and Fridays. You must reserve early by calling (809) 440-0531/2213.

2. World Wide Watersports offers a half-day Sailing & Snorkeling Trip which leaves daily at 1:30 PM, returning at 5 PM from the Grand Anse Beach. The trip includes sailing to a coral reef for snorkeling, lunch, rum punch, and a limbo dance party with plenty of Calypso music. The cost is $40 per person and it can be reserved by calling World Wide Watersports at (809) 444-1339.

3. The *Grenadian Rhum Runner* offers the best "booze cruise" on the island. The barge-type boat leaves the port of St. George's at 1 PM from a dock across from the Fire Station on the Carenage and returns at 4:30 PM. The cruise takes you to Morne Rouge beach for 1 1/2 hours in the sun, where you can try the variety of watersports available. Bring along extra cash if you are interested in watersports; the cost is additional to the cruise. The *Rhum Runner* includes complimentary rum and fruit punch, snorkel equipment with a $10 deposit, and all the fun you can handle dancing and partying. The cost is $20 per person. Make reservations at (809) 440-2198/3422.

4. Morning and afternoon trips on a **glass bottom boat** are available through World Wide Watersports every hour from 9 AM to 5 PM. View the coral reefs swarming with tropical fish, sea fans, and underwater plantlife for $10 per person. The boat leaves from the Grand Anse Beach, and reservations can be made by calling (809) 444-1339. Take a trip on the glass bottom boat, then relax for the rest of the day on the beautiful beach of Grand Anse.

5. For the adventurous hiker, **Henry's Safari Tours** offers a guided and informational hiking tour ideal for a cruiser's short time in port. The island tour takes you to the Concord Valley to see the cascading waterfalls where you can take a guided hike for 90 minutes past the first waterfall, explore the spice plantation, or simply enjoy the river. The next scheduled stop is the Nutmeg Processing Plant in Gouyave, then on through the Central Mountain Range. Henry's Tours follow the seldom-used roads winding through plantations, the tropical rain forest, and picturesque volcanic valleys. The return trip to St. George's takes you to the Grand Etang Lake and National Park Visitor's Center, home of the Mona monkey exhibit. The entire tour takes between five and six hours and costs $35 per person for a group of two without the hike at Concord Valley, or $33 per person including the hike. With 3 or more people on the tour, the cost per person is less. For more information and reservations contact Dennis Henry at (809) 444-5313.

Beaches

1. The most popular beach, always alive with activity, is **Grand Anse**. Located to the left of St. George's, it is a five-minute taxi ride from the pier. Hotels line the beach and offer a multitude of watersports, but the best organization on the beach is to the right side of the Ramada Renaissance Hotel (facing the water). World Wide Watersports has every type of watersports equipment available for rent, and provides the best in professional service and attitude. The beach has an assortment of restaurants for lunch, and the hotel pool areas have rest room facilities. Grand Anse is a two-mile stretch of beach with room for every visitor to find a private piece of sand. It is also swarming with locals trying to sell everything from spice baskets to a cool drink. If you aren't interested, a firm no will be sufficient.

2. Morne Rouge is a smaller cove located 10 minutes from St. George's, over the hill from Grand Anse. The beach is home to the *Rhum Runner* party cruise and has a variety of watersports available when the "booze cruise" comes to the beach. A small restaurant is on the beach–perfect for lunch–and afterwards you can find a little more privacy further down the beach. Do not bring valuables with you to the beach.

3. A hidden piece of paradise is located 20 minutes from St. George's at the estate property, **La Sagesse**. The beach cove here is perfect for privacy, peace, and tranquility. There are actually three beaches on the property, two of which are within a short hiking distance from the guest house and restaurant. You can literally escape the "real world" here as you enjoy the natural wonders of the plantation. The Nature Center, dedicated to increasing environmental awareness, gives an overview of the natural environment surrounding the property. A guided tour of the area is also possible (see Self-Guided Tours) and lunch at the restaurant is worth the taxi ride out to the estate. Spend the whole day exploring, or make it part of an island tour.

Grenada Beach Chart:

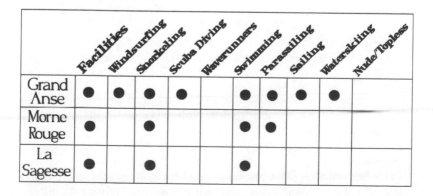

	Facilities	Windsurfing	Snorkeling	Scuba Diving	Waverunners	Swimming	Parasailing	Sailing	Waterskiing	Nude/Topless
Grand Anse	●	●	●	●		●	●	●	●	
Morne Rouge	●		●			●	●			
La Sagesse	●		●			●				

Island & Ocean Sports

All rates are quoted in U.S. dollars

Golf:
The Grenada Golf Club, just above Grand Anse, offers a 9-hole golf course perfect for cruise passengers arriving in St. George's. The lush greens and beautiful surroundings make a golf adventure on Grenada a unique experience. The green fees are $12 and club rentals are $8 for the 9 holes. Full clubhouse facilities, golf instruction, and refreshments are available. Contact (809) 444-4128 to reserve tee times, or take a taxi to the main entrance for a round of Caribbean golf.

Tennis:
The Ramada Renaissance Hotel on the beach of Grand Anse has courts available for hourly games of tennis. A five-minute taxi ride will bring you to the main entrance of the hotel where you can play a set of tennis, then enjoy all the amenities on the beach. Contact the Ramada at (809) 444-4371/4372 for current rates and court reservations, costing approximately $15 per hour.

The ocean sports listed below are available through World Wide Watersports.

Windsurfing:
Rentals are available for $15 per hour, with additional instruction and lessons offered for beginners. The calm seas off Grand Anse are ideal for learning to windsurf.

Sailing Sports:
Hobie Cats are rented for $25 per hour, dinghies and kayaks are $15 per hour, and pedal boats are $10 per hour. All sailing equipment is offered with instruction, and is the most adventurous way to enjoy a day at sea.

Water-skiing:
Speed boats offer water-skiing and knee board skiing at a rate of $15 per person for 30 minutes. Instruction is also available, and the more people, the more fun.

Parasailing:
Try a flight through the air with Sky Ride, offering a 20-minute ride for $20. Sky Ride operator Trevor Renwick offers flights from the

beach near the Ramada, or you can make reservations by calling (809) 444-4222.

Scuba Diving And Snorkeling:
Beautiful coral reefs await scuba divers, but you should not touch or remove sealife from the ocean to protect the reefs for other divers and snorkelers. Snorkeling equipment is offered for rent at $10 per set for a half-day, requiring a refundable deposit. Scuba diving for certified divers, including equipment, costs $30 for a single dive, and $45 for a dive to the sunken cruise ship *Bianca C*. A two-tank dive costs $50 per person and explores the coral reefs surrounding the St. George's area. Call ahead for reservations and confirmation of dive trips available.

World Wide Watersports is opening its new dive facility this year and is the most professional operator on the beach. There are two other dive operators on Grand Anse offering–Dive Grenada at the Ramada Renaissance, and Grand Anse Aquatics at the end of the beach. These groups offer quality equipment, but they utilize small boats which may be uncomfortable for certified divers on a two-tank dive. Contact world wide watersports first and, if you are unable to arrange a dive, contact one of the others.

One-Day Itinerary

Grenada offers the opportunity to escape the hustle and bustle of everyday life, to simply enjoy the beauty of nature. The "one-day" itinerary is designed for a day exploring the natural side of Grenada.

Cruise passengers with only one day on Grenada should hire a taxi for the two trips described. The total cost of the taxi for one to four persons will be $41. Drivers are always available near the pier area, and some be willing to bargain for a round-trip to the Bay Gardens and the La Sagesse estate. The sites, driving time from one location to the next, and round trip taxi fares from St. George's are listed below in U.S. dollars.

Bay Gardens	5 7 minutes	$16 round-trip
La Sagesse estate	20 minutes	$25 round-trip

What to Bring:
Comfortable walking shoes, a bathing suit, a towel, and sunscreen are essential items for La Sagesse Nature Center and beaches. A

camera with a flash is also vital for capturing views of the beautiful flowers at the Bay Gardens. It rarely rains on Grenada, but you may wish to bring along a light jacket and hat to guard against the showers.

Directions:
Refer to the island map for numbers corresponding with the suggested sites described.

1. The journey begins at 9 AM with a taxi ride to **Bay Gardens**. Keith St. Bernard, the proprietor of the gardens, will guide visitors through his magnificently grown and maintained floral paradise. Spend up to an hour wandering through the shaded pathways and see how many different plants and flowers you can recognize. Also have Keith point out the many spices growing in their natural state, like nutmeg, cinnamon, pepper, and others.

2. Have the taxi driver take you along the coastline, through a large banana plantation, out to the nearly hidden **La Sagesse** estate. Have the driver return at 2:30 PM, or plan to hire another driver for the return trip to St. George's.

If you arrive between 10 AM and 2 PM, you may take a guided nature hike around the property to learn about the environmental systems that make up the beach, coastline, mangrove, and coral reefs. La Sagesse has three beach areas to explore, and the hiking trails and banana plantation also make interesting side trips. Spend the next four hours enjoying La Sagesse and plan to have lunch at the restaurant, which prepares the best seafood or continental cuisine for their guests. The atmosphere is very relaxed, and should allow you to escape your troubles for the day.

3. Either take the pre-arranged taxi at 2:30 PM, or call for another driver to take you back into downtown **St. George's**. The National Museum and shops just off the Carenage are interesting places to spend 30 minutes to an hour. Wander around the historic port, or have an afternoon drink at the Nutmeg Restaurant along the Carenage until your cruise ship departs.

The total day on Grenada should last between six and seven hours, and before departing the island be sure to buy some spice baskets for friends and family at home.